In Nature's Honor

In Nature's Honor

Myths and Rituals Celebrating the Earth

Patricia Montley

SKINNER HOUSE BOOKS

BOSTON

Printed in the United States.

Cover art by Julie Baer, *Great Meadows and Butterflies*, 2002, 23½" x 23½", mixed media gouache on wood panel, © 2002 Julie Baer, www.juliebaer.com
Cover design by Gopa & Ted2, Inc.
Text design by Suzanne Morgan

ISBN 1-55896-486-X

Library of Congress Cataloging-in-Publication Data
Montley, Patricia.
  In nature's honor : myths and rituals celebrating the earth / Patricia Montley.
    p. cm.
  Includes index.
  ISBN 1-55896-486-X (alk. paper)
  978-1-55896-486-0
  1. Nature--Religious aspects. I. Title.
  BL65.N35M67 2005
  203'.8--dc22

                                                                2005006837

5 4 3 2 1
08 07 06 05

Note: We have included several websites in the Selected Bibliography for the convenience of our readers, although we recognize that websites are not permanent and that the URLs may become invalid after the book is published.

We gratefully acknowledge permission for the following materials:

"Gather the Spirit," used by permission of Jim Scott (www.jimscottmusic.com).

"Sing of Living, Sing of Dying," used by permission of Thomas J. S. Mikelson.

"Autumn Psalm of Contentment," by Edward Hays © 1988 by Forest of Peace Books, an imprint of Ave Maria Press Inc., P.O. Box 428, Notre Dame, IN 46556. Used with permission of the publisher (www.avemariapress.com).

Recipes adapted from *Witch in the Kitchen: Magical Cooking for All Seasons*, by Cait Johnson, Destiny Books, an imprint of Inner Traditions International, Rochester, VT 05767. Copyright © 2001 by Cait Johnson (www.InnerTraditions.com).

Agosto/August from *Canciones, 1921-1924/Songs, 1921-1924* by Federico Garcia Lorca © Herederos de Federico Garcia Lorca. Translation by Alan S. Trueblood © Herederos de Federico Garcia Lorca and Alan S. Trueblood.

Continued on page 378.

For Sally,
my best critic,
and dearest.

Contents

Introduction

Our home lives are filled with rituals—practices that are faithfully enacted with comforting regularity: the nightly bath, the bedtime story, the "How-was-your-day?" supper talk, the sharing of coffee over the morning paper. Some may be more elaborate: the summer trip to the beach, the Halloween costume party, the extended-family Thanksgiving dinner, the exchange of holiday gifts, the fourth of July picnic.

In temples, churches, or mosques, ceremonial acts prescribed by tradition involve the whole faith community. Many of these include the reading and singing of meaningful or poetic passages, often from texts considered sacred, performing symbolic acts, using symbolic objects, eating or drinking symbolic food, testifying to certain beliefs, making promises to live a certain way. While they are an important part of everyday life, these rituals have a formality that takes us out of "everyday" time and place and puts us in a place deep inside our spirits where we long for meaning and connection—to the transcendent in ourselves, in the universe, in others. When repeated every week, every year, every generation, rituals become a source of comfort and continuity, something that connects us to our near and distant ancestors and descendants.

Historically, many rituals mark the changing of the seasons. Others emphasize the relationship of humans to nature: rites of purification, sacrifice and fertility, rites that honor the gods and goddesses identified with nature's processes.

Thus the seasonal markers, the solstices and equinoxes, are occasions for rituals and festivals around the world. We light fires to provide symbolic (and in some cases, actual) illumination and warmth. Water becomes a means of ritual purification. Food becomes sacred by the sharing of it—at altars or at family tables. We offer sacrifices or gifts to our gods or to one another in their honor.

But why have people throughout history marked the passing of the seasons with religious rituals? For believers in a personal deity, ritual might be viewed as the dramatized version of prayer directed at a divine figure who, if pleased by our endeavors, will bless us. For those who are less sure about a personal deity, an understanding of the purpose of ritual might be found in considering its functions. Ritual enables us to live our daily lives more mindfully—and possibly more morally. Ritual transforms us. Ritual provides a way of passing on our spiritual values.

In *Children of the Morning Light*, storyteller Manitonquat recounts a tale the Wampanoag people tell their children that stresses the importance of appreciating the sun. It encourages them to welcome Grandfather Sun in the morning and say a grateful goodbye in the evening. Do adult members of the tribe really believe that the sun hears and understands them? Surely not. Why then do they greet the sun each day and celebrate rituals marking the solstices? Some of *us* may celebrate the Winter Solstice, letting go of the old year and welcoming the new. In her Solstice ritual in *Spiral Dance*, Starhawk proclaims,

> We turn the wheel to bring the light.
> We call the sun from the womb of night.

But do any of us believe that the return of the sun literally depends on our calling it? Again, surely not.

Yet perhaps our power to summon the sun, to affect the germination of the seed or the quality of the harvest, is real in the same way all the myths are true and all the gods and goddesses are real. They

speak to us of a psychological truth that transcends logic and sur-
passes reason. They are in the realm of faith and metaphor. They are
beyond fact and therefore beyond contradiction.

What is not beyond fact is that we have come to imagine ourselves so far from dependent on the natural world that we freely
abuse and exploit it. Would we use solar energy for nuclear
weapons if we envisioned the sun as Grandfather? Would we plunder the earth, pollute the water, puncture the protective ozone
layer, level the rain forests, and drive whole species of animals to
extinction if we regularly and ritually acknowledged the beauty
and power of the natural world, our dependence on it, and its dependence on our good treatment?

If we celebrate planting and harvesting rituals and thus grow
more mindful of the sources and importance of our food, isn't the
next step to become more informed of our government's policies
regarding food distribution worldwide? And with this awareness,
are we not more likely to take action to eliminate hunger in our
own and other countries?

If we ritually acknowledge the Spring Equinox and celebrate in
myth and music the many vegetation gods who died and were
buried in the earth as seeds—only to rise as fruit and flower and
grain—will we not better appreciate the vernal revival of nature?
Will we not better understand that there is a time to be born and a
time to die? This is the true power of ritual.

But ritual does more than affect the way we live our daily lives.
Performing a ritual together transforms us from a group of individuals into a community because the ritual represents the values
we share, and this sharing forms the basis of our togetherness. If
we gather at the neighborhood park or garden for a Spring
Equinox ritual that includes planting seedlings, we are professing
our investment in the neighborhood, our agreement that it is important to care for the earth we live on, and our belief that doing
this caretaking together is better than doing it separately. If we
gather for a Fall Equinox ritual and give thanks for the harvest,
singing, "To those in need of food for body and for soul may we

give of our store, that they and we be whole," we are publicly professing a communal commitment to sharing our resources and, further, admitting that our own well-being depends on it.

If we repeat these words and gestures year after year, provided we do so mindfully and honestly, then we gradually become more protective of our shared environment, more appreciative of our neighbors, and more active working with them to care for the poor and the place we all call home. In short, we are transformed into a community. And this too is the true power of ritual.

Ritual is also a way of passing on our spiritual values to the next generation. If, together with our children, we honor the memory of our beloved dead at a Samhain or All Souls ritual, we are teaching them the importance of the life well lived and the legacy it leaves. The way we teach our children values is living by our values. If an action is worth a hundred words, a ritual is worth a hundred lectures. A lecture speaks primarily to the mind, while a ritual has the power of symbol. It goes directly to the imagination, where it explodes into a myriad of meanings and motivations. Surely our young people hunger for such an experience.

In addition to serving these functions common to all communal rituals, seasonal rituals offer something more, an enhanced awareness of the beauty and power of the natural world and of our connection to something larger than ourselves.

Anthropologists tell us that ritual is a mode of behavior exhibited by all known societies; because of this universality, it is actually a way of defining humans. We are beings who create ritual. Without it, we are less than human, condemned to the prosaic half-life of literalism. With ritual, we appreciate the poetry of the world around us and the world within us.

The religion of early peoples celebrated the ways in which they were bound to the elements of earth, air, fire/sun, and water. Whether the seasons are the four we know, or the two delineated by the Yoruba (dry and rainy), or the three recognized by the Egyptians (flooding, growing, and dry), or some other set, the earth rotates around the sun and the amount of light changes from day to day and affects all living things. Sometimes the ancients personified the elements and seasons as goddesses or gods, whom they called upon in gratitude and entreaty.

More recent, monotheistic religions rejected these elemental/seasonal deities, depersonalizing our connection to the earth. And the industrial revolution all but completed our withdrawal from the natural world. Thanks to technology, in "developed" countries, most of us now are sealed off from nature. The bonfires that once honored the sun gods have given way to electricity, which has, for most of us, all but eliminated anxiety at the approach of the long, dark cold of winter. The harvesting of crops, which were once attributed to the grain goddesses, has been taken over by agribusiness, extinguishing the fear of famine. Water for drinking and cleansing is at our fingertips, the supply largely monitored by municipalities. We live and work and drive in climate-controlled environments. Unless we garden as a hobby, we never put hands to soil. Because we do not come close to the awareness of our dependence on the elements that early peoples had, we do not honor these life sources as they did.

In recent decades the environmental movement, research in ancient goddess religions, and the growing respect for nature religions as practiced by the Native Americans in this country and the Celts in Europe have worked together to generate a resurgence of interest in seasonal rituals that celebrate the earth and our connection to it, which must be acknowledged as not just physical but also profoundly spiritual. It is the purpose of this book to explore that connection and offer ways to celebrate the seasons.

We are accustomed in the United States to reckoning our seasons by the solstices and equinoxes. Winter begins on or about December 21; spring, March 21; summer, June 21; and autumn, September 21. But this system is not universal and certainly not ancient. These astronomical markers work for us as delineators because they generally represent our *thermal* seasons. But the old agrarian communities of Europe had climates more attuned to the *solar* seasons. Meteorologist Keith Heidorn defines these on his

"Weather Almanac" website. If we divide the year into four solar seasons, the quarter having the greatest potential solar energy and longest days would be solar summer and the quarter with the least potential solar energy and shortest days would be solar winter. In between, the sun "springs" from the short days of winter into the long days of summer, and then "falls" back.

In this system, the beginning of November marks the arrival of winter; the beginning of February, the start of spring; the beginning of May, the opening of summer; and the beginning of August, the onset of autumn. The ancient Celts, among others, observed these solar seasons and identified these four markers as *quarter days* because they divided their year into four parts. A similar system is observed in China. In the first week of February, the Chinese celebrate the beginning of spring (*Li Chun*), which is also their New Year. The beginning of summer (*Li Sya*) is early May, the beginning of autumn (*Li Chyou*) is early August, and the beginning of winter (*Li Dung*) is early November. Some earth-centered religions celebrate the solstices and equinoxes as quarterly dividers of the year, but observe as well the markers of the solar seasons, sometimes referring to them as *cross-quarter days*.

This book is concerned with rituals marking the openings of both the thermal and solar seasons. Thus the eight chapters cover the two solstices, the two equinoxes, and the four quarter days.

Each chapter starts with a history of the seasonal marker, its cultural and mythological foundations, and ways in which it has been celebrated from ancient to modern times. Suggestions are then offered for specific activities and practices that individuals, families, or small groups can use to celebrate the season. The chapter concludes with a formal ritual appropriate for faith communities or other gatherings. Each ritual is a scripted text, providing explanatory narration, litanies of seasonal blessings, dramatic enactments, songs, and readings of myths, poems, and essays, as well as suggestions for ceremonial food and symbolic actions appropriate to the feast.

The book's structure lends itself to multiple approaches. Certainly reading it cover-to-cover in one sitting is acceptable! So too is reading each chapter in sync with its season. But you don't have to start at the beginning. If you pick up the book for the first time in early March, you can begin with the chapter on Spring Equinox.

The rituals take thirty to sixty minutes, depending on the number of participants. While songs and readings and other components are included, these should be treated as suggestions. Lyrics have been provided for more than forty songs. Many have melodies that readers will recognize and be able to sing without musical notation. While many of the lyrics provided are original, the melodies can be found in various hymnals. Some selections are popular songs or classical pieces that have been written and recorded by professional artists. For these, readers may wish to obtain the sheet music or CDs identified in the Music Resources section. This section also lists websites where you can listen to audio files of the music. Certainly those sponsoring the ritual should feel free to substitute other (especially original) music and readings, using whatever elements would make the experience most meaningful for the participants.

One way to adapt the rituals for the particular needs of your community is to use spontaneous rather than scripted litanies. Instead of the service leader speaking the words provided in the litanies in this book, you may wish to invite people to call out their own suggestions during the ceremony. Or you can collect suggestions in advance, perhaps combining them with the words offered here and/or generated by those who are preparing the service.

Another type of substitution is also encouraged. My own experience of the seasons is grounded in the mid-Atlantic coast of the United States. Blooms and birds, trees and wildlife, climate and colors in my neighborhood may be different from yours. I invite you to consider your own experience of nature as you read.

I sincerely hope that people of all religions or no religion will use and enjoy this book. It is intended for anyone who appreciates the beauty of the earth, the strength of our bond with it, and the joy and comfort that can be ours in claiming and proclaiming that bond.

Winter Solstice and the New Year

December 21-22

A world without warmth, a world without light. It's what our ancient ancestors feared most. Perhaps as the first humans traveled farther and farther from their tropical homes, they noticed with increasing anxiety that days grew shorter and nights longer. As their food supply dwindled—with the earth seemingly barren and many animals in hibernation—and as the temperature plummeted, so did their spirits. What if the light disappeared altogether? What if the sun abandoned them, leaving them to scrabble for existence in a cold, dark world?

The Seasonal Calendar

Eventually humans came to understand that the tilt of the earth on its rotational axis and its continuous revolution around the sun result in the annual seasons. In the northern hemisphere, the sun appears to reach its maximum height—thus producing the greatest number of daylight hours—on June 21 or 22, Summer Solstice. The minimum elevation—producing the least number of daylight hours—is on December 21 or 22, Winter Solstice. Since both events mark the moment when the pattern reverses itself, the sun seems for a few days to "stand still." Hence the term *solstice*, from the Latin *sol* ("sun") and *stare* ("to stand still").

Ancient peoples around the world perceived these solstice events, as well as the Spring and Fall Equinoxes, to be so momentous that many of them created mammoth structures to mark them. Richard Heinberg describes many such structures in *Celebrate the Solstice*. Their respective websites also provide factual details. The Newgrange burial mound in Ireland, for example, was built nearly seven thousand years ago in such a way that the sun shines directly through an opening above the main entry into the heart of the tomb only at dawn on Winter Solstice. The same is true of the chambered passage mound on Gavrinis Island in Brittany, France. England's Stonehenge, with its circle of massive standing stones constructed some five thousand years ago, is a marker of both solstices. Maes How, on the Orkney Islands north of Scotland, built around 2700 BCE, is another burial chamber that marks the Winter Solstice, admitting the last rays of the setting sun through its entrance passage. The standing stones of Kintraw in Argyll, Scotland, as well as Long Meg and Her Daughters in Cumberland are also oriented to the Winter Solstice sunset.

Hundreds of such megalithic structures that mark the solstices and equinoxes have been discovered throughout Europe. Other such natural observatories have been identified in Asia, Indonesia, the Middle East, Africa, and the Americas. In the ancient Near East, Heinberg tells us, "The axis of the smaller Temple of Ra-Hor-Ahkty, attached to the great hall at Karnak, is oriented to sunrise on the Winter Solstice," as is the window of the High Room of the Sun in the same temple complex. The Temples of Thebes and Abydos are likewise oriented.

On the other side of the world, in the ancient Inca capital of Cuzco, the *Coricancha* or Sun Temple, which contained the famous solid gold sun disks, was oriented toward the Winter Solstice sunrise. Farther north, the Chumash people of California marked the Winter Solstice with exquisite rock art. For example, at Burro Flats, "a complex collection of animal and geometric images is shaded throughout the year by a canopy of rock," but at dawn on Winter Solstice, "a triangle of sunlight cuts to the center of a series of concentric rings before shrinking back to the base of the prepared rock surface." A similar Winter Solstice phenomenon can be seen when two daggers of sunlight frame a spiral petroglyph at the top of Fajada Butte in Chaco Canyon in New Mexico.

Mythology and History

The sacredness of this hour of the sun's return has been honored not just in structures but in stories. Mythology suggests that the ancients overcame their fear of the sun deserting them with sympathetic magic. Diverse tales tell of sun deities who withdraw their life-sustaining energy from earth and must be coaxed out of hiding each year like a new baby from its mother's womb. In *The New Book of Goddesses and Heroines*, Patricia Monaghan identifies some of these. The Cherokee Sun Unelanuhi locks herself in her house, grieving for her dead daughter, and can be enticed to smile only by the music and dancing of young people. Bomong, sun goddess of the Minyong of India, covers herself with a gigantic rock at the death of her sister; only when a carpenter revives the sister does the goddess emerge, to the singing of all the animals. The Finnish Paivatar is captive in a dark cave guarded by a witch, whose henchmen must be vanquished by a poet before the sun can be freed. Heima, sun goddess of the California Miwok, remains shut up in her stone house until doves with slingshots hurl stones through the wall, frightening her into rising from the smoke hole.

Perhaps the most famous sun deity is Amaterasu Ōmikami, whom even modern Japanese emperors have claimed as an ancestor. Ashamed at the bad behavior of her brother, this "Heaven Shining Great August Spirit" hides in a cave, leaving heaven and earth in darkness. To entice her forth, Joseph Campbell tells us in *The Masks of God: Oriental Mythology*,

> The eight million spirits of the Plain of Heaven assembled trees before the cave, bedecked with jewels, lighted bonfires, and laughed aloud with such uproar at a raucous dance . . . that the goddess in her cave, becoming curious, opened the

door to peek out. They held a mirror before her, the first she had ever seen; she was drawn out, and the world again was alight.

In *O Mother Sun!* Monaghan theorizes that the stone basins in the cavern at Newgrange might have been filled with water at the Solstice, thus becoming mirrors in which the rising sun could admire her beauty and, like Amaterasu, be enticed to return.

Apparently our ancestors believed that at Winter Solstice, the sun can be wooed out of hiding only with music and dancing, singing and poetry, "jeweled" trees, bonfires, and laughter. Perhaps we still believe it. Otherwise why would we practice our sympathetic magic in the dark of December? Why string our evergreen trees with lights and bedeck them with sun-shaped "jewels"? Why light bonfires in our hearths and set candles in our windows? Why shoot fireworks into the black sky, dance raucously, and laugh aloud on New Year's Eve? Why gather in Times Square, a crowd of strangers pressing for community, and count the seconds till the great illuminated ball makes its slow descent, bringing the bright promise of possibility? Because it is the birthday of the sun!

The Winter Solstice event is so important that it has been celebrated in diverse cultures all over the world for millennia—often associated with a deity of light who conquers darkness or a deity of plenty who vanquishes need.

In some cases, the imagery is of death and rebirth: the death of the old solar year and the (re)birth of the new solar year, in the form of a divine child who is born of a goddess or of a "virgin" human mother impregnated by the primary god. As Marina Warner points out in *Alone of All Her Sex: The Myth and the Cult of the Virgin Mary*, "The virgin birth of heroes and sages was a widespread formula in the Hellenistic world: Pythagoras, Plato, Alexander were all believed to be born of woman by the power of a holy spirit." According to the Roman biographer Suetonius, the emperor Augustus was miraculously conceived when his mother was impregnated by the god Apollo.

If the births of these human heroes warranted such extraordinary circumstances, how much more miraculous must the births of the sun gods have been? In ancient Egypt, the goddess Isis gives birth to Horus, "the Light of the World." His Persian counterpart, Mithra, is born of the goddess of waters, Anahita, the "Immaculate One," said to conceive from the seed of Zarathustra. In ancient Greece the harvest god Dionysus, son of the human Semele and divine Zeus, is ritually sacrificed, eaten, and reborn as an infant. Although the god was originally represented by a man, a goat was later substituted for the sacrifice.

According to the Christian writer Epiphanius, as late as the fourth century CE in Egyptian Alexandria celebrants kept an all-night vigil on the eve of January 6, followed by chanting and a procession with a gold-star-marked image. At this feast of the goddess Kore they proclaimed, "Today the Maiden . . . gave birth to the Aeon!" This Greek term for "vital force" or "life" has aptly come to mean "an age, an eternity." The annual birth of the sun god/year god exemplifies the "myth of the eternal return," early peoples' belief in the cyclical nature of the world.

For those so miraculously conceived, it is not surprising that even the midwife would be divine. Lucina, the Sabine goddess of light, was combined with the Roman Juno, and as Juno Lucina, goddess of childbirth, she brought children into the world. In his "Fourth Eclogue," Virgil prays for Emperor Augustus, believed to be Apollo's son: "O chaste Lucina, smile favorably, for your own Apollo is now king." The Church's assignation of December 13 as the feast of its Saint Lucy bears inadvertent homage to this pagan midwife of the wondrous sun-child born at Yule. In a Swedish ritual on Saint Lucia's Day, the oldest daughter in the family wears a white gown and a crown of lighted candles, symbolizing the returning sun.

The deities honored at Winter Solstice were associated not only with the returning sunlight but also with the plentiful harvest that it would eventually bring. In ancient Rome, the Saturnalia began as a celebration of the feasts of the divine couple Saturn, god of agriculture, on December 17, and Ops, goddess of plenty, on December 19. Eventually the festival was extended from December 17 to December 24. It was a time to honor the gods and implore their protection of winter crops, a time to celebrate the New Year (though the very early Romans marked the New Year at the Spring Equinox).

At the time of Winter Solstice, the births of so many gods and heroes were celebrated—including Apollo, Attis, Baal, Dionysus, Helios, Hercules, Perseus, Theseus, and Mithra—that in the third century, Emperor Aurelian established a single festival for all of them on December 25 and called it the Birthday of the Unconquered Sun (*Sol Invictus*). The cult of the sun god Mithra, whose birth was attended by adoring shepherds, originated in Persia but spread rapidly in the Roman Empire and was a fierce rival of the burgeoning Christianity. In 274 CE, Mithraism was declared the official religion of the Empire, but by the fourth century, with the conversion of Constantine, Christianity had won out.

Christ mass, the Christians' celebration of the birth of their god of light, has an ambiguous history. Biblical scholars agree that the birth date of Jesus of Nazareth is unknown and further admit that, if its connection to census-taking is to be believed, a winter date is unlikely since spring (after the birth of new animals) or fall (after the harvest) is a more plausible time for taking the census and collecting taxes. On the other hand, Ronald Hutton, in *The Stations of the Sun: A History of the Ritual Year in Britain*, contends that the Roman census reported in Luke's gospel is "historically implausible," but believes that the stories of Christ's nativity make sense on a mythological level

> as archetypal representations of the birth of a hero, at the junction of many worlds: engendered partly human and partly divine, coming into life at a place neither a house nor the open air, belonging partly to humans and partly to animals, and in a strange land, and adored by people living upon the margins of society.

Many communities in the early Church celebrated Christ's birth on January 6, the same date the pagans celebrated Aeon's birth and a date still honored in the Greek Orthodox Church. But there was not universal agreement. In an attempt to substitute a Christian celebration for a pagan one, in the fourth century Pope Julius I designated December 25 as Christmas, a date that coincided with the Festival of the Unconquered Sun.

Although it took time for this celebration to become universal, by 1100 Christmas was the major festival of all Europe. However, the festivities were so merry and the symbols and practices in use so reminiscent of Saturnalia that sixteenth-century reformers forbade some of the more colorful revelries such as plays, processions, and dancing. In England, the celebration of Christmas was forbidden by an act of Parliament in 1644 and the day was designated as a fast day. Businesses were required to remain open. Plum puddings were denounced as pagan. With the restoration of Charles II to the throne, many of the Christmas customs were revived, but conservatives persisted in referring to Yuletide as "Fooltide."

Across the Atlantic, Christmas was officially banned in Boston for some twenty years during the seventeenth century. The Puritan rector of Harvard College, Increase Mather, condemned it as a heathen celebration, an excuse for "excess of wine [and] mad mirth." Even today, a number of evangelical Christian sects refuse to celebrate Christmas because of its pagan origins. Nevertheless the vast majority of Christians commemorate Christ's birth on December 25 and have no objection to symbols and practices whose use by pre-Christian and non-Christian peoples is seen as confirming their universality and thus enhancing their value.

The universality of the Winter Solstice is reflected in celebrations of the event around the world and throughout human history. The Celts celebrated the birth of their sun god Bel with games and revelries. In China during the Shang dynasty (1500–1100 BCE), according to Heinberg, the emperor "symbolically renewed the world order" at the solstices. For three days prior to the Winter

Solstice, he underwent ritual purification by abstaining from certain foods, sexual activity, and even music. Just before Solstice dawn, the emperor processed to the Round Mound in Beijing's Temple of Heaven, accompanied by royalty, officials, musicians, and dancers. There he knelt in the center of a series of concentric stone circles (the center of the universe) and prayed facing north. Then he lit a fire, read an account of the previous year, and "made ceremonial sacrifices to heaven . . . of incense, jade, and silk," as well as "a portion of . . . human flesh from a sacrificial victim."

Among the ancient Incas, the emperor played a key role in the Winter Solstice ritual. The Incas enacted the drama of their sun god Inti at the festival of Inti Raymi. E. C. Krupp, in *Echoes of Ancient Skies*, describes the first part of this day's ritual. Before sunrise on Winter Solstice (June), the emperor and other high-ranking leaders went to a ceremonial plaza in Cuzco, where they removed their shoes out of respect for the sun. When the sun appeared, they crouched "and blew respectful kisses to the glowing golden disk." The emperor then lifted two golden cups of a sacred drink brewed from fermented corn. One was offered to the sun (poured into a basin and then onto the ground), and the other was shared with the participants.

Not all New Year rituals take place at Winter Solstice. Some ancient civilizations, including the Mesopotamians, Sumerians, Babylonians, and oldest Romans, celebrated the New Year at Spring Equinox. In *Cosmos and History*, Mircea Eliade describes the four-thousand-year-old ceremonial for the Babylonian New Year, celebrated at the Equinox. In this twelve-day event, the king, representing the deity, restored the world order. But first there had to be a regression to the chaos that preceded creation: The social order was overturned, a mock king was crowned, and the real king dethroned. This prepared the way for "a new and regenerated human species." Then the creation story was read and the victory of the god Marduk over the forces of chaos enacted. After the community fasted and the king endured a ritual humiliation, the "festival of fates" was celebrated: Omens for each of the twelve coming months were decided (the equivalent of creating the coming year). Then the king, restored to his rightful position and signaling the return of order—or rather, the regeneration of a new order—engaged in a ritual mating with a slave or prostitute in the service of the temple. This represented the sacred marriage of Marduk and his consort Sarpanitu and was believed to ensure the fertility of the land. For Eliade, the Babylonian New Year ritual is an example of

> an attempt to restore—if only momentarily—mythical and primordial time, "pure" time, the time of the "instant" of Creation. Every New Year is a resumption of time from the beginning, that is, a repetition of the cosmogony. . . . At the end of the year and in the expectation of the New Year there is a repetition of the mythical moment of the passage from chaos to cosmos.

A recurring theme common to these ancient New Year rituals is renewal of the earth and its people, brought about through the formal acknowledgment of the passing of the old order and the establishment of the new order.

Contemporary Celebrations Around the World

In many Winter Solstice rituals this renewal is accomplished through purification—by fire, water, or noise. Contemporary celebrations, while diverse in their particulars, reveal a common enthusiasm for welcoming the return of the light. Lighting bonfires to help assure the victory of light over darkness, Iranians celebrate *Shabe-Yalda*, the birthday of the sun, which had its origins in Zoroastrianism, the state religion that preceded Islam. The Kalash people of Pakistan also light bonfires and conduct ritual purifications at their feast of *Chaomas* to honor the god Dezao. The Tibetan Feast of *Dosmoche*, which celebrates the dying year, features an elaborately decorated magical pole, which is torn down at the end of the five-day festival. The Chinese feast of *Dong Zhi* marks the turning point from the darkness and cold of yin to the light and warmth of yang—a time for "doing the winter" (*Ju*

Dong) by being optimistic, wearing new clothes, giving gifts, and eating extravagant meat dishes. At their New Year festival *Shogatsu*, the Japanese decorate the entrances to their homes to welcome the year-god Toshigami-sama. In shrines and temples, big bells are rung to drive away evil thoughts. Through o-harai, the Shinto Great Purification rite performed on December 31, believers are cleansed of all pollution and prepared for relationships with their *kami*, or divine spirits.

In *Book of the Hopi*, Frank Waters describes a Hopi Winter Solstice ritual, Soyal, which begins with the blessing and purification of sacred water, corn, and altars and proceeds with recitations and dances. The Hawk Maiden, symbolic mother of the people, offers seeds symbolizing the yet-to-be-born and a dancer impersonating Mui'ingwa, the god of germination, spins the sun shield in a gesture intended to reverse the sun's movement in the sky and thus begin a new year.

Although Hindus use a lunar calendar, many Indians celebrate the solstices. A popular custom in northern India is the ceremonial clanging of bells to drive out evil spirits. On *Makara Sankramana*, Hindus welcome the returning sun and see it as the opportunity to replace the darkness of falsehood with the illumination of wisdom and the coldness of human selfishness with the warmth of generosity. Wiccans, following in the traditions of the ancient Celts, celebrate Winter Solstice as one of their eight major *sabbats*, or seasonal feasts.

Jews around the world observe the Festival of Lights, *Hanukkah*, which celebrates the cause of religious freedom championed by the Maccabees, who recaptured Jerusalem in 166 BCE and rededicated the temple that had been taken over by Hellenistic pagans. Commemorating a miraculous sustaining of light from lamps whose oil never ran out, *Hanukkah* is a moveable feast determined by both lunar and solar events. It begins on the twenty-fifth day of the Hebrew month of Kislev, three days before the new moon closest to the Winter Solstice, thus occurring at the darkest time of the year. Arthur Waskow suggests in *Seasons of Our Joy* that in choosing this time, the Jews were capturing a pagan solstice festival that had won wide support among partially Hellenized Jews, in order to make it a day of God's victory over paganism. Even the lighting of candles for *Hanukkah* fits the context of the surrounding torchlight honors for the sun.

Extended Feasts

A Midrashic tradition suggests an even older origin of Winter Solstice feasting: When Adam experiences the first darkening of the earth as the days grow shorter and shorter, he fears that he has done something wrong and will soon be without light altogether as a result. So he prays and fasts for eight days. But when the sun starts to return and the days lengthen, he understands that this is the way of nature. He celebrates his relief by feasting for eight days.

So it seems that from Adam on, humans had the sense to know that one day is not enough time to celebrate a major feast. Thus we have the eight days of Saturnalia, the eight days of Hanukkah, the twelve days of Christmas, etc.

During Saturnalia the army rested, commerce and schooling were suspended, criminal executions were stayed. It was a time to make merry and enjoy the company of family and friends. People decorated their homes with greenery, kept lamps burning against the evil spirits of darkness, visited neighbors with gifts to celebrate the New Year. Some donned masks and hats and danced through the streets, a tradition we still know as mumming. Slaves were allowed to speak freely and were served by their masters at table. Goodwill prevailed. Work is limited during Hanukkah as well; it is forbidden during the time the candles are burning on each of the eight nights.

Waverly Fitzgerald identifies several such extended commemorations on her "School of the Seasons" website: Babylonians viewed the twelve days between the Winter Solstice and the New Year as the time of struggle between chaos and order. Like the Romans, the Hindus, Chinese, and Celts all saw this period as a time for reversing the order of things and relaxing social rules, a practice that ultimately had the effect of strengthening the established order. In medieval England, all work was suspended during the twelve days of Christmas. The ancient Greeks attributed the halcyon days—the two weeks of fine weather that bracket the Winter Solstice—to the magical powers of the kingfisher, who calms the sea so she can hatch her young.

Clearly this is a time for giving birth—to offspring, to ideas, to resolutions. It is a magical time, a "time out" when normal activities and rules are suspended, a time for turning away from the hubbub of daily life, a time for reassessing our goals and values, a time for determining how our lives might be better and how we might help to make the lives of others better. Our own tradition of New Year's resolutions reveals the hope we harbor for the possibility of new life—a new way of living that is healthier, more meaningful, more creative, and more generous.

Children

It is not surprising that the birthday of the sun god, the divine child, has also been a day to honor human children. One such honor is reflected in the practice in twelfth-to-sixteenth-century England of selecting a choirboy to play the role of bishop. According to Hutton, on the Feast of St. Nicholas (December 6) or the Feast of the Holy Innocents (December 28), in parishes all over the country, these boy bishops, attired in Episcopal robes and miters, would lead the procession—blessing spectators and collecting contributions for the churches—and then conduct the services, except for the Mass. This role reversal of adults and children provided a much more controllable rite of reversal than some others related to social or economic class. In addition, it reflected the spirit of Christmas, with its celebration of the birth of a divine child and the biblical emphasis on the innocence of children.

Another way of honoring children was to shower them with gifts and sweet treats, special pleasures, and entertainments. On the day after Saturnalia, the Romans celebrated Juvenalia, the day on which they feasted their children and gave them good luck charms. Buddhists celebrate Children's Day at this darkest time of the year, understanding that, like the newborn sun, the children of a community represent the promise of a brighter future. In the Christian tradition, offering gifts to children may have been inspired by the biblical account of the three wise men's gifts of gold, frankincense, and myrrh to the infant Jesus.

The tradition of the gift-bearing Santa Claus has a long history. In "Celebrating Winter Solstice," Selena Fox reminds us that he is a folk figure with multicultural roots:

> He embodies characteristics of Saturn . . . , Cronos (Greek god, also known as Father Time), the Holly King (Celtic god of the dying year), Father Ice/Grandfather Frost (Russian winter god), Thor (Norse sky god who rides . . . a chariot drawn by goats), Odin/Wotan (Scandinavian/Teutonic All-Father who rides the sky on an eight-legged horse), Frey (Norse fertility god), and the Tomte (a Norse Land Spirit known for giving gifts to children at this time of year).

The Pennsylvania Dutch call him Belsnikle, a clear linguistic link to the Celtic sun god Bel. Santa's eight reindeer, with their many-branched antlers are a reminder of Herne, the Celtic Horned God. Given the prehistoric cave drawings in Lascaux, France, the Horned God may well be the oldest male deity in Western history—the one whose impregnation of the earth mother assures the rebirth of spring. Santa's sleigh may be a descendant of the solar chariot or boat in which the dying sun god makes his exit. It is no coincidence that Santa lives in the North Pole. The north is traditionally the land of the dead, the home of the spirits taken there by the god of the dying year.

Pauline Campanelli, author of *Wheel of the Year*, likens Santa's method of entering and leaving a house to that of "faeries who entered and left their mounds via the smoke-hole," or "the witch who ascended her chimney on her broomstick," or "the universal shaman who flew in spirit through the smoke-hole of his tent."

The name Santa Claus is believed to be a corruption of Saint Nicholas, whose legendary life and deeds, as Fitzgerald reminds us, made him the patron of marriageable girls, pawnbrokers, bankers, children, butchers, vat-makers, thieves, sailors, bakers, and two countries (Russia and Greece). It is puzzling how this fourth-century bishop of Myra in Asia Minor was transformed into the rotund hero of our childhoods.

In many European countries, Saint Nicholas is credited with distributing gifts of nuts and sweets to good children and sometimes taunting naughty children with a switch. But this Saint Nick, according to Campanelli, is seldom depicted in the traditional clothing of a bishop:

> In Russia, Santa Claus wears a coat of dark fur; in France, as Pierre Noel, his coat is white; and as Father Christmas in England, it is red. In Germany he is called Weinachtsmann and his coat is sometimes patched. Our own American version of the jolly fat man in the red suit was created by Thomas Nast, a cartoonist born in 1840.

In all his manifestations, Saint Nicholas is always pictured as an old man with a long white beard symbolizing wisdom and old age. It is also possible that "Saint Nick" is a variation of "Old Nick," another name for Woton, the Anglo-Saxon god who shares features of the Celtic Holly King.

Although the particulars vary, one thing remains constant in this history of seasonal gifting, the importance of the old blessing the young. The dying year leaves treats to sweeten the New Year. But the greatest gift—symbolized in the children themselves—is hope.

Yule Customs

Another name for the Winter Solstice festival is Yule, though there is some controversy about the etymology of the term. A common belief is that *Yule* derives from the Norse *iul* or the Anglo-Saxon *hweol*, both meaning "wheel," as in "wheel of the year," which is the sun. Another theory is that *Yule* comes from the Scandinavian *Jul*, a midwinter feast honoring Odin, whose nickname was Jolin (pronounced "yolin"). But according to *The American Heritage Dictionary*, *yule* (or *yole*) is a Middle English word derived from the Old English *geol* or *geohhol*, a twelve-day pagan winter festival.

The customs of this season revolve around producing and celebrating light and heat, the elements that we miss most in midwinter. One of the oldest customs—possibly dating back to the Roman Saturnalia or beyond—is burning the Yule log. A large log is often chosen earlier in the year—of long-burning wood if available, for it is believed the celebration will last as long as the Yule log burns. In some places, the log is brought into the home at dusk on Solstice Eve, carved with sun symbols, decorated with holly and ivy, and placed in the hearth with ceremony, where it is ritually lit with a splinter of the preceding year's Yule log, which has been kept for this purpose. The symbolism is rich; the blazing log may be seen as the sun god within the fiery womb of the mother goddess. And the ritual works its sympathetic magic: All gather and gaze, visualizing the return of the sun and warmer days, for the Yule log is the counterpart of the bonfires lit at Summer Solstice. The ashes are believed to bring good luck and are sprinkled on the crops as fertilizer and even scattered about the house for protection. And a piece of the unburned log is kept to light the next year's log, providing a sense of continuity. This practice was eulogized by seventeenth-century English poet and clergyman Robert Herrick:

> Come bring with a noise,
> My merry, merry boys,
> The Christmas Log to the firing:
> While my good Dame she
> Bids ye all be free,
> And drink to your heart's desiring.
> With the last year's Brand
> Light the new Block and,
> For good success in his spending,

On your psaltries play,
That sweet luck may
Come while the Log is tending.

More common even than the Yule log as a symbol of this season is the evergreen, the tree that remains vigorously verdant despite cold and darkness, the tree that does not lose its leaves and thus seems to be immortal. Many ancient cultures—including the Egyptians, Chinese, and Hebrews—had sacred trees that symbolized eternal life. Campanelli tells us,

> In ancient Greece, the fir was sacred to Artemis, the Moon Goddess who presided over childbirth. The Gaelic word for fir also applies to the palm, the birth tree of Egypt and Babylonia. To the ancient Celts, certain sacred trees were called "Bele-Trees" or "Billy-Glas," meaning evergreen or immortal trees, and they are probably associated with Bel, the Sun God reborn at Winter Solstice.

The Romans had pine groves attached to their temples. On the eve of a holy festival, a priest would harvest one of the sacred pines, decorate it, and bring it to the temple for ceremonial use. In pagan Europe, tree worship was common, and even after the coming of Christianity, survived there in the Scandinavian practice of putting up a tree for the birds during Christmas time and in using evergreens to decorate the barn and house at the New Year in hope of warding off the devil. Germans set a Yule tree inside the house or at its entrance. Eventually decorations were added and most choices for these were fruits, nuts, and flowers—things people hoped would be plentiful in the New Year with the sun's return.

Like the evergreen tree, other persistently green plants are associated with the season. Holly and ivy are traditional favorites in Europe. Winter Solstice is a time of cosmic reversal, sometimes imagined by early peoples as a struggle between two opposing forces, the waning sun and the waxing sun. The victory of the latter over the former is celebrated in story and symbol. In Norse mythology, Frey is the sun god born at Winter Solstice; his rival is Njord, who rules the other half of the year. In some Celtic traditions, the Holly King represents the dark and dying year, while the Oak King represents light and rebirth.

In a mysterious fifteenth-century poem cited by Hutton, the ivy contends with the holly for a position of honor in the hall. The holly wins out and the ivy is relegated to decorating the outside porch. Another carol, "Holvyr and Heyvy," reflects the belief that "holly represented the male and ivy the female." Yet another (still popular) medieval carol, "The Holly and the Ivy," whose refrain celebrates "the rising of the sun," concludes the rivalry between the two with "the holly bears the crown." Perhaps not coincidentally, the Chinese celebrate the rebirth of *yang*, the masculine principle of nature corresponding to light, fire, life, and movement, at Winter Solstice, and that of *yin*, the feminine principle corresponding to darkness, water, death, and stillness, at Summer Solstice.

Barbara Walker suggests another symbolism for holly in *Women's Rituals*:

> It was originally named for the dark underground Crone-goddess Holle, or Hel, from whose womb the sun arose. The red berries of the holly symbolized the Goddess's holy blood, shaper of all life. . . . The evergreen leaves of the holly represented ongoing life, retaining vitality through the winter, with an implied promise of immortality.

Making seasonal wreaths of evergreens, holly, and ivy, symbolizing the wheel of the year, is an ancient tradition. Mary Harrington reports in an *Audubon Newsletter* article that the original Norse/Germanic Yule wreath "was made of iron and decorated in evergreens with a candle placed in the center to represent the returning sun." Gertrud Mueller Nelson, author of *To Dance with God*, describes how people in the North left their fields for the winter, put away their tools, removed the wheels from their carts, decorated them with greens, and hung them in their halls as a reminder that it was time to withdraw from the demands of everyday life and turn inward. She sees this as the possible origin of the Christian Advent wreath, a circle of greenery with four candles, one lit on each of the four Sundays that precede Christmas.

Another plant associated with the Winter Solstice is mistletoe, which Pliny reports was sacred to the Druids when it grew mysteriously on their sacred tree, the oak. They supposedly cut it off with a golden sickle and dropped it onto a white cloth spread out below, assuring that it would not touch the ground and lose its special healing and protective powers. Harrington tells us that the Norse believed that enemies who met under mistletoe would throw down their weapons and kiss as a sign of peace. People would hang it on the doorways of neighbors to indicate grievances were forgiven. Mistletoe was considered an effective medicine for treating delirium, epilepsy, and heart disorders. Some sources add infertility, claiming its white berries are a symbol of semen. Because it produces berries in winter, like holly, when other plants seem barren, it is a sign of hope. Its berries are favored by a number of birds, including the robin, although they are poisonous to humans.

While Yule fires and decorated trees may help to entice the new sun out of hiding, the myths and traditions suggest that the coaxing is not complete without music and dancing, singing and poetry, laughter and feasting. Together with dressing up, visiting friends, giving gifts, and putting on plays, these are the very things that lift our own spirits as well, making the long, cold winter nights bearable and reminding us of the pleasures of life and the joy in loved ones. The Roman Saturn (Greek Cronos, Father Time) was, as our term *saturnine* suggests, a gloomy, taciturn deity, one not above eating his rival children. The only way to drive him out and welcome the New Year was to dispel the forces of gloom with revels.

As befits a time of reveling, many traditions involving food and drink are associated with Winter Solstice. One of the best known, from southern England, is *wassailing*. The term comes from the Middle English *waeshaeil* (Old Norse *vesheill*), meaning "to be in good health." It is applied to both the toast itself ("Be hale!" or "To your good health!") and to the drink used in the toast, which was commonly wine mulled with spices, roasted apples, and sugar.

A variation of wassailing is categorized by Hutton as a type of "saining" ritual, one "intended to safeguard people and property against the powers loose in that time of darkness and also during the coming year." Possibly descended from pre-Christian practices, this involved a group of young men going into the orchard with a bowl of wassail and blessing the fruit trees (or the best one as representative of all) by rapping them with sticks, sprinkling them with the cider, dipping bread in the cider and placing it in the branches, and/or saying or singing an invocation that generally included some variation on this eighteenth-century one:

> Here's to thee, old apple tree,
> Whence thou mayst bud
> And whence thou mayst blow!
> And whence thou mayst bear apples enow!

After this they would let out a great howl or shout (accompanied in some places by the firing of guns) and enjoy the wassail themselves.

A wassailing custom described by Hutton provided a similar rite for livestock. A group of men and women would take a bowl of wassail decorated with greenery into the stall of the best ox and pass it around. Sometimes a cake or a basket containing one was put on the animal's horns as he was toasted with a rhyme like this one from Herefordshire:

> Here's to thy pretty face, and to thy white horn,
> God send thy master a good crop of corn,
> Both wheat, rye and barley, of grains of all sort,
> And next year, if we live, we'll drink to thee again.

In yet another variation of wassailing, "poor people seeking hospitality" carried a decorated wassail bowl, symbol of peace and communality, from house to house, sometimes singing carols. In return for the drink and entertainment, they received a substantial meal of "white bread, cheese, and minced pies."

Every culture that celebrates Winter Solstice has its own traditional foods for the occasion. Not surprisingly many are fruits and sweets. Fruits are both a special luxury in the winter and a reminder of the plentiful harvest it is hoped the sun's return will bring. The Japanese eat sun-colored *umeboshi* (pickled sour plums) at New Year's to ensure good health. In the West, fresh oranges, another sun symbol, are a popular treat, often found in the toes of children's holiday stockings. Although the Chinese celebrate the New Year at their spring festival rather than at the Solstice, it too features oranges as the traditional gift of those visiting the homes of friends and family.

The custom of making and giving sweets is an ancient one. The Romans gave their friends jars of honeyed dates and figs to bring sweetness in the New Year. For the same reason, we give fruitcakes soaked in rum or sugar cookies shaped like the sun or like an evergreen tree or Santa. When we set fire to the brandy atop our plum pudding, we are mimicking the sun's rebirth. The French, with their celebrated talent for pastries, prepare a Yule log treat—a cake roll covered in chocolate icing and decorated with sugar holly leaves. Without electric light or central heating, our ancestors relied for warmth on the hearth at this darkest, coldest time of the year and on the cheer provided by festive food and drink. We may be more comfortable than they, but we are still susceptible to depression caused by darkness (seasonal affect disorder) and know the value of raising the blood sugar level!

One way to celebrate the Solstice and to drive off dreariness and depression is music. Playing or singing favorite carols together can salute the sun, lift the spirits, and provide warmth and camaraderie. We have a wealth of songs to choose from. Many in our tradition were written as Christmas carols and are sung to celebrate the birth of Christ. With adjusted lyrics—such as those appearing in the ritual at the end of this chapter—they can also be sung to celebrate the sun's return.

For many today, Winter Solstice marks not only the return of the sun but the return of family members from homes or schools in other parts of the country or world to celebrate with loved ones and welcome the New Year together. At such a time, family and community rituals are important, as are personal rituals of renewal. Following are some suggestions for rituals that can be performed alone or with family or friends.

WAYS TO CELEBRATE

Honor the balance between dark and light.

☽ On Solstice Eve, value the dark. On this longest night of the year, before the light overcomes the dark, sit in the dark (alone or with others) and think about the importance of darkness. Bless mushrooms that grow in the dark and honeysuckle that sends its luscious scents into the night. Be grateful for the darkness that soothes us to sleep, the darkness that animals require for hibernation. Give thanks for sheltering dark places: the rich earth where seeds germinate, the caves that harbored our ancient ancestors (and where some of our sun gods were born), the cellars that keep us safe from tornadoes, the wombs that provide our first nourishment. Acknowledge the darkness of suffering, which can deepen our appreciation of life and strengthen our connection to one another.

☽ Be mindful of the light. In the period between Summer and Winter Solstice, track the sun. Notice its rising or setting point in the sky each day. On Winter Solstice it will be the farthest south. Or pick a place in your home (a stretch of carpet, the kitchen table, your desk) and notice the time of day when the sun moves across it. If you have a solar-sensitive outdoor light, note the time when it goes on each evening; all other things (clouds, fog) being equal, it will turn on earliest at Winter Solstice.

☽ Dance with your shadow to acknowledge your dark side. The Balinese celebrate the New Year at Spring Equinox. On its eve, they conduct rituals of purification: washing of sacred icons, exorcising of demons with chanting or banging of gongs, carnival processions with effigies of evil spirits that are then burned—all in the interest of ridding their lives of negative energy. But on the day itself, on Nyepi, all is quiet. No one leaves the house; there is no fire, no electricity, no love-making, no work. The Balinese believe this most important of their Hindu feasts should be a day of introspection and reflection. Give some quiet thought to the transition from the old year to the new.

Say goodbye to the old year and welcome the new.

⑥ Let go of things that are hurtful. Acknowledging them in the presence of others can sometimes be a kind of exorcism. Or write them on a piece of paper, fold it up, and burn it in the hearth (or in a metal bowl if you have no hearth). Make peace with the people who have disappointed you or whom you have disappointed. Forgive. Ask forgiveness.

⑥ On Solstice Eve, carve sun images on a Yule log and burn it in the hearth. If you don't have a fireplace, flatten the log slightly on one side so that it won't roll, drill four holes in it for the four seasons (or eight for the eight days of Saturnalia, twelve for the twelve days of Christmas, or thirteen for the thirteen lunar months of the year), and put red candles in the holes. Weave greens around the bottoms of the candles. Put the log in a place of honor, gather family or friends around, and light the candles. Perhaps a different person could light each one and identify a hope she or he has for the coming year. As the candles burn, talk with one another about your hopes for the coming year and about the ways you can bring more light into the world.

Decorate your home for Solstice.

⑥ When you bring greenery into the house, hang some around the mirrors, calling attention to them. As you pass each mirror during the days of Yuletide, look at your image and remember the story of Amaterasu, the Japanese sun goddess who, enchanted with her beautiful image, came out of hiding to greet it. Bring your best self out of hiding.

☺ Using pastel crayons or paints or snippets of colorful pictures from magazines, create a mandala representing the sun and all the things we enjoy because of it. Or simply celebrate spheres by making a painting or collage of all things round—balls, oranges, grapes, plums, soy nuts, peas, tomatoes, garbanzo beans, eyes, globes, stones, rolling hills, young girls' breasts, pregnant women's stomachs, protons, bubbles, marbles, onions, pearls, milk duds, castors, jawbreakers, doughnut holes, dandelions, poppy seeds, etc. Or make a large mobile of the sun and hang it from the ceiling.

☺ Decorate an evergreen tree. Drink mulled cider and listen to seasonal music while decorating the tree. So much the better if there is a family member who plays the piano or another instrument. String cranberries and popcorn—in hope for a good harvest for the coming year—and drape them on the tree. Make a sun symbol for the top of the tree. Use colored paper, felt, pipe cleaners, balsa wood, or wire to make images of birds or fruits or musical instruments to decorate the tree—symbols of things that will beckon the sun. As you hang ornaments from years past that have special meaning, remember aloud the person or event the ornament brings to mind.

Appreciate nature's winter offerings.

☺ Greet the solstice sunrise. Sing a song such as "Morning Has Broken," "Here Comes the Sun," "You Are My Sunshine," or simply, "Happy Birthday." Offer a yoga salute-to-the-sun.

☺ Meet with friends on a mountaintop to dance the sun up and welcome it out of hiding with poetry, song, and hot drinks. Or do it in your backyard.

☺ Take a walk in the woods at midday. Notice how different the trees and the paths are in winter. Acknowledge the slumbering life around you.

Celebrate the season dramatically.

֍ Enact the story of one of the sun deities, such as Amaterasu hiding and being cajoled from her cave with dancing, or angels urging the shepherds to find the newborn Jesus, or the battle of the Oak King and the Holly King.

֍ Honor all the newborns in your family or neighborhood. Gather all the children, pets, plants, and representations of projects (manuscripts, videos, blueprints, songs, recipes, designs, reports, photos, etc.) that have been born or made during the year. Acknowledge them as a blessing. Celebrate them with sweet treats, singing, and dancing.

Give gifts to celebrate the sun's return and the New Year.

֍ Make inexpensive gifts for family members and friends such as their favorite foods or holiday treats, simple articles or tree ornaments made from found objects or scraps of wood or fabric, or coupons for your time and energy to wash the car, mend clothing, play your musical instrument, run errands, fix dinner or clean up when it isn't your turn, design a website, mow the lawn, plant/weed/mulch the garden, clear the gutters and spouts, paint, polish, repair, clean, decorate, do laundry, do income taxes, give massages, or write or address cards for elders. Give whatever talents or abilities you have that others could use or enjoy.

֍ Make corsages of holly sprigs and red ribbons to give to family members or guests.

֍ Make a house for the birds in your neighborhood. Or make a birdfeeder with pine cones, peanut butter, and birdseed. Or put up a commercial feeder and keep it filled with seeds through the winter.

꙰ Give gifts to the poor in your area and around the world. Donate clothing and bedding to shelters. Volunteer to cook or serve food in a soup kitchen. Volunteer your building, decorating, or cleaning skills for those who need housing through Habitat for Humanity or a similar organization. For holiday gifts to friends and relatives, contribute in their name to organizations that help the poor; for example, buy a farm animal for a family in Cambodia through Heifer International.

Enjoy a seasonal feast.

꙰ Welcome family and friends to your home. Invite your friends for a potluck dinner, encouraging all to bring dishes that feature winter vegetables or suggest the sun in shape or color: squash casserole, quiche, soufflé, rolls or a round loaf of bread, citrus salad topped with sunflower seeds, pumpkin pie, etc. Decorate the table with large red candles circled with greens.

꙰ Prepare a bowl of wassail. Try this recipe from Cait Johnson's *Witch in the Kitchen* for "a large gathering of moderate drinkers, or a small one of serious revelers."

WASSAIL

In a large soup pot, gently heat the following ingredients:

1 gallon (or more) apple cider
1 large cinnamon stick, broken into pieces
13 allspice berries (one for each full moon of the year)
1 apple, sliced crosswise to reveal a pentacle within each slice
1 small whole orange, organic if possible, studded with
8 whole cloves (one for each festival of the year)

Then add: Irish whiskey, other whiskeys, or even burgundy or claret if you wish and maple syrup or brown sugar to taste. Start by adding a cup or so of alcohol to your wassail and taste to determine the potency you're after, adding more and tasting until you get it right or you're beyond worrying about it. Do not allow wassail to boil unless you want to lose the alcohol. Serve steaming hot in mugs. Cut a lemon or orange crosswise (revealing "rays" emanating from the center) and float the slices in the wassail. Or float one grapefruit slice to represent the sun and create the rest of the solar system by cutting other fruit (oranges, apples, pears, berries) into round slices of varying size to represent the planets.

⚉ Host a ritual in your home that includes any of the following: recognizing the occasion with a short explanation of Winter Solstice; a quiet time for acknowledging the blessings and disappointments of the old year and expressing hopes for the New Year; lighting the Yule log or Yule wreath; sharing seasonal poems or readings, which can be provided by hosts or brought by guests; singing carols; lighting (or decorating) the evergreen tree; and ritual sharing of seasonal food and drink.

WELCOME THE RETURNING SUN

A WINTER SOLSTICE RITUAL

Prior to the ritual, an evergreen tree is set up and strung with lights. The gathering place is darkened. During instrumental music, the following participants slowly enter in this order and take their places: Candlebearer, with large, lighted candle; Turners 1 and 2; Lighter; Readers 1-7; Leader; Narrator. All but the last two will also act as Servers where indicated.

Narrator　Welcome to our celebration of Winter Solstice. The choir will sing the first hymn through and then please join us in singing the song again.

　　　　　The choir sings the following words to the melody of "Greensleeves." Then All repeat.

Choir   What night is this, so long and dark,
          on which we feel such a yearning—
          as earth is sleeping, her seedlings keeping,
          while toward the sun she's turning?
          This, this is Solstice night
          when dark surrenders to the light.
          Hope! Hope for all who live.
          This night the sun is born anew.

Acknowledging the Seasonal Change

Narrator Please be seated. In the beginning was the light of the
          sun, which gives life to all that grows, plants and ani-
          mals and humans alike. And the people saw that in the
          cycle of the seasons, the days grew shorter and colder as
          the sun seemed to withdraw, and the days grew longer
          and warmer when the sun began its return. And the
          people celebrated the day that marked the beginning of
          that return. This day—December 21 [*or 22, if applica-
          ble*] in our calendar—is what we in the northern coun-
          tries call the Winter Solstice. It is a time for reflecting
          on the blessings and challenges of the old year, a time
          to prepare our minds and hearts for the New Year. It is
          a time to strive for peace.

Reader 1 If there is to be peace in the world,
          There must be peace in the nations.
          If there is to be peace in the nations,
          There must be peace in the cities.
          If there is to be peace in the cities,
          There must be peace between neighbors.
          If there is to be peace between neighbors,
          There must be peace in the home.
          If there is to be peace in the home,
          There must be peace in the heart.

                                                        —Lao-Tse

Leader (*pausing for a moment of silence after each statement*) Peace in the heart begins with letting go. As the old year departs, so do its sorrows. Let us silently, in our hearts, acknowledge and release those sorrows.

We forgive those who have hurt or disappointed us. May their offenses be gone with the old year.

We ask forgiveness of those we have hurt or disappointed. May we resolve to behave more kindly in the New Year.

Let us give thanks in our hearts for the blessings of the old year, especially for the people who have enriched our lives.

Meditation music

Extinguishing the Old Fire

Narrator The dwindling of the sun's light in autumn is a reminder that even as the old year dies, so must all living things. So must we. Many times. Like the serpent that sheds its skin, we shed our old selves that we may grow into new ones. The Winter Solstice marks the beginning of this new life—whose growth is symbolized in the waxing of the daylight. For this reason, the celebration in many ancient cultures included the ritual extinguishing of the old fire—symbolized here in this candle—and the rekindling of the new fire. All are invited to participate in this ritual by reading responsively.

Candlebearer comes forward with lit candle.

Leader As the old year passes,

Candlebearer blows out the candle that symbolizes the old fire, and puts candle out of sight after All respond.

All   May the hurtful be forgotten, the good remembered.

Lighting the New Fire and Turning the Wheel of the Year

A large cart wheel decorated with seasonal greens has been set flat on a table on a small lazy Susan. Four large candles are set in it, symbolizing the four seasons.

Narrator   The circle of the Yule wreath here symbolizes the wheel of the year, the complete cycle of the four seasons, represented by four candles. In some old agrarian cultures in the North, people left their fields for the winter and put away their farming tools. They took the wheels from their carts, decorated them with greenery, and hung them in their halls as a reminder that it was a time to withdraw from the demands of everyday life, a time to turn inward, to acknowledge the feelings of cold and loss, the feelings of fear and longing, to await, in a spirit of hope, the return of the sun, which itself was sometimes called the wheel of the year.

Our ancient ancestors believed they played an important role in turning the wheel of the year. They understood that their ritual celebrations helped the seasons to change, encouraged the sun on its journey. Some of them erected great monuments to mark that journey. If we enlightened moderns are too sophisticated for such beliefs, is it not our loss? The same science that has shattered these beliefs has made it possible for us to puncture the protective ozone layer, to pollute the air and water, to plunder the earth, to use the sun's energy for nuclear weapons. Is it not time to return to reverence for the earth, to play our part in caring for it, to engage in the changing of the seasons . . . to turn the wheel of the year?

Lighter and Turners cross to wheel. Lighter stands behind

the Yule wreath with a taper. Turners stand on either side of it.

Narrator   We invite you to join in turning the wheel, reading responsively.

Leader   As we kindle the new fire,

Lighter lights the first candle.

All   We have hope for many blessings in the New Year.

Turners turn the wheel clockwise one quarter.

Leader   We turn the wheel, disperse the gloom.

Lighter ignites second candle.

All   Call forth the sun from the rich earth's womb!

Turners turn the wheel one quarter.

Leader   We turn the wheel of death and birth.

Lighter ignites third candle.

All   We change the seasons of the earth!

Turners turn the wheel one quarter.

Leader   We turn the wheel to beckon the light.

Lighter ignites fourth candle.

All   We summon the sun from the womb of night!

Narrator   Please stand and light your own candle from the new fire as it comes to you. May the fire of longing in our hearts be a beacon to the fire of the sun, summoning its return.

Music plays as Servers light their candles from the new fire, then light candles of all participants. Narrator begins speaking when all candles are lit.

Narrator   As we share this light of the new fire, let us sing a wel-
              come to the returning sun.

              *All sing the following words to the melody of "O Come, O
              Come, Emmanuel." During the second verse, the electric
              lights gradually come up. At the end of the song, the
              Narrator extinguishes candle and all follow this lead.*

All sing   O come, O come, the hope of all who live,
              and to the earth your warmth and nurture give.
              All people wait and trust that this night
              will bring the fruits of our desire to light.
              Rejoice! Rejoice! The wheel is turning still,
              and soon our hearts with solstice light will thrill.

              O come, thou light which shines on everyone,
              who keeps your healing warmth away from none.
              Teach us, like you, to warm the earth
              and sing the praise of every creature's worth.
              Rejoice! Rejoice! We turn the wheel once more,
              and with the change of seasons, Earth restore.

Litany of Seasonal Blessings

Narrator   Please be seated. There is so much to be grateful for at
              this time of the year. Please join now in a litany of
              seasonal blessings. We invite you to respond with
              "Blessed be!"

Leader   For all people on whom the sun shines, whether
              women or men, poor or rich, old or young, wherever
              they live, whatever they believe, whomever they love,

All   Blessed be!

Leader   For the music of Yuletide and all those who compose
              and play it,

All   Blessed be!

Leader   For the songs of Yuletide and all those who write and sing them,

All   Blessed be!

Leader   For the feast day meal and all who prepare it and all who share it,

All   Blessed be!

Leader   For snow and ice and sledding and skiing and skating,

All   Blessed be!

Leader   For warming fires and warming homes, for Yule logs and candles and electricity,

All   Blessed be!

Leader   For evergreen trees and holly and ivy and mistletoe,

All   Blessed be!

Leader   For Santa Claus, Saint Nicholas, Belsnikle, Grandfather Frost, Pierre Noel, Father Christmas, and all the gifts they bring,

All   Blessed be!

Leader   For loving families and good friends,

All   Blessed be!

Leader   For infants and puppies and kittens and newborns of every species,

All   Blessed be!

Leader   For a peaceful world for them to grow up in,

All   Blessed be!

All sing "Dona Nobis Pacem."

For suggestions on a spontaneous litany rather than a

scripted one, see page xvii.

Celebrating the Solstice Tree

Narrator   Here in the heart of winter, when the daylight hours are shortest, we long for assurance that spring will return, that once again the warm sun will nurture growing things and make the earth green, giving us fruit and flowers. In this time when foliage has all but disappeared, we look to the trees whose evergreen boughs offer us the gift of hope.

Reader 2   For a tree there is hope, even if it be cut down, that it will sprout again, and that its tender shoots will not cease. Even though its roots grow old in the earth, and its stump die in the dust, yet at the first whiff of water, it may flourish again and put forth branches like a young plant.

                                                                    —Job 14:79

Narrator   As we listen to the next reading, let us look at and appreciate the beauty of our own evergreen tree.

Reader 3   May the blessing of light be on you (*tree lights go on*),
                   light without and light within.
             May the blessed sunshine shine on you and warm
                   your heart
             till it glows like a great peat fire, so that strangers may
                   come and
             warm themselves at it, and also friends.

                                                         —traditional Irish blessing

Narrator   Please stand for the singing of "O Solstice Tree."

             All sing the following words to the melody of "O Tannenbaum."

All sing   O Solstice Tree, O Tree of Life,
             your roots go deep down in the earth!

O Solstice Tree, O Tree of Life,
your branches reach to heaven!
Your boughs so green in summer time
stay bravely green in winter time.
O Solstice Tree, O Tree of Life,
you give us hope eternal.

O Solstice Tree, O Tree of Life,
how brightly shine your candles!
O Solstice Tree, O Tree of Life,
assuring our renewal!
They are the stars, the moon, the sun,
providing light for everyone.
O Solstice Tree, O Tree of Life,
how brightly shine your candles!

Honoring the Sun Deities

Narrator   Please be seated. The sacredness of this hour is celebrated in special places around the world. In Ireland, for example, the prehistoric Newgrange burial mound was constructed so that the light enters its inner chamber only at Winter Solstice dawn.

Leader   The Incas of Cuzco housed their brilliant solid gold sun disks in the innermost shrine of the Sun Temple, which was oriented toward the Winter Solstice sunrise.

Narrator   The Chumash [*SHOO-mash*] Indians, producers of magnificent rock art, created a series of complex shapes in Burro Flats, California. The shapes are always shaded by a rock canopy except on the morning of Winter Solstice, when a triangle of light illuminates them.

Leader   We honor our ancient ancestors, who celebrated the Solstice in structures and in stories as well, for the myths of many cultures provide explanations for this seasonal celebration. One such story is that of the Japanese sun goddess Amaterasu [*AH-mah-tay-RAH-soo*].

Dancers enact the following story as it is read. After the story, a traditional Japanese melody plays while dancers exit.

Reader 4   The shrine of Amaterasu Ōmikami, "Heaven Shining She," is the holiest Shinto shrine in all Japan. The sun goddess watches over the building of irrigation canals, guides the fields of growing rice, and presides over the great Weaving Hall of Heaven, where women weave the sacred tapestries. Her brother Susanowo is assigned dominion over the sea, but in spite of this honor, he is jealous of his sister's greater power, so he blocks the canals and stomps upon the rice plants until all lies in chaos. Then the angry Susanowo murders a piebald colt and heaves its body into the celestial weaving house, where it strikes the looms, which fall upon the women, sending several to the Land of the Dead.

At this, Amaterasu is filled with rage. But refusing to fight on such a demeaning level, she decides instead to withdraw her warmth and light. Thus she retires to the Cave of Heaven and pulls the great door tight behind her so that the world is in darkness, the people are frightened, and no rice can grow. The other deities decree that Susanowo must be banished from the heavens. But how to tempt Amaterasu from the cave?

Finally they conceive a plan. The playful goddess Ama No Uzume dances a wild dance before the entrance of the cave. She makes movements and faces that bring such laughter from the others that Amaterasu hears them inside. Curious, she opens the door a crack and peers out. The dance grows wilder. The laughter grows louder. Amaterasu grows more curious, until at last the golden sun goddess emerges to find out the cause of such merriment. At that moment she finds herself staring into the sacred golden mirror. Her brilliant image in the mirror is so intense that she takes a closer look. At this moment, Ama No Uzume quickly closes the door to the cave. Thus the sun goddess returns to the world—and with her the light that provides life for plants and animals and people. This story is told at every Winter Solstice as the days that have darkened earlier each night reverse into their mirror image and each succeeding day's light lasts moments longer.

—adapted from Merlin Stone

Narrator   On this night, virgin mothers of many times and cultures around the world have given birth to sun gods. In remembering them, we honor our ancestors who held this night sacred. As we call upon them now, we invite you to respond with "Praised be the light!"

Leader   In ancient Persia, Anahita, the "Immaculate One," mother goddess of waters, gave birth to the sun god Mithra.

All   Praised be the light!

Leader   In ancient Greece, Kore, the maiden goddess, gave birth to Aeon, the life force.

All   Praised be the light!

Leader   In ancient Rome, Juno Lucina, goddess of childbirth, brought children to light.

All   Praised be the light!

Leader   In medieval Mexico, the Aztec Coatlicue [coh-ah-TLEE-cooeh] gave birth to Huitzilopochtli [wee-tsee-loh-POCH-tlee], the high-flying sun.

All   Praised be the light!

Leader   In West Africa, Nana Buluku gave birth to the sun god Liza.

All   Praised be the light!

Leader   In Bethlehem, the Virgin Mary gave birth to Jesus, "the Light of the World."

All   Praised be the light!

Narrator   From the Winter Solstice on, the sun rises higher and higher in the sky. With this festival, we celebrate the regenerative cycle of the earth, the hibernation of the animals, the intense energy of the seeds as they germinate. It is a time for us to feel our inner power, to nurture our growing strength, to rejoice as our ancient forebears did in the waxing light. Please stand and sing with joy.

All sing the following words to the melody of "Joy to the World."

All sing   Joy to the world!
The sun returns.
Let all the earth rejoice.
Let every heart
bid welcome to the light.
And heaven and nature sing.
And heaven and nature sing.
And heaven, and earth, and nature sing!

Welcome the sun's
returning rays
to warm and light our days.
Let all who live
upon the earth
exult in joyful praise,
exult in joyful praise,
exult, give thanks, in joyful praise!

Celebrating the Taste of Life

During this last song, Servers come forward with trays of sun-shaped sugar cookies and small cups half-filled with spiced cider.

Narrator   Our ancestors around the world celebrated this joyful season with gifts of sweet treats to friends and neighbors. Let us celebrate our hope for good things in the New Year by reminding ourselves of how sweet life can be.

Leader   In medieval times, many communities followed the tradition of wassailing at Winter Solstice. In the hope of assuring a good harvest, the wassailers carried a bowl of spiced cider into the apple orchard. They selected a representative tree, sprinkled it with cider, and offered a blessing such as this one sung in the Cornworthy district of England:

Reader 5   So here my old fellow I drink to thee
and the very health of each other tree.
Well may ye blow, well may ye bear
blossom and fruit both apple and pear.
So that every bough and every twig
may bend with a burden both fair and big.
May ye bear us and yield us fruit such a store
that the bags and chambers and house run o'er.

Leader   That we too may be abundantly productive in the coming year, let us celebrate this Winter Solstice and our own rebirth by toasting one another with wassail.

Narrator   We invite you to come forward for a sweet cake and a cup of nonalcoholic wassail. Please return to your seat with them, and when all have been served, we'll toast one another and enjoy these treats together.

Choir sings the following words to the melody of "Morning Has Broken" and continues with other music as needed until all have been served and returned to their seats.

Choir   Darkness has vanished;
           morning is dawning.
           Black night is banished;
           sunlight appears.
           Welcome the new day;
           welcome the sunrise.
           Let the morn's new rays
           cast out all fears.

           Gone is the old year,
           come is the new one.
           Gone are the old tears,
           gone with the night.
           Kindle a new flare
           deep in your heart's core.
           Cherish the glow there,
           make it grow bright.

Narrator   Please stand and read responsively. (*holds up a cookie*)

           In shape of sun, behold the cake
           that in the hearth of love we bake.

All   In spite of darkness, pain, and strife,
           taste and savor the sweetness of life.

           All eat cookies.

Leader   (*raising a cup of wassail*) The wassail at the apple tree
           assured its rich fertility.

All   May we who toast each other here
           bear good fruit in the coming year!

           All toast and drink, then sing "Here We Come A-wassailing"
           through twice.

All sing   Here we come a-wassailing,
           Among the leaves so green.
           Here we come a-wandering,

So fair to be seen.
Love and joy come to you.
And to you your wassail too.
May life bless you and send you a happy New Year,
May life bless you and send you a happy New Year.

Narrator   Please be seated. We have rejoiced in the return of the sun; we have welcomed the waxing light. And yet still the nights are long, and even the days are cold—and colder yet to come, we know. In the face of this harsh reality, we struggle to believe in the resurgence of life, to answer the questions of our doubting hearts.

Reader 6   Where are the swallows fled?
Frozen and dead,
Perchance, upon some bleak and stormy shore.

Reader 7   O doubting heart!
Far over purple seas
They wait, in sunny ease,
The balmy southern breeze,
To bring them to their northern homes once more.

Reader 6   Why must the flowers die?
Prison'd they lie
In the cold tomb, heedless of tears or rain.

Reader 7   O doubting heart!
They only sleep below
The soft white ermine snow,
While winter winds shall blow,
To breathe and smile upon you soon again.

Reader 6   The sun has hid its rays
These many days;
Will dreary hours never leave the earth?

Reader 7   O doubting heart!
The stormy clouds on high

Veil the same sunny sky,
That soon (for spring is nigh)
Shall wake the summer into golden mirth.
   —Adelaide Anne Procter, "A Doubting Heart"

Giving Gifts of Holly

All sing the following words to the melody of "God Rest Ye Merry Gentlemen" while Servers distribute sprigs of holly to all.

All sing Two brothers, twins, who rule the year
     contend on Solstice Day,
     deciding who will claim the earth,
     whose power will hold sway.
     Now comes the night to celebrate,
     that magic time of year:
     let us bring in the light and turn the wheel,
     turn the wheel,
     Let us bring in the light and turn the wheel.

     The Holly King of Winterwood
     rules over all that's stark:
     the mysteries of death and loss,
     and all that's deep and dark.
     But now his reign draws to a close,
     his power waning dim.
     Let us bring in the light and turn the wheel,
     turn the wheel,
     let us bring in the light and turn the wheel.

     The Oak King, Lord of Greenwood
     rules over all that's light:
     the mystery of growing things,
     and all that's new and bright.
     And now his power waxes strong—
     he woos and wins the earth.
     Let us bring in the light and turn the wheel,

turn the wheel,
let us bring in the light and turn the wheel.

Narrator   As this song suggests, one seasonal tradition imagines the Winter Solstice as a time of struggle between the old year symbolized by the Holly King and the new year symbolized by the Oak King.

Leader   Another tradition has it that holly was originally named for the dark underground crone-goddess Holle, or Hel, from whose womb the sun arose. The red berries of the holly were her holy blood, the source of all life. The evergreen leaves represented ongoing life and the promise of immortality. Let us wear our sprig of holly, symbol of fertility, as a sign of our potential for creativity in the New Year.

Narrator   Let us stand and sing the praises of this wondrous plant.

All sing "Deck the Halls."

All sing   Deck the halls with boughs of holly, fa la la-la-la, la-la-la-la!
'Tis the season to be jolly, fa la la-la-la, la-la-la-la!
Don we now our gay apparel, fa la la-la-la-la, la-la-la-la!
Troll the ancient Yuletide carol, fa la la-la-la, la-la-la-la!

See the blazing Yule before us, fa la la-la-la, la-la-la-la!
Strike the harp and join the chorus, fa la la-la-la, la-la-la-la!
Follow me in merry measure, fa la la-la-la-la, la-la-la-la!
While I tell of Yuletide treasure, fa la la-la-la, la-la-la-la!

Fast away the old year passes, fa la la-la-la, la-la-la-la!
Hail the new, ye lads and lasses, fa la la-la-la, la-la-la-la!
Sing we joyous all together, fa la la-la-la-la, la-la-la!
Heedless of the wind and weather, fa la la-la-la, la-la-la-la!

Leader   We invite you to join us after the ceremony for refreshments and fellowship and on your way out to deposit your cups and your candles in the containers provided.

Narrator May the returning sun illumine our minds and warm our hearts. May we walk in the light and give birth to good ideas and worthy projects in the New Year. May the solstice light shine in all of us.

          Instrumental music

Imbolc, Purification and Candlemas

February 1-2

With Winter Solstice only six weeks behind us and Spring Equinox yet seven weeks away, darkness still rules in the northern hemisphere, though the light is slowly, perceptibly gaining. For some of us, the winter by now feels too cold and too long. We yearn for light and warmth. We are tired of looking at the gray sky through a web of stark branches that appear barren and brittle. We are weary of a landscape that seems a monochromatic brown.

Yet appearances deceive. Beneath the remaining patches of snow, the leafmeal of last autumn labors quietly, seeking its natural bliss, intent on its moist metamorphosis. On surprisingly sturdy tree limbs, tiny, tight buds of hope are crowning. Nature is not dead, only sleeping—and soon to awaken.

The Seasonal Calendar

In many northern European countries, nature is already awakening and showing early signs of spring. The aspen and blackthorn are starting to flower in England. Ewes are giving birth in Ireland, where crocuses and daffodils begin to dot the meadows. It's time to plow and sow. Although in the United States we think of spring as beginning in March at the time of the Vernal Equinox, this is largely a twentieth-century American shift. In many other places and in earlier times, spring was welcomed at the start of February.

The Celts celebrated the awakening of the earth after winter as Imbolc or Imbolg (both pronounced "imolk") or Oímealg or Óimelc (pronounced "imelk"). This was one of their quarter days dividing the year into four seasons. Most scholars agree that the meaning of the word is related to sheep's milk, which makes sense, given that Imbolc welcomed their lambing season, when ewes began to lactate. Surely the arrival of this milk and the cheese it could provide would have been cause for celebration at a time when stored grains from the last year's harvest might have been running low. By extension the feast celebrated all mothers' milk, the very act of breastfeeding, and the institution of motherhood.

Eric Hamp suggests in an article in *Studia Celtica* that the word *Imbolc* derives from a lost Indo-European root term for "purification" and speculates that the feast of Imbolc was a purification festival. A medieval quatrain cited by Pamela Berger in *The Goddess Obscured* seems to support this:

Tasting every food in order,
This is what behoves at Imbolc
Washing of hand and foot and head,
It is thus I say.

The French scholar Joseph Vendryes suggests that the washing could have been related to the purification ceremonies the Romans undertook in February to rid the land and its people of impurities before the planting that marked their New Year in March.

Berger supplies yet another linguistic possibility. Since "in Old Irish the prefix *im-* means 'around' or 'about,' and *bolc* or *bolg* means 'belly,'" the word *Imbolc* might "reflect an ancient ritual of going around the arable field (symbolic belly of the mother goddess)," a ritual that would have been appropriate for this time of tilling and sowing.

Mythology and History

The maternal deity in this case would be Brigid, mother goddess of Ireland, who "breathes life into the mouth of dead winter," according to Alexander Carmichael's *Carmina Gadelica*. In a series of ancient myths, she is variously identified as the mother of the Dagda (the Great Father of the Celts), as his wife/consort, and as each of his three daughters. Unlike other ancient triple goddesses, whose manifestations as maiden/mother/crone reflect the seasonal changes in the life cycle of the agricultural year and of humans, the three sister-Brigids were of the same age, with each having a distinct purview. This triune Brigid appears as a goddess of inspiration, healing, and metal-working, and she is therefore the patron of poets, physicians, and artisans—functions essential to any primitive culture. Displaying a spectrum of patronage that was both inclusive and ironic, she was also invoked by women in childbirth for a safe delivery and by soldiers on the battlefield for victory over enemies.

But Brigid's veneration was not limited to Ireland. Barbara Walker reminds us in *The Woman's Encyclopedia of Myths and Secrets* that Brigid was "older than Celtic Ireland, having come with Gaelic Celts from their original home in Galatia." As the titular divinity of the Brigantines, who occupied parts of France, Spain, and the British Isles, she was the equivalent of Juno Regina, Queen of Heaven.

Brigid may be older still. Patricia Monaghan, author of *The New Book of Goddesses and Heroines*, claims Brigid may have taken on some aspects of the ancient seasonal goddess of pre-Celtic peoples, called the Cailleach. She describes a series of stories in Scotland in which the Cailleach held a maiden named Bride prisoner in the mountains:

> But her own son fell in love with the girl and, at winter's end, he eloped with her. [In another version, her brother rescues her.] The hag chased them across the landscape, causing fierce storms as she went, but finally she turned to stone and

Bride was freed. In such stories, which may date back as far as 2,000 to 3,000 years, Brigid becomes a surrogate for a spring/summer goddess whose rule over the land alternated with that of the fall/winter hag.

Monaghan also believes that the name Bridestones—given to the massive sandstones used in Neolithic monuments such as Stonehenge and Avebury—suggests that this was the name of an ancient primary goddess. Perhaps Bride's identification with the Cailleach might also be evidenced in the legend that these very monuments—like the mountain ranges—were stones dropped from the Cailleach's apron.

Walker identifies the Cailleach with the Hindu Kali, the dark crone-goddess of death and destruction, noting the similarity in their names and functions. The term itself means an old woman or hag, or in some interpretations, "a veiled one," referring to the goddess's "most mysterious manifestation as the future, Fate, and Death—ever veiled from the sight of men," since none could know how he would die.

Part of the Cailleach's mystery was that she was a shape-shifter, now running in the forest with the wild animals, now sending thunderbolts from the heavens, now creating snow or frost over the land with her magic wand, which many tried to steal, though none could outwit her. One famous tale recounted by Merlin Stone in *Ancient Mirrors of Womanhood* tells of three Scottish brothers who sat by the fire one night roasting the catch from their hunt. A filthy old beggar woman appeared and asked to share their food and fire. The first two refused, but the youngest complied and offered her half his blanket as well. Thus did he come to "spend the night with the Cailleach, the Queen of the Faeries—never regretting for a moment that he had been so kind."

In the Irish version of this tale, "The Adventures of the Sons of Eochaid Mugmedon," the brothers are five and it is they who request nourishment—water from an old hag who guards the well. She will barter it only for a kiss (or, presumably, the ritual mating that this implies), and when the youngest brother, Niall, delivers, he is rewarded with the kingship of Tara, for he has proved his worthiness by valuing more than appearances.

But the hoary Cailleach of winter becomes the maiden Bride of spring, who inevitably grows into the hag again, only to be transformed into the maiden again the following spring. Thus do the seasons of the goddess's life—like our own—reflect those of the earth.

Variations on Brigid's name in the different lands where she was venerated include Brigit, Bridget, Bride, Brighid, Brid, Brig, Brigantia, Brigandu. The Irish name has been variously interpreted to mean "high," "exalted one," "firebrand," or "fiery arrow." Many scholars believe that the seat of her worship was at Kildare in the province of Leinster, where druid priestesses kept a perpetual fire burning in her honor.

The goddess was associated not only with fire and with the earth as bringer of spring but also with water. In Roman times she was invoked as the nymph goddess, and Julius Caesar called her the Gaulish Minerva. (At Minerva's spring festival, the Quinquatria, the arts and crafts were celebrated and the arms, horses, and trumpets of the Roman army were ritually purified.) Brigid's connection to water is further evidenced in the rivers named for her, among them the Braint in Anglesey, Wales, and the Brent, in Middlesex, England. According to the *Carmina Gadelica*—a collection of Celtic folk prayers, charms, rituals, and omens—the ancients made sacrifices to the triple goddess Brigid at the meeting of three waters. Further, her sacred wells were believed to house healing waters.

This same source tells us that one of Brigid's primary symbols was the serpent. Her regeneration of the earth on the feast of Imbolc was reflected in the use of serpent effigies in her rituals, as well as in a poem recorded there:

Today is the Day of Bride,
The serpent shall come from the hole,
I will not molest the serpent,
Nor will the serpent molest me.

In *Celtic Mysteries*, John Sharkey proposes that Brigid's sanctuary at Kildare may have been a cult center for the serpent. Certainly the association of fertility goddesses with the ever-changing serpent who repeatedly sheds its skin, thus giving birth to a "new" life, is a common one. Ancient goddesses, from the Hindu Anata to the Chinese Mat Chinoi to the Egyptian Isis, were associated with the serpent. Given the symbolism, it is tempting to see in the legend of Saint Patrick driving the snakes from Ireland an attempt to rid the new Christian god of his rival goddess, even as the demonizing of the serpent in Genesis reflects the rivalry between Yahweh and the Mesopotamian serpent deities.

Another of Brigid's symbols, appropriate to her role as mother-goddess, was the cow. In *The Serpent and the Goddess* Mary Condren reminds us that the sacred cow (now a term of derision) "symbolized the sacredness of motherhood," and its milk "was one of the earliest sacred foods throughout the world, equivalent to our present day communion." Not only the perfect food, providing nourishment and comfort, cow's milk was believed to have curative powers as well. The Irish actually used it for baptism into the twelfth century, when the practice was banned. So honored was motherhood in Brigid's domain that rape, which might result in *forced* motherhood, was punished with the utmost severity. It may be that belief in Brigid's desire to protect women from rapists is what inspired the stories of her inventing the whistle.

Such an exalted goddess—as powerful as fire, as purifying as water, as nurturing as earth, who protects mothers and soldiers alike, who guards the herds and flocks, inspires the keepers of the culture, and provides maternal nourishment in every possible way—would not likely be abandoned by her people. The Christian missionaries of the fifth century were wise enough to see this, so instead of condemning her, they "converted" her.

The Brigid canonized by the Christian church was supposed to have lived in the fifth century, yet her two earliest biographers didn't write until the seventh. Donál Ó Cathasaigh in "The Cult of Brigid:

A Study of Pagan-Christian Syncretism in Ireland," explains that neither of them can be credited with an historical account. Broccan, a devotee of the saint, composed a Latin hymn eulogizing her life and works but provided no chronologies or verifiable facts. These are also lacking in the prose *Life of Brigid* written by Cogitosus, a monk who lived at Kildare, once a pagan sanctuary but by his time a thriving monastery with a mill, a metallurgy studio, and a scriptorium for copying and storing manuscripts. Since proclaiming the sanctity and miracles of his foundress would only have enhanced the reputation of his institution, he had every reason to be partial.

According to Cogitosus and subsequent biographers who relied on and embellished his work, Brigid was the daughter of a pagan chieftain, Dubhthach, and his Christian slave woman. When his wife grew jealous of her pregnant rival, she insisted her husband send the woman away. He sold her to a druid, in whose house she gave birth to Brigid. Later when the girl returned to her father as a domestic, the wife again grew jealous. At her insistence, Dubhthach tried to marry Brigid off. The king of Leinster might have taken her if the girl's radiant beauty hadn't been outweighed by her penchant for giving away her father's valuables, as well as household goods and foodstuffs, to the poor and disabled. Other suitors, apparently able to make their peace with this generosity, pursued her. But she managed—sometimes with the help of a miracle that left her grotesquely but temporarily disfigured—to deter them all. Instead, with seven other virgin companions, she dedicated herself to the religious life, founded a community at Cill-dara ("Church of the Oak"), and was even consecrated a bishop. Ó Cathasaigh reminds us that as abbess, Brigid would have "had responsibility for tradition-bearing (poetry), healing, and metalwork."

The stories are replete with astounding miracles. While she was still in the womb, it was prophesied that she would "shine in the world like the sun in the vault of heaven." At her birth, which was attended by angels, a pillar of flame hovered over the house.

(Two centuries later, a hymn would identify her as "golden sparkling flame" and entreat her to lead the way to "the eternal kingdom, the dazzling shining sun.") As a babe, she was nourished on the magical milk of Otherworld cows, and when she was left sleeping in the stable, the cow dung ignited in a burst of light. Her power over nature continued as an adult. She hung her cloak on a sunbeam; she moved a felled tree that no one else could budge; at her bidding a river sank to allow her passage; she tamed a fox and a wild boar; a pitcher of water that dropped from her hands neither spilled nor broke.

Her dealings with humans were also marked by miracles. She cured a frigid woman at the husband's request and made the fetus of a pregnant nun disappear. Like the Jesus of the gospels, she cured the deaf, the blind, and the possessed, as well as lepers, lunatics, and paralytics. To the truly needy, she was a savior. But she wasn't above punishing those who were ungenerous or deceitful. A man carrying salt who refused to share it with her found it turned to stone on his back. And a rich man pretending to be a beggar who cheated her out of several sheep found them back in her fold the next morning.

Famous as a mediator, she drew a film over the eyes of feuding brothers so they were unable to hurt each other. On one occasion, boys untrained in music suddenly became skilled harpists at her urging. But her most common feats were her "miracles of plenty." Her cows gave milk three times a day. She changed water (in some versions, her bathwater!) into beer. She multiplied foodstuffs, most popularly ale, bacon, and butter, and whatever she dispensed was replenished.

And the miracles continued after her death. As late as the twelfth century, it was reported that in honor of Saint Brigid an eternal flame was kept alive in the fire sanctuary at Kildare where earlier, some scholars believe, the same fire had burned for the goddess Brigid. Nineteen nuns each took a turn keeping vigil through the night, and on the twentieth night, the story goes, Brigid herself must have taken a turn, for the fire was always burning bright on the following morning. Even today, the faithful make pilgrimages to her sacred wells, streams, and shrines, hoping for miraculous cures or nourishing grace.

Similarities between the goddess and the saint abound. They are both powerful figures associated with fire and water, with nurturing milk and the animals that provide it, and with the sanctuary at Kildare. They share a role as patron of healing, poetry, and metalworking. They even share a name. But perhaps most importantly, Ó Cathasaigh contends, they share a maternal significance, for she who was "mother of the gods" was transformed into "the second Mother of Christ," "Mary of the Gael," and "Mother of the High King of Heaven," all titles given (however anachronistically) to Saint Brigid. Faced with the lack of "ascertainable facts" in the testimony of the saint's early biographers, Ó Cathasaigh believes that they converted myth and saga into "pseudo-historical tradition," modifying the Celtic religion over time, grafting the name and functions of the matriarchal deity onto the saint. He concludes,

> The goddess of poetry, healing, and the metal arts thus became the Christian patroness of learning, healing, and domestic arts. Because the celibate monks could not transfer the strong sexual/maternal qualities of the Celtic Brigid to her Christian counterpart, they virginized her, identified her with the Mother of Christ, and hailed her as "Protectress of Ireland."

The traditions associated with the feast of Imbolc, which were practiced all over Ireland as recently as the nineteenth century, further emphasize the connection between the goddess and the saint. Ó Cathasaigh describes some of these. One custom involved young boys called "Biddies" (a nickname for Brigid) dressing up a *churndash* (the plunger used to agitate milk in the butter churn) in women's clothing and carrying it from door to door, begging for gifts. The churndash, in addition to representing the milk itself, was the initial version of an effigy of the saint later carried in procession from one household to another.

One practice involved leaving a cloth, called Brigid's cloak, in the open on the eve of Imbolc so that it might acquire healing powers. The cloth would then be applied as needed during the year and was believed especially effective in curing barrenness and illnesses related to childbirth. Throwing a cake of bread or a sheaf of oats against the doorstep on this night was believed to drive away hunger. This was thought to ensure an ample food supply. A second cake was left outside as an offering to the saint or as food for the needy.

Perhaps the most ritualized custom grew up around the belief that Brigid, if summoned, would visit and bless households on the eve of her feast. At nightfall, a young girl carrying a bundle of straw or rushes (which had been left outside the house for this purpose), knocked three times on the door of the home, each time asking for admission in Brigid's name. After the third time, the family bid her welcome and the parents gave prayerful thanks for the health of the household and its animals. Then all set about weaving crosses from these materials while offering traditional prayers. (The design of these crosses varied with the location, though they commonly had four equal arms joined as a swastika, a shape found in prehistoric European art. Some scholars interpret this as a sun symbol, the four arms representing the sun's rays, and see "Brigid's cross" as evidence of her status as a sun goddess.) After a festive meal that included an abundance of dairy products, the crosses were placed in the thatch of the roof and in the barn as a protection for humans and animals. Remnants were strewn on the floor or made into a tick mattress in case the saint wanted to extend her visit through the night. Sometimes a girdle or hoop was made of the rushes, and family members and their livestock passed through it to guard against illness or disease.

Ronald Hutton, author of *The Stations of the Sun*, also describes these customs and adds that in the seventeenth century in the Hebrides, the practice was to make a "Bride's bed," to dress a large sheaf of oats in women's clothes, lay it in a basket, set a wooden club (a peeled wand of birch or willow, for example) next to it, and then summon the saint to her bed. If the residents found a footprint or the mark of the wand in the ashes of the fire the next morning, they took it as an indication of Brigid's visit and a sign that the crops would be plentiful. The figure was carried in procession by young women wearing white, who visited the houses in the village to receive decorations for the image or cakes with butter and cheese for themselves. When finished, they set the figure in a place of honor and enjoyed the food. The young men of the village—after begging for admission and paying respects to the image—joined them and all danced till dawn. The event closed with all singing a formal hymn—"Beauteous Bride, foster mother of Christ"—and giving any food that was left to the poor. Hutton believes that in the islands and some Irish communities, the rites of February 1 were "designed to give a particular prominence, and dignity, to the women of a community. . . ."

In "The Festival of Brigit the Holy Woman," Séamus Ó Catháin sees in aspects of the cult of Brigid her role as a fertility figure comparable to the god Lugh, her counterpart celebrated at Lughnasa, August 1, the opposing spoke on the wheel of the year. Ó Catháin also describes the three-part activity carried out on Imbolc Eve, though in his account (from County Mayo) the man of the house, rather than a young girl, demands entrance for the sheaf of straw wrapped in cloth that he carries. The man orders those inside to kneel, open their eyes, and admit Brigid. Ó Catháin interprets this as symbolically ordering them to "be prepared to submit themselves to the process of insemination and possible impregnation through the good offices of the goddess who rules over such matters." The centerpiece of the feast is butter, the product of churning, an act that is "an imitation of sexual intercourse," representing creation, with the butter itself standing for the "much hoped for product of sexual union." Finally, the third stage of the ritual, the weaving of straw, "is dominated by the symbolism of the cross . . . perceived in folk tradition as possessing the potential to promote fertility," representing as it does the "tree of life." Ó Catháin concludes that the festival's interpretation implies regeneration and reproduction, the special purview of Brigid.

Ó Cathasaigh notes that the saint's devotees honor her by making pilgrimages to holy wells, sacred streams, and ancient ruins associated with her life and legends. Most popular is the one, still attracting thousands of followers, that leads to her shrine at Faughart, the town where she was supposed to have been born. Perhaps not coincidentally, the Hill of Faughart is near the site of megalithic tombs and is associated with heroes of the ancient sagas. Though the exercises conducted at the shrine have been Christianized, "the prescribed ablutions in the stream" on whose bank she is believed to have knelt "and the prayer circuits round the large stones and the ubiquity of the antiquarian monuments hint at elaborate pre-Christian [druidic] rituals." Thus to Imbolc's association with lactation and milk is added its connection to even more basic life-liquids, for the pilgrimage undertaken at this time "celebrates a stream (symbolic of amniotic fluids) once sacred to a pre-Christian community." Though the Christian church appropriated the pilgrimages to honor its saint, the very nature and timing of the pilgrimages point to an earlier origin:

> The spring rite, signaling, as it does, rebirth in nature and new growth in the fields, certainly cannot be as recent as Christianity. Fertility and guardianship of the land were, after all, the domain of the Gaulish Brigid. . . . In the rituals associated with Brigid, there are vestiges of an ancient maternal deity who provides abundance and who heals and protects.

That these rituals included purification rites should come as no surprise.

February derives its name from the Latin *Februa*, the Roman festival of purification celebrated on February 15. Also known as Lupercalia, this festival was staged at the foot of the Palatine Hill, where Romulus and Remus, legendary founders of Rome, were believed to have been suckled by a she-wolf. W. W. Fowler provides a description and various interpretations of this extremely primitive ritual in *The Roman Festivals of the Period of the Republic*. After the sacrifice of goats and a dog and sacred cakes made by Vestal Virgins, two young men of high rank had their foreheads ritually smeared with the sacrificial blood, which was then wiped off with wool dipped in milk. They were then required to laugh, strip naked, and partake of the sacrificial feast. After this, attired only in the goat skins cut into strips, they ran around the base of the hill, using these strips—called *februa*—to strike those women who, desiring to become pregnant, stepped into their path.

One explanation for the application of the bloody knife, the cleansing with milk ("the source of life"), and the laughing is that these symbolic acts signified "the death and revival of the Vegetation-spirit," which comes to life again each spring. Fowler sees the running of the naked youths around the Palatine as "a beating of the bounds and a rite of purification and fertilization." In ancient times, the day itself was called *Februata* (from *februum* or "purification"). In particular, the striking with thongs of goatskin may have been perceived as both a purification and fertility ritual. Participants may have believed that infertility was caused by evil powers and could be exorcised by symbolic whipping, leaving the subjects cleansed from hostile influences and newly energized by natural forces. (Ritual whipping to encourage fertility has also been a custom among the Latvians. On the morning of Spring Equinox, according to Mara Mellena of the Latvian Institute, those who rise earliest in the household awake the others by "switching" them with steamed birch branches to encourage fertility and assure health and success. In Slovakia, on Easter Monday it is still the custom for young men to throw water on young women and "switch" them with braided willow wands.) The popular Lupercalia festival was celebrated until 494, when, according to Fowler, Pope Gelasius I established in its place the Christian Feast of the Purification of the Virgin Mary.

The event memorialized by the Christian feast was Mary's observance of a practice prescribed by Mosaic law. Leviticus 12 describes a woman who has given birth as "unclean" for forty days after the delivery of a male child and for twice as long if the child is female. At the end of this period, during which she is excluded from the sanctuary, she is to bring a lamb or a dove "for a sin offering." Then "the priest shall offer them up before the Lord to make atonement for her, and thus she will be clean again after her flow of blood." That Mary complies with this precept is attested to in Luke 2:22-38, where it is reported that Mary presents herself and her newborn at the temple in Jerusalem. Here she is purified by the sacrifice of doves and offers her son to be "consecrated to the Lord." Here also the holy man Simeon prophesies that the child will be "a light of revelation to the Gentiles," suggesting a theological universalism dear to the heart of this evangelist.

According to the *Catholic Encyclopedia*, which contests the assertion that the feast was established as a replacement for Lupercalia, this biblical event was commemorated in Jerusalem as early as the fourth century on February 14, forty days after January 6. It was simply called "the fortieth day after Epiphany," January 6 being the date then observed as the birthday of Jesus. From Jerusalem, it spread first to the Eastern Church, then to the Western Church; in the last quarter of the century, when the Roman feast of the nativity was set on December 25, it was celebrated on February 2. The new title of Purification of the Blessed Virgin Mary appeared for the first time in the seventh century, at the end of which Pope Sergius I introduced a procession for this day. In most dioceses in the Middle Ages the feast had an *octave*, which extended the celebration for a week and signaled its importance in the liturgical calendar. In the eleventh century, the blessing of candles became associated with the feast. This ritual included a solemn procession representing the entry of Christ, "the Light of the World" into the temple, as well as the singing of Simeon's canticle, which acknowledges the Christ child as "a light of revelation."

Hutton reviews the history of the feast of the Purification and points out that it "had a tremendous emotional appeal in the north." While in the Mediterranean world, its main theme was purification, "its importance further north, where winters were darker and colder, was primarily as a celebration of returning light." This is evidenced in the imagery of light and darkness, of renewal and rebirth found in the services commonly used in the British Isles of the late Middle Ages for the Feast of the Purification. By this time, the candles themselves were venerated objects. After they were blessed, parishioners carried them in procession around the church after Mass, then burned them before a statue of Mary or took them home for use in times of danger or sickness.

> From this ceremony the feast took its popular British name of Candlemas; it marked the formal opening of spring and of the month which drives the darkness from the afternoon and (in England at least) usually restores the first flowers to the earth and the first buds to the trees.

Fueled by this emotional appeal to folks eager to welcome spring, the processions accrued a dramatic cast of characters supplied by various guilds: Mary herself, her husband Joseph, the prophet Simeon, the three kings, and an assortment of angels, saints, bishops, and emperors. Musicians and municipal banquets were not far behind. However, with the Protestant Reformation's disapproval of "superstitious" acts, the blessing of candles— though not the feast itself—was abolished in England and Scotland. In Catholic Ireland, the feast of the Purification supplemented Brigid's Day.

The popularity of the feast of the Purification had less to do with its commemoration of a scriptural event than with "the manner in which it fulfilled profound seasonal needs," for the rituals of cleansing are typically employed in preparation for a fresh start, associated with springtime. For people who endure a cold, dark winter, the rites of spring are not to be denied. Under duress from reformers, formal rituals were not eliminated but transmuted into folk customs. For example, people in Dorset, deprived of their church processions, exchanged candles as gifts on the feast.

Communities of the border districts of Scotland lit fires on the hills. In Wales, on the eve of the Virgin's Feast of the Candles, Candlemas carolers went singing door to door. In eighteenth-century Caernarvonshire, carolers were admitted to view a candlelit living tableau of Virgin and Child once they had answered a series of riddles. Here they sang to her again and toasted her with the drink provided. Hutton notes that both the Welsh and the Irish customs had become ways to pay respect to womanhood and concludes, "This may reflect a pre-Christian tradition in these Celtic areas, or it may have been the natural result of the convergence of the two festivals of Brigid and Mary."

In *Festivals of Western Europe*, Dorothy Spicer records a variation on the Candlemas carolers in Luxemborg-Ville that was practiced as recently as the mid-twentieth century. School children took blessed candles to the elderly and shut-ins who were unable to make it to church for the blessing—and in return they were given coins and tasty treats. The boys and girls went from house to house, carrying their lighted candles and singing,

> Open, open, we come with your candle.
> The wax we hold is blessed.
> None of us will be naughty today,
> For each child brings sacred vows.

> We hope that all your life
> You will see the light of the sun.
> Open, open here is the light
> With each child's sacred vows.

> We hope that in this life
> Neither mind nor soul will darken,
> And that for you in heaven above
> There will be everlasting light.

While the last verse reflects the Christian tone of the practice, perhaps the second verse hints at an earlier heritage, a welcoming of the sun whose return wakens the earth and its inhabitants to new life.

Contemporary Celebrations Around the World

Although Europeans and North Americans have marked the beginning of February as Imbolc, the Feast of the Purification, Candlemas Day, or even Groundhog Day, many people in the Far East, the Middle East, and South America celebrate with a variety of other festivals at this time of year.

The Chinese New Year, or Spring Festival, is determined by the lunar calendar. It begins with the new moon of the lunar New Year. In the solar calendar, this would be late January or early February. As with the Celts, the Chinese celebrate the earth's awakening at this time, which marks the beginning of the plowing and sowing season. The celebration lasts for fifteen days and includes both religious and secular rituals. Professor Wolff-Michael Roth of the University of Victoria, British Columbia, provides a breakdown of the two-weeks' activities on his website, "Chinese New Year." On the first day, people welcome the gods of the heavens and earth; on the second, they pray to all the gods and also to their ancestors. During the next two days, men pay their respects to their fathers-in-law. On the fifth, there is no visiting; everyone stays home to welcome the god of wealth. During the next five days, everyone visits the homes of friends and relatives as well as temples, where they pray for health and good fortune. There are family reunion dinners, featuring special foods, more prayers, and offerings to Yu Di, the supreme god of Chinese mythology. The culminating event is the Lantern Festival, for which houses are decorated with colorful lanterns and sweet or savory rice dumplings are eaten.

In preparation for New Year, Chinese families set out platters of oranges—symbols of happiness—and candied fruit, arranged on a "tray of togetherness" to start the New Year sweetly. They write good wishes (for health, happiness, long life, etc.) on vertical red scrolls and hang these on the walls. They also attach great importance to flowers as signs of nature's reawakening and bring vases of blossoms or floral decorations into their homes. It is a tradition, when visiting, to take a bag of oranges or tangerines and replace treats that are eaten from the candy tray with *lai see*, small red envelopes containing coins for children.

The Chinese New Year is a time to thoroughly clean house, pay debts, get haircuts and new clothes, and light firecrackers at midnight to send out the old year—for which purpose all doors and windows are opened as well—and welcome the new.

In nearby Japan, the Spring Setsubun ritual marks the transition from winter to spring on February 3. Jim Metzner reminds us in "Pulse of the Planet" that farmers of a millennium ago celebrated the arrival of spring by offering beans to the god who taught them to cultivate rice. Today the bean throwing continues in temples, where sumo wrestlers or other celebrities whose birth sign is that of the current year lead the ceremony. They throw the beans while chanting, "Out with devils! In with good luck!" Misfortune is driven away and replaced by good fortune. The demons of bad luck and the cherubs of good luck are sometimes impersonated by people—especially children—wearing masks and enacting the replacement. Families toss roasted beans throughout their homes, exorcising evil spirits; then each family member eats the number of beans corresponding to his/her age. As the website of the American School in Japan points out, it is a ritual of purification and renewal reminiscent of spring cleaning in Western countries.

Eyewitness Masamichi Tanaka describes an elaborate Setsubun ritual as it took place in 1981 in the city of Ayabe at a sanctuary of Oomoto, a spiritual movement that began in 1892. At this event, priests lit altar candles with a sacred flame and purified both the food offerings and the congregation with a special wand. The chief priest then prayed for a good harvest, as well as for remission of sins and peace on earth. Young maidens danced to bells and *koto* music. Worshippers chanted a prayer of purification and wrote their names on slips of rice paper called *hitogata*. (Originally these were paper dolls that people rubbed themselves with, thus transferring their sins onto the paper.) Finally, their path lit by lanterns, the priests and matrons in white kimonos carried the jars containing these *hitogata* to the river, where the jars were shattered and the names dropped into the waters for cleansing.

Cleansing figures largely in the Indian festival of Mahashivratri, which occurs on the fourteenth night of the dark half of the month of Magh (February-March), just before the new moon. It celebrates the union of Lord Shiva, who danced the universe into existence, and Sati, the divine mother. Devotees fast all night in temples where young girls sing devotional songs in honor of the god who saved humanity from destruction. When the Ganges River threatened to overflow, Shiva walked beneath it, directing its water to sift through the seven sections of his hair, which thus divided it into seven holy rivers. The Janak Community Center of New Delhi provides an online description of the feast. Worshippers bathe at sunrise in the Ganges or other holy water, offering prayers to the sun, Vishnu, and Shiva. Thus purified, they dress in clean clothing and carry water to the temple. Here they ring the temple bells and bathe the Shiva linga, a large phallic pillar symbolic of the creative force, in water, milk, and honey. Then they decorate the linga with garlands of flowers and offer incense sticks and food, especially bael leaves, which are believed to have a cooling effect on the hot-tempered Shiva, who on this day brings special blessings to his devotees.

The water deity Yemaya is celebrated at this time as well (sometimes called Ymoja, Yemoja, Imanje, or Yemanja). Monaghan tells us that in her original homeland of Africa, Yemaya "was the Yoruba goddess of the Ogun River, where she was said to be the daughter of the sea into whose waters she empties." Yet at the same time she was revered as the "mother of waters"—Mama Watta—because she gave birth to all the world's waters. "Even as she slept, she would create new springs, which gushed forth each time she turned over." According to Michael Jordan's *Encyclopedia of Gods*, the waters of her sacred Ogun River are considered a remedy for infertility.

Yemaya traveled on slave ships with the African diaspora to the peninsula of Bahia, Brazil, where she is still honored as goddess of the sea, giver of all life, and patron of fisherfolk. Here, though the primary religion is Catholicism, many practice *Candomblé*, a mixture of traditional African religion, Catholicism, and Brazilian spiritualism. In the Candomblé pantheon, Yemaya is associated with Mary, and her feast is the same as that of the Purification of Mary, February 2. In the fishing center of Salvador, Bahia, the festival begins at daybreak, when the goddess is invoked by drummers, chanters, and dancers. These last include priestesses who dance into a trance state, in which they are believed able to make contact with divine or deceased spirits. Meanwhile thousands of people bring their gifts of flowers, soap, perfumes, and candles to Yemaya's shrine. These are put into baskets and taken in procession to the seashore, where fishermen load them onto their little boats, carry them out to sea, and "offer" them to the goddess in the hope that she will bless the people who live on her shores.

Other February festivals, though not overtly religious in nature, celebrate the arrival of spring. For example, in 1999 the month-long Hala was established in Kuwait primarily as a tourist attraction. Today Hala is celebrated with social, economic, and entertainment events, including indoor ice-skating, raffle drawings, shopping mall extravaganzas, museum exhibits, poetry readings, concerts by military bands and popular musicians, and fireworks.

In Baguio, the summer capital of the Philippines, natives and some million tourists alike celebrate the week-long February flower festival of Panagbenga, a Malayo-Polynesian term for "season of blooming." The opening ceremonies include an extravagant parade of flower-floats that transform the main thoroughfare into a living garden.

The Chiang Mai Flower Festival in Thailand, scheduled for early February, the most beautiful time of the year there, features a floral-floats parade, a Miss Flower pageant, cultural events, agricultural exhibitions, and competitions for flowers, garden arrangements, and international foods.

Whatever their religion or race, people the world over are happy to celebrate the arrival of spring. That many of these cele-

bratory rituals include rites of purification should be no more surprising than the common practice of fasting before feasting.

Anthony Aveni, author of *The Book of the Year*, reminds us that
"moved by earth rhythms, our ancestors attributed magical powers to plants and animals that changed their behavior at key points
in the year's cycle." He cites a number of proverbs that identify the
start of February as such a key point, demonstrating its association with weather predictions. For example,

> If Candlemas Day is bright and clear,
> there'll be two winters in the year.

Here's one that clearly connects weather prediction to the
habits of animals:

> The badger peeps out of his hole on Candlemas Day, and
>   when he finds it's snowing, walks abroad,
> but if he sees the sun shining, he draws back into the hole.

In the United States, Badger's cousin Groundhog plays the
same role on February 2, to predict the weather and thus indicate
when spring will really begin. Since the Middle Ages, many have
subscribed to the belief—with dwindling seriousness—that hibernating animals test the weather on this day and that we might depend on them as predictors of spring's arrival. For the Irish it was
a hedgehog on St. Brigid's Day. In the Pyrenees it was a bear.

> Before it became scarce in most of Europe, the hibernating
> bear antedated both the badger and the groundhog as the
> great inspiration for the rite of spring. His emergence from
> hibernation was actually thought to accelerate nature's awak-
> ening. Because of his strength, cunning, and intelligence,
> people thought the bear their equal—even their ancestor.
> Scandinavians believed people could change into bears
> (whence our word "berserk") and that donning a bearskin
> would help a warrior acquire the bear's power and stamina.

Whether marked by fauna or flora, the arrival of spring in February has always been something to celebrate.

In many parts of the United States, we recognize little of spring in February. Whether our Punxsutawney Phil sees his shadow or not, many of us feel that warm days are still a long way off. Yet the earth beneath our feet is full of life and the limbs of the bleak, brown trees dream of green.

WAYS TO CELEBRATE

Honor the animals.

🔥 Every year at this season bald eagles convene along the upper Skagit River in Washington State to feed on salmon that have spawned and are about to die. In the first week of February, binocular-bearing humans convene to watch these majestic birds and celebrate the Bald Eagle Festival with breakfast, lectures, and music. Have breakfast with the birds in your own backyard or neighborhood (though the weather may require a window between you and them). Fill the bird feeder and your own cereal bowl and see what happens. It might help to open the window or venture outside and play a few notes on your flute, recorder, penny whistle, or kazoo.

🔥 Adopt a pet from the pound, or join the walk-a-dog program.

🔥 Donate time or money to the Society for the Prevention of Cruelty to Animals or your local animal shelter.

🔥 Give your dog a bath or a nice, long walk.

Honor mother's milk.

🔥 Coddle a nursing mother. Clean her house, provide a carry-in dinner, or offer to baby-sit.

⑥ Do you have a family member, neighbor, or friend who has lost a child to war, illness, or accident during the past year? Send her a comforting treat or a pot of flower bulbs to let her know you are thinking of her.

⑥ Take the mothers in your family out for a milkshake, hot chocolate, or Bailey's Irish Cream.

Celebrate milk.

⑥ Take a milk bath.

⑥ Make buttermilk pancakes or sour cream coffee cake for breakfast.

⑥ Make a cream soup and sourdough bread for lunch or dinner.

⑥ Have a custard or custard pie, a hot milk sponge cake, crème brûlée, ice cream, cream puffs, éclairs, or cheesecake for dessert.

⑥ Invite your friends over for a potluck meal featuring milk dishes.

Celebrate Goddess/Saint Brigid, patron of poets, smiths, and healers.

⑥ Write a poem describing the season, perhaps after taking a walk in the woods or park.

⑥ Try your hand at metalworking, jewelry-making, or another craft.

⑥ Give an aloe plant to a mother with young children. The juice of its leaves can be used to soothe minor burns.

Celebrate fire, a method of purification and source of inspiration.

⑥ Clean your fireplace and/or kitchen oven. Then set a candle on the clean hearth or on the stove and welcome inspiration.

✹   Try this recipe from Cait Johnson's *Witch in the Kitchen* for a soup that provides a quiver of fiery arrows to the palate.

_____

BRIGID'S BROTH OF INSPIRATION

Ingredients:

2 tablespoons olive oil
3 leeks, white parts only, washed well and cut into ½-inch
    rounds
1 red bell pepper, diced
1 medium carrot, diced
2 teaspoons paprika
¼ teaspoon (or more) cayenne
6 cups vegetable broth or water
sea salt to taste
handful of garlic-mustard greens, coarsely chopped
1 to 2 cups croutons
sour cream as topping
sprouts for garnish

In a large soup pot, heat the olive oil. Add the leeks, red pepper, and carrot and heat, stirring occasionally, until barely tender. Sprinkle vegetables with paprika and cayenne to taste. As you sprinkle, visualize Brigid's fiery energy filling the pot; the cheery orange-red color is a warming reminder of her vivid hair and of the sun that is slowly bringing the frozen earth back to life. Cover vegetables with vegetable broth or water and sea salt to taste. Bring to a boil and cook, covered, for 15 minutes. Add a handful of garlic mustard greens. Use a field guide and search your own yard, if possible (garlic mustard is usually up and growing, even at this chilly time of year). If garlic mustard is not available, substitute parsley or watercress. As you stir these into the broth, think of the green of the new plants just beginning to sprout and grow outdoors. This same green vitality is now a part of your soup. Continue cooking for 2 or 3 minutes. Place several croutons into individual bowls, ladle soup into bowls, and top each serving with a dollop of sour cream. Arrange 2 or 3 of the sprouts on the sour cream.

Imitate Brigid's generosity.

⚭ Volunteer at a homeless shelter.

⚭ Help prepare a meal at a soup kitchen.

⚭ Write letters to your congressional representatives urging them to introduce or support legislation that would provide health care coverage for all.

Celebrate the stirring of life.

⚭ What plan or project or idea has been gestating in you that is now ready for testing? Make the birthing effort now; bring it to light.

⚭ February is a month when Americans honor political activists who brought revolutionary ideas to light: George Washington, Abraham Lincoln, Susan B. Anthony, and Martin Luther King Jr. Read a biography of one of these heroes or their speeches. Consider what political action you might take to further their ideals.

Purify your space.

⚭ Clean out closets, cabinets, and drawers. Get rid of junk and excess "stuff" from your attic, cellar, or garage. Donate usable items you no longer need to charity.

⚭ Clean your workspace. Organize your file drawers and your computer files. Delete old e-mails. Clear your desktop.

Purify your heart.

⚭ Make peace with someone who is critical of you.

⚭ Light a candle. Play some meditative music. Quiet your mind with deep breathing. Then think about the strengths and weaknesses of your personality. Write on slips of paper the negative traits you would like to replace with more positive ones. Burn each slip. (Light it with the candle flame and then drop it into a metal container or fireplace.) As the paper burns, think about one concrete action that would put you on the road to developing the positive trait you want to replace the burning one. This ritual can be private or done with family members, support groups, etc. If it would be helpful in strengthening resolve and if those involved are comfortable doing so, the traits and resolutions could be read aloud.

Appreciate the taste of clean water.

☽ Buy a bottle of spring water. Pour a glass slowly, listening to its sound and observing its clarity. Drink it slowly, savoring the taste. Describe the experience in words (or music).

☽ Investigate the quality of the drinking water in your municipality or region. If it's good, write a letter or e-mail of gratitude and encouragement to your mayor. If it's not good, write one urging a plan for improvement.

Appreciate the healing power of water.

☽ Visit a spa with spring water if there is one near you, or treat a friend who has recently undergone a loss to the comfort of such an experience.

☽ Relax in a hot bubble bath.

☽ Clear out your nasal passages over the steam from the tea kettle (carefully!).

☽ Visit the nearest bay, lake, river, or stream. Celebrate Yemaya, the mother of waters, by drumming or dancing at the shoreline or on the bank.

☽ Contact your state representatives and encourage them to save your local body of water from pollution and/or join a volunteer organization dedicated to this mission.

🖢 Arrange to take a group of children on a field trip to your local water purification plant.

🖢 Listen to Debussy's *La Mer*.

🖢 Read Rachel Carson's *The Sea Around Us*.

🖢 Write a poem in praise of your favorite body of water.

🖢 Describe in your journal a favorite childhood memory associated with water.

Use water mindfully.

🖢 Wash the car, paying attention to the difference the "bath" makes.

🖢 Give your plants a generous drink and watch the soil absorb the water. If you live in a cold climate and there is still snow on the ground, bring a handful inside, put it in a bowl and watch it melt, appreciating the transformation. Consider if there is anything "frozen" in you that needs to melt and flow. Use the melted snow to water your plants.

🖢 Wash windows—or at least the one you look out the most. Appreciate the improvement.

🖢 If you don't already have one, install an efficient showerhead. Or get one as a gift for someone who would like one.

🖢 Install low-flow faucet aerators. According to the website of the Center for the New American Dream, our water supply is rapidly diminishing

> as human populations swell and inefficiently drain precious aquifers. For every thousand of us who install faucet aerators and high-efficiency showerheads, we can save

nearly eight million gallons of water and prevent over 450,000 pounds of carbon dioxide emissions each year!

Celebrate Candlemas.

☙ Burn a candle in honor of the heat still hidden in the earth, waiting for spring.

☙ Eat dinner or make love by candlelight.

☙ Burn a sweet-smelling candle as you take a bath or read poetry or meditate.

☙ Make candles. Directions for many methods and variations are available on the Internet.

Start spring planting.

☙ If you live in a warm enough climate, start planting your garden.

☙ If you live in a colder climate, set seeds in pots and put them on a sunny sill in your home until it's warm enough to transplant them outside. Meanwhile, look at your garden site and visualize green and growing things.

RENEW THE EARTH AND OURSELVES

AN IMBOLC/PURIFICATION RITUAL

All sing the following words to the melody of "Praise God from Whom All Blessings Flow."

All sing In greening lands begins the song,
     Which deep in human hearts is strong.
     In cheerful strains our voices raise,
     To fill the whole spring world with praise.

Narrator For those of us who live in cold or even temperate climates, February is a time of faith—faith in the power of life, in the cycles of nature. Although the sun reversed its course at Winter Solstice, there are still more hours of darkness than light each day. Yet we have faith that the light will wax stronger. Because, after all, it always has.

Leader The deciduous trees are a dreary expanse of brown against the gray sky, their sap asleep in frozen roots. Yet we have faith in the greening to come. The ground is cold—in some places still patched with snow. Yet beneath it, silent seeds are germinating, poised for awakening. We have faith that spring will come. Because, after all, it always has.

Narrator Sometimes it is February in our hearts, times of dreary, colorless sameness when we are bored with our lives, or times when the darkness and cold of loneliness or stress or failure seem unending, and we doubt we can endure it much longer, or times when we are frozen in our losses, when we despair of ever loving again, of ever being truly joyful, or of finding meaning in our lives. Yet we must have faith that spring will come. Because, after all, it always has.

Leader The wheel of the year turns. Seasons change. Darkness gives way to light, which wanes into darkness. Birth and death and birth and death and birth. Each has its season, and each season is a necessary part of the whole. It is the way of all nature. Let us embrace it with faith.

Reader 1 A Light exists in Spring
Not present on the Year
At any other period—
When March is scarcely here

A Color stands abroad
On Solitary Fields

That Science cannot overtake
But Human Nature feels.

It waits upon the Lawn,
It shows the furthest Tree
Upon the furthest Slope you know
It almost speaks to you.

Then as Horizons step
Or Noons report away
Without the Formula of sound
It passes and we stay—

A quality of loss
Affecting our Content
As Trade had suddenly encroached
Upon a Sacrament.

—Emily Dickinson

All sing "This Is the Truth That Passes Understanding," words by Robert Terry Weston.

All sing   This is the truth that passes understanding,
             this is the joy to all forever free:
             life springs from death and shatters every fetter,
             and winter turns to spring eternally.

Celebrating the Breath of Life

Narrator   For North Americans, spring does not officially begin until March 21. But in many of the northern European countries, people are already enjoying the first signs of spring: flowers on the blackthorn and aspen, crocuses and daffodils in the fields, and new lambs in the pens. For them it is time to plow and sow. The ancient Celts thought of the approximate midpoint between Winter Solstice and Spring Equinox—February 1 in our calendar—as the beginning of spring. They told a story of the old hag of winter, who gives way to the young maiden of spring. The maiden is their mother goddess Brigid, or Bride, who breathes life into the mouth of dead winter.

Three Dancers enact the story following as it is read.

Reader 2   In ancient Scotland—and perhaps even now—the beautiful young maiden Bride spends the winter imprisoned within Ben Nevis, the highest mountain in all the land. Her jailer is the Cailleach [*CALL-y'ach*], the blue hag, who brings darkness and seeming death and destruction over everything. Her gray, bristly mane is like the tail of a wild horse. Her green teeth are sharp enough to sever an oak branch. Her nose is crooked and hollow, her eyes dark and smoky, her body spotted and diseased, her whole appearance loathsome. Her footsteps cover the ground with frost, and her fingers channel the cold wind and storms.

But one day when all the people have grown weary of winter and tired of the Cailleach's tyranny, Bride's brother, the young god Angus, comes to her rescue. Their father, the Dagda, is the god of fertility and agriculture. Seeing her brother approach, the girl prepares for her escape. She jumps onto his white horse, and quickly they ride off. The wretched hag chases them across the mountains and valleys, all the while causing fierce storms as she goes. But the young ones are stronger and faster and sustained by the warmth of their affection. Finally, exhausted and out-paced, the old woman of winter moves more and more slowly, until at last she stops altogether and eventually turns to stone. Thus the young Bride, goddess of spring, is free to bless the land with warmth and light, which from this time until summer grows stronger and stronger. And so Brigid reigns until the seasons change again.

—adapted from *The Cycle of Kings*

Narrator   Thus does Brigid breathe life into the mouth of dead winter. In some variations on the story, Brigid does combat with the Cailleach. In others, the Cailleach journeys to a magic well at dawn on the first day of spring and upon looking at her image reflected in it or drinking from it, she is transformed into the maiden.

Leader   How to breathe life into that which seems dead? No easy task. Cup your hands together and hold them to your mouth. (*Pause.*) Inhale deeply. Now breathe a long, slow breath into your hands. Then close your hands together, holding the breath inside. How warm and alive it feels.

What transformation awaits us? What is wintering in us that needs to be breathed into life? What seeds are germinating? What ideas are hibernating? At its core the earth is warm, and that warmth is now rising. So too are our spirits. Let us silently consider how we might be receptive to the stirrings of the spirit.

Silent meditation, followed by the Choir singing "On the Dusty Earth Drum" by Joseph S. Cotter Jr.

Choir   On the dusty earth drum beats the falling rain;
now a whispered murmur, now a louder strain.

Slender, silv'ry drumsticks on an ancient drum
beat the mellow music bidding life to come.

Chords of life awakened, notes of greening spring,
rise and fall triumphant over everything.

Celebrating the Return of the Sun

Narrator   By February 1, the daylight lasts noticeably longer than at Winter Solstice, confirming that the fiery sun has indeed begun its return journey. Not surprisingly, Brigid is associated with fire. One of the meanings of her name is "firebrand" or "fiery arrow." Scholars believe that Druid priestesses at the goddess's sanctuary in Kildare, Ireland, kept a perpetual fire burning in her honor, a fire that Catholic nuns continued to keep when the goddess was converted to saint and her sanctuary to a monastery. Stories of the saint's life also retained the fire imagery: A pillar of flame hovered above the place where she was born and she was believed to hang her cloak on a sunbeam. Like her divine counterpart, the saint was the patron of metalworkers, at home near the blacksmith's furnace. On the eve of her feast, the faithful ritually invited her into their homes and considered themselves blessed if the next morning they found the mark of her footprint in the ashes of their hearth.

Leader   From the fourth century, Christians also commemorated at this time the biblical event of Mary presenting herself in the temple to be purified after the birth of her son Jesus. On this occasion, according to the gospel account, the prophet Simeon hailed the child as "a light of revelation." By the eleventh century, perhaps in recognition of Simeon's acclamation, the blessing of candles became associated with the feast, which came to be known as Candlemas, a feast that had strong appeal in the colder, darker northern countries, where it was primarily a celebration of returning light. In the border districts of Scotland, people lit fires on the hills. In some places in Scotland and Ireland, bonfires were used to burn an effigy of the Cailleach, symbolizing the death of winter.

Narrator   And at this same time, halfway around the world the Chinese celebrate their New Year, or Spring Festival, when the earth awakens. Their rituals and customs include a Lantern Festival and a fireworks display to send out the old year and welcome the new.

Leader   For some of our ancestors, the fires on their hilltops
           and the flames of their candles beckoned the sun, drew
           it closer. We may no longer share this belief. But we can
           still appreciate fire as a symbol not just of the physical
           light and warmth we hope for with the return of the
           sun but also of spiritual enlightenment and the
           warmth of kindness and generosity.

           We invite you to come forward and light a candle
           in the spirit of appreciation for the light and warmth of
           the sun and in the hope of a more enlightened mind
           and warmer heart.

           A container of sand has been set out to receive the burn-
           ing candles. While instrumental music plays, a Lighter
           lights one candle and stands with it to provide light for
           the others. Each participant comes forward and takes a
           small candle from a basket held by a Server, lights it from
           the candle of the Lighter, places it in the container of
           sand, and returns to her/his place. If necessary, there can
           be two containers of sand, two Basket Holders, and two
           Lighters, and directions given for the flow of traffic. The
           Leader waits for all to return to their places before speaking.

Leader   With minds and hearts open to the fire of inspiration,
           there are no limits to the imagination, as evidenced by
           this poem by William Butler Yeats, "The Song of the
           Wandering Aengus."

Reader 3   I went out to the hazel wood
           Because a fire was in my head
           And cut and peeled a hazel wand
           And hooked a berry to a thread
           And when the white moths were on the wing
           And moth-like stars were flickering out
           I dropped the berry in a stream
           And caught a little silver trout

When I had laid it on the floor
I went to blow a fire aflame
But something rustled on the floor
And some one called me by my name
It had become a glimmering girl
With apple blossoms in her hair
Who called me by my name and ran
And faded through the brightening air

Though I am old with wandering
Through hollow lands and hilly lands
I will find out where she has gone
And kiss her lips and take her hands
And walk among long dappled grass
And pluck till time and times are done
The silver apples of the moon
The golden apples of the sun

Celebrating the Water of Purification

Narrator   Brigid—whether goddess or saint—was an elemental
figure, associated not only with the earth as bringer of
spring's fertility, with the air as breath of life, and with
the fire as summoner of the sun but also with water as
a source of purification and healing. In Roman times
Brigid was invoked as "the nymph goddess," and there
are rivers in all the British Isles named for her. Further,
the water from her sacred wells was thought to have
healing powers. Some of the saint's legendary miracles
were related to water, including her famed ability to
change it into beer! Even today, the faithful make pilgrimages to her sacred wells and streams, where they
ritually cleanse their hands and hearts.

Leader   Scholars remind us that ritual cleansing often precedes
significant cultural and religious events, especially

those that mark seasonal changes. The ancient Romans, for example, engaged in February purification rites to cleanse the land and its people before the planting in March, when they observed their New Year.

Narrator   The Japanese celebrate the end of winter at the beginning of February with the celebration of Setsubun. In a late twentieth-century ritual at an Oomoto sanctuary, participants prayed for purification and wrote their names on pieces of rice paper, which they put into jars that were ritually carried by priests to the river where they were released to the cleansing waters.

Leader   Cleansing is at the center of the Indian festival of Mahashivratri in February or early March. It celebrates the god Shiva, who divided the Ganges into seven holy rivers at the time of creation. Worshippers bathe in the Ganges at dawn, then carry its sacred water to the temple, where they bathe the Shiva linga, a large phallic column that symbolizes the god as creative force.

Narrator   On February 2, the people of the African diaspora in Bahia, Brazil, honor Yemaya, mother of waters, giver of all life. At daybreak, drummers, dancers, and chanters invoke her as long lines of worshippers form, bearing flowers and other gifts that are carried out to sea by fishermen and there offered to the goddess.

The Choir or a Soloist sings "O Yemaya" by Aeona Silversong. The song can be accompanied by Drummers and/or Dancers.

Choir   O-oh, Yemaya, Imaja, Yemaya;
or Soloist   You are the Goddess of the Sea,
    and the Mother of all that be.
    O-oh, Yemaya, Imaja, Yemaya;
    You walk the white-capped wave,
    and the salt spray is your kiss.

Your dress of white and blue,
and the seaweed is your hair.
O-oh, Yemaya, Imaja, Yemaya;
The Goddess of the Sea, and Mother of all that be.

Leader   Yes, the sea is "the mother of all that be," for it is from the sea that all life came. Let us give thanks and praise for all the earth's waters—waters that nourish and cleanse and heal.

Give thanks for all the waters that be,

All   For bays and gulfs and shining seas!

Leader   For rivers that flow like meandering snakes,

All   For wells in the desert and great mountain lakes.

Leader   For vastness of oceans unparagoned,

All   For each fishing hole and tiny frog pond.

Leader   For Atlantic, Pacific, and the blue Aegean,

All   For the Baltic, the Bering, and the Caribbean.

Leader   For the Nile and the Niger and Amazon,

All   For the Mississippi, Missouri, and Yukon.

Leader   For the Rhine and the Rhone and the Rio Grande,

All   For the Tigris, Euphrates, and sacred Ganges.

Leader   For the Thames, the Seine, the Shannon, the Po,

All   For the Darling, the Uruguay, and the mighty Congo.

Leader   May these giving waters—and all the rest,

All   With our careful tending be ever blest!

Narrator The best way to prepare for the coming of spring is to commit ourselves to the care of the earth's waters—

without which there could be no spring, no life, no world as we know it. For as the poet Gerard Manley Hopkins exclaims,

> What would the world be, once bereft
> Of wet and of wildness? Let them be left,
> O let them be left, wildness and wet;
> Long live the weeds and the wilderness yet.
>
> —"Inversnaid"

But rites of purification do more than prepare the earth for seasonal transitions; they also prepare our human hearts for the many changes they undergo. The Hebrew psalmist prays, "A clean heart, create for me, O God, and a steadfast spirit renew within me." The Christian Jesus promises, "Blessed are the clean of heart, for they shall see God." How shall we clean our hearts to prepare for the experience of the transcendent? How shall we purify our spirits that we might discern the direction of our growth?

The cleansing of the earth and the cleansing of our hearts are connected. It is in attempting the one that we accomplish the other.

Leader   With faith in this possibility we invite you to join us in a purification ritual. Servers stand ready with pitchers and basins at their stations. When you come forward, place your hands, palms up, over the basin. The Server will pour a few drops of water on your fingertips and speak the first line of the invocation by Buddhist monk and peace activist Thich Nhat Hanh:
   Water flows over these hands.
You respond with:
   May I use them skillfully
   to preserve our precious planet.

Each station might include three Servers: one to hold the

*basin, one to pour from the pitcher, and one to offer a
small paper towel for drying. There should also be a basket for discarding the towels. A small table might substitute for the basin holder. Or if the participants are few
and this part of the service short, the same Server might
hold a small pitcher in one hand and a small basin in the
other. Silence is recommended so that everyone present
can hear the litany of familiar voices committing the
community—member by member—to the task. When
all have returned to their places, everyone sings "I've Got
Peace Like a River" by Marvin V. Frey.*

All sing   I've got peace like a river,
I've got peace like a river,
I've got peace like a river in my soul.
I've got peace like a river,
I've got peace like a river.
I've got peace like a river in my soul.

I've got joy like a fountain,
I've got joy like a fountain,
I've got joy like a fountain in my soul.
I've got joy like a fountain,
I've got joy like a fountain,
I've got joy like a fountain in my soul.

I've got tears like the raindrops,
I've got tears like the raindrops,
I've got tears like the raindrops in my soul.
I've got tears like the raindrops,
I've got tears like the raindrops,
I've got tears like the raindrops in my soul.

I've got love like an ocean,
I've got love like an ocean,
I've got love like an ocean in my soul.
I've got love like an ocean,

I've got love like an ocean,
I've got love like an ocean in my soul.

Celebrating Mother's Milk

Narrator   The Celts divided their year into four seasons and called the first day of each a quarter day. The name they gave to the February 1 quarter day was Imbolc [*IM-olk*]—an appropriate one since the name means "ewe's milk" and this was the time when ewes began to lactate and lambs were born. It was, in fact, a festival that celebrated all mothers' milk and motherhood itself.

The Celtic goddess Brigid was called on by women in labor and invoked to cure barrenness. One of her symbols was the sacred cow, whose milk was thought to be the most nourishing and healing of foods. Biographers of *Saint* Brigid—called Bride—claimed she was nursed on the milk of a sacred Otherworld cow and that her miracles included curing a frigid woman. But her most famous miracles involved the multiplication of food. Her cows gave milk three times a day. Whatever stores she gave to feed the poor were magically replenished. Her butter churn was never empty. She was so associated with milk that the churndash—the plunger used to agitate the milk—came to be her symbol at Imbolc, whose ritual feast centered on dairy products. In the nineteenth century Alexander Carmichael visited the Scottish Highlands and collected oral reports of folk customs practiced there. Here is an excerpt from a prayer to Brigid he recorded.

Reader 4   We shall have flesh,
We should have that
We should have that.

The cheek of hen,

Two bits of barley,
That were enough,
That were enough.

We shall have mead,
We shall have spruce,
We shall have wine,
We shall have feast.
We shall have sweetness and milk produce,
Honey and milk,
Wholesome ambrosia,
Abundance of that,
Abundance of that.

We shall have harp,
We shall have harp,
We shall have lute,
We shall have horn.
We shall have sweet psaltery
Of the melodious strings
And the regal lyre,
Of the songs we shall have,
Of the songs we shall have.

The calm fair Bride will be with us. . . .

And the Spirit of peace
And of grace will be with us,
Of grace will be with us.

—*Carmina Gadelica*

Leader   Milk played an important role in the February purification rites of the Romans. At their festival of Lupercalia,
two high-ranking young men had the blood of sacrificial animals ritually applied to their foreheads and then
wiped off with wool dipped in milk. Scholars believe
this cleansing with milk, "the source of life," symbolized
the revival of life in the spring.

Narrator Milk is used in the Indian festival of Mahashivratri, when the *Shiva linga*—symbol of the male creative force—is bathed not just in the water of the Ganges but also in milk, a symbol of the female life force.

Leader Scientists tell us that breast milk is a complete, versatile, and perfect food, with each species of mammal producing a version uniquely designed for the nutritional needs of its young. In addition, it carries antibodies from the mother's immune system, helping the infant to resist disease.

Narrator The nursing mother has been venerated through the ages. We see her in the glorified breasts of stone statues of prehistoric clans and in the wood and clay carvings of primitive tribes. We see her in the three-thousand-year-long worship of Isis, often depicted suckling her son, the god Horus. We see her in the early Renaissance fascination with the *Maria Lactans*, the nursing Madonna. If we sense the sacredness of this image, perhaps it is because we appreciate the reality it conveys with such simple yet awesome power. Our mothers feed us with their very bodies—even after our birth. What act could be more generous, more loving, more divine? What liquid could be a clearer symbol of love and kindness?

Leader We invite you to come forward for a cupful of milk. Please return to your seat with it, and when all have been served, we'll toast one another and enjoy it together.

If needed, give traffic directions here. It might be announced that lactose-free milk is available. Servers hold trays of small cups, half full of milk. If possible, these Servers are nursing mothers or pregnant women. Participants come forward for milk and return to their places with it while instrumental music plays. When all have returned to their places the Narrator holds up a cup of milk.

Narrator   Behold the nourishment complete
That comforts and protects.

All   (*holding up cups*) Give thanks for milk, so warm
and sweet,
That human life connects.

Leader   The gift of love, the food of life—
May we who taste it here

All   Turn hearts and hands away from strife
And hold all beings dear.

All drink and then sing the following words to the melody of "Come, Thou Font of Every Blessing."

All sing   Source of life, this food of mothers,
Warm and white and nourishing.
Joins us to all humankind and
Gives us joy in flourishing.
Gifts of love and gifts of caring,
May we learn to share with all
Sisters, brothers, the world over,
And all creatures great and small.

Sharing Gifts

Narrator   If, indeed, we hold all beings dear and are joined to all humankind, then surely we must share what we have with those who have less. If we do not, how can we call ourselves "connected"? How can we consider ourselves part of the great web of life? The legendary Saint Brigid was famous—indeed, infamous—for her generosity to the poor, as we shall hear in the next reading, "The Giveaway" by Phyllis McGinley.

Reader 5   Saint Bridget was
A problem child.
Although a lass
Demure and mild,
And one who strove
To please her dad,
Saint Bridget drove
The family mad.
For here's the fault in Bridget lay:
She would give everything away.

To any soul
Whose luck was out
She'd give her bowl
Of stir about;
She'd give her shawl,
Divide her purse
With one or all.
And what was worse,
When she ran out of things to give
She'd borrow from a relative.

Her father's gold,
Her grandsire's dinner,
She'd hand to cold
And hungry sinner;
Give wine, give meat,
No matter whose;
Take from her feet
The very shoes,
And when her shoes had gone to others,
Fetch forth her sister's and her mother's.

She could not quit.
She had to share;
Gave bit by bit
The silverware,

The barnyard geese,
The parlor rug,
Her little niece
's christening mug,
Even her bed to those in want,
And then the mattress of her aunt.

An easy touch
For poor and lowly,
She gave so much
And grew so holy
That when she died
Of years and fame,
The countryside
Put on her name,
And still the Isles of Erin fidget
With generous girls named Bride or Bridget.

Well, one must love her.
Nonetheless,
In thinking of her
Givingness,
There's no denial
She must have been
A sort of trial
Unto her kin.
The moral, too, seems rather quaint.
WHO had the patience of a saint,
From evidence presented here?
Saint Bridget? Or her near and dear?

Leader Perhaps we are no match for Brigid, and our generosity does not quite try the patience of our families and friends. Yet still, in our best moments even we unsaintly mortals know the joy that comes from giving.

  Spring, though on its way, is not quite here for many of us. We encouraged you to come today [*tonight*] with blankets and bedding [*or clothing*] for the poor. We invite you now to come forward and deposit your gifts in the containers provided. (*Indicate where these are.*) After the ritual, they will be taken to [*name of local shelter*].

Participants bring offerings forward while the Choir sings "For All That Is Our Life," words by Bruce Findlow.

Choir   For all that is our life we sing our thanks and praise;
               for all life is a gift, which we are called to use
               to build the common good
               and make our own days glad.

               For needs which others serve, for services we give,
               for work and its rewards, for hours of rest and love;
               we come with praise and thanks
               for all that is our life.

               For sorrow we must bear, for failures, pain, and loss,
               for each new thing we learn, for fearful hours that pass:
               we come with praise and thanks
               for all that is our life.

               For all that is our life we sing our thanks and praise;
               for all life is a gift which we are called to use
               to build the common good
               and make our own days glad.

Narrator   (*when all have returned to their places*) We have cele-
               brated the breath of life, which is beginning to warm
               our world. We have welcomed the returning sun with
               fire. We have purified our hands and hearts with water
               for service of the earth. We have drunk together the
               milk of human kindness. We have shared our goods
               with the poor.

               We now invite all to share with one another good
               wishes and fellowship after the ritual.

May the sun that warms the earth soften our hearts,
and the returning light brighten our spirits.
May our animosities melt like snow in spring,
and our joy in life be as that of new lambs.

All sing the following words to the melody of "For the Beauty of the Earth."

All sing   For the warmth within the earth,
For the bright, returning sun,
For the creatures giving birth,
For the milk that freely runs,
We our joyful voices raise,
Singing hymns of grateful praise.

For the water and the fire,
Cleansing elements of old,
For the love that hearts desire,
For the caring deeds untold,
We our joyful voices raise,
Singing hymns of grateful praise.

Spring Equinox

March 21-22

Snowdrops have opened their umbrellas, crocuses are welcoming bees, rays of ready-to-burst forsythia sway the breeze, and daffodils are on their greening way. Young mothers and old grandfathers are pushing carriages. Kids are searching out jump ropes and hopscotch chalk, dusting off skateboards and scooters, reaching for baseball bats, tennis rackets, and lacrosse sticks. Teens are oiling rusty bikes, washing winter off salty cars. Sap stirs in the still-bare maple, where a plump robin lands on a bud-tipped branch. Chipmunks scramble out of their winter homes. Everything is new again: It's spring.

The Seasonal Calendar

The earth is warming, the light is gaining dominance. On Winter Solstice, the sun is at its lowest path in the sky, making it the short-est day of the year, the one with the fewest daylight hours. From then on, the sun's path rises in the sky until it reaches its peak at the Summer Solstice in June, providing us with the longest day of the year. Halfway between, around March 21, the sun's path crosses the celestial equator, which divides the sky into northern and southern celestial hemispheres. At this point, we have twelve hours of day and twelve of night. Hence the term *equinox*, or "equal night." Whether we live in Australia or Angola, Amsterdam or

Afghanistan, Antarctica or America, on this day we share a common experience: We all have an equal amount of light and dark.

The early Romans divided the year into lunar months of twenty-nine or thirty days, which eventually fell out of sync with the seasons. Julius Caesar replaced it with a solar calendar of 365 days—plus an extra in leap years—and declared Spring Equinox to be March 25. In 1582 Pope Gregory XIII revised the calendar again and established the Vernal Equinox as March 21.

Although they lacked our sophisticated astronomical instruments, early peoples were well aware of this event—the harbinger of their returning food supplies—and as with the Winter Solstice, they celebrated it in formidable structures.

The earliest known of these is the five-thousand-year-old cluster of cairns, Loughcrew, located forty kilometers from Newgrange in Ireland. Here a beam from the sunrise on both equinoxes enters a chamber in one of the cairns and illuminates the backstone, on which are carved solar symbols that clearly reveal its astronomical function.

The ancient Egyptians built their Great Sphinx and pyramids at Giza and the surrounding temples of Osiris and Isis, as well as the pyramids at Memphis, Sais, and Tanis, oriented toward the equinox sunrise.

This same orientation is found in the ruins of the temple in the ancient Near Eastern city of Heliopolis (now Baalbek, Lebanon). Given the strong influence of the Canaanite religion on the invading Israelites, some scholars see the influence of this structure on that of Solomon's famous temple at Jerusalem, which was also oriented to the equinox sunrise. Richard Heinberg, in *Celebrate the Solstice*, notes,

> Each Spring Equinox, at the time of the ancient agricultural festival of sowing, sunlight was allowed to penetrate the length of an open passage from the doorway of the temple over the high altar and into the Holy of Holies. It was on this occasion, and this occasion only, that the High Priest entered the *sanctum sanctorum*.

There is even some evidence to suggest that witnessing this penetration formed part of the ritual associated with the festival.

The Americas are also home to structural equinoctial markers. In the Aztec capital of Tenochtitlan, the Temple Mayor functioned as an observatory that announced the equinoxes. The Pyramid of the Sun, constructed two thousand years ago by the people of Teotihuacan, near Mexico City, marks both solstices and equinoxes, as does the Mayan temple group at Uaxactun. The ceremonial pyramid, El Castillo, built by the ancient Mayans in Chichén Itza (Mexico), displays the descent of the plumed serpent-god Kukulkan-Quetzalcoatl. During the afternoon of both equinoxes, the sun's light on the architectural features of the pyramid's façade creates a series of triangular shadows that suggest the slow, downward slithering of a snake until it joins the carved serpent's head at the base of the steps. Some scholars think this snake image was associated with fertility rituals.

Farther north, some thousand years ago, the mound builders of the Mississippi Valley moved more than fifty million cubic feet of earth to create ceremonial pyramids. The one that has come to be called Monks Mound, in Cahokia, is the largest prehistoric earthen work in North America. Its four terraces rise to a hundred feet and cover fourteen acres, and it is oriented toward the equinox sunrise.

Stone structures used as calendars to mark the equinoxes (among other astronomical events) are also found in North America. These include Calendar One, a natural amphitheater in Vermont, and Mystery Hill in New Hampshire, whose megalithic standing stones have earned it the title America's Stonehenge.

Mythology and History

If Winter Solstice marks the birth or rebirth of the sun deities, Spring Equinox marks the birth or rebirth of the vegetation deities. The myths associated with this time of the year not only explain the origin of the changing of the seasons but in some cases provide the bases for the rituals used to celebrate it.

The two equinoxes coincide in the Amazon with the beginning of the rainy seasons. Heinberg reports that the Desana and Barasana Indians who live there believe that at the time of creation, the "Sun Father fertilized the world at its center by there erecting a perfectly vertical rod. It was from this spot that the first people emerged." Because this spot happens to lie almost exactly on the equator, the sun is directly overhead on each Spring and Fall Equinox and an upright staff casts no shadow. The Indians believe "the Sun's rays are again directly penetrating the Earth, making the world fertile and new." Thus is the world created and re-created.

Some re-creation myths involve the death and resurrection of a vegetation god. The oldest of these myths on record is that of Inanna, the Sumerian goddess worshipped as Queen of Heaven and Earth, whose sacred marriage to her son/lover, Dumuzi the shepherd, assures the fruitfulness of the land and its animal and human inhabitants.

Inanna sets out to visit her sister Ereshkigal, Queen of the Underworld. Her descent takes her through seven gates, at each of which she must give up an article of clothing, an ornament of her queenship: first her crown, then her jeweled earrings and necklace, then her cloak, shoes, and belt, and finally her very dress, until she is at last stripped of all adornment and must face her dark-haired sister, the dark side of herself, completely naked.

When Ereshkigal turns her skull-eyes upon her sister, Inanna dies and is impaled upon a meat hook to rot. When she doesn't return to earth after three days, her servant appeals to the god Enki, Inanna's father, who sends help. But Inanna is allowed to return to her kingdom only if she can find someone to take her place among the dead. She passes up those who have mourned her absence as possible substitutes. But when she discovers Dumuzi sitting upon her throne, unconcerned with his loss and happy with his newly assumed position, she appoints him to be her replacement. Thus Dumuzi, the god of vegetation, also "dies"; he is forced to spend part of every year beneath the earth, fertilizing it. In his absence the rivers dry up and the desert grows parched. But upon his return, after his decaying flesh has fed its germinating seeds, the earth once again bears fruit.

In Babylonia, the couple was known as Ishtar and Tammuz, and one version of their story is somewhat different. Tammuz is gored by a wild boar and, mortally wounded, is taken to the Underworld, where he is spellbound in sleep until Ishtar descends to awaken him. While he sleeps, so does life above the earth. Inanna and Dumuzi (under various names) were worshiped widely in the Mesopotamian world for over three millennia, from 3500 BCE to 200 BCE.

Isis and Osiris were worshiped for about four centuries into the Christian era. Isis is the "throne of Egypt," from whose lap the pharaohs rule. Osiris is her brother-consort, ruler of the Underworld and god of the Nile and of vegetation, the germ of life buried but revived by the power of the goddess.

The pair have a wicked brother, Seth, whose jealousy drives him to seal up Osiris in a chest and throw it into the Nile. As it floats down to the sea, Isis cuts her hair in mourning and searches the country for her dead lover's body. Meanwhile the chest comes to the shores of Byblos, where it rests in the roots of a tree that quickly grows up around and conceals the coffin. The local king discovers the fragrant tree and orders it cut down to serve as a column in his palace. Isis learns what has happened, retrieves the column, and takes it back to Egypt, where she cuts away the wood, opens the coffin, and breathes momentary life back into Osiris. In that fleeting moment when his loins live again, Osiris impregnates Isis with a son, Horus, who will rule Egypt. Mourning the loss of Osiris yet again, Isis hides his body and in due course gives birth to Horus.

Finding his brother's body, Seth takes violent action against Osiris a second time, cutting his body into fourteen pieces and scattering them around the country, hurling his phallus into the Nile, where it is devoured by a fish. Isis once again sets out on a search for her lost lover. She recovers and reassembles his remains—

all but the phallus—and fans life back into Osiris with her great wings, enabling him to assume his role as ruler of the Underworld. She makes replicas of his missing phallus and plants them about the country. In each burial place, the Nile's flooding waters fertilize the land and produce rich crops. (In another version of the myth, she plants the various body parts where she finds them, with the same results.) So each year in Egypt, Isis's tears of mourning make the Nile overflow, and its waters unite with the body of her dead lover Osiris to assure the fecundity of the land.

Another search for the lost loved one is found in Homer's "Hymn to Demeter." In the long-ago time of eternal spring, Demeter, the mother goddess of agriculture and fertility, makes all things grow. One day when her daughter Kore ("the maiden") is gathering flowers, the earth opens, and Hades, ruler of the Underworld, abducts her. Her screams to her father Zeus go unheeded. Distraught Demeter searches wildly for her lost daughter. When she discovers that Zeus has approved the abduction, she withdraws from Olympus in grief and rage, thus causing universal famine. Faced with this ongoing catastrophe, Zeus relents.

Daughter is restored to mother, whose joy again unleashes earth's fertility. But because Kore has eaten the pomegranate, food of the dead, while in Hades and has thus made the transition from innocence to knowledge, she assumes the role of Persephone, Comforter of the Dead, and so must return to the Underworld for part of each year. In her absence, her mourning mother weeps the world into winter. (Persephone's Norse counterpart is Freya, whose absence from the earth during fall and winter has the same effect.)

But it must be so, for as Anne Baring and Jules Cashford assure us in *The Myth of the Goddess*, "Persephone is the seed that splits off from the body of the ripened grain, the mother, when, sinking beneath the earth, she returns in the spring as the new shoot."

Adonis is another mythological figure who divides his time above and below the earth. In one version of this myth, Adonis is born of the virgin Myrrha, a temple woman, in the same cave in Bethlehem that will later be claimed as the birthplace of Jesus. In another version, he is conceived when Myrrha tricks her king-father into impregnating her. Once pregnant, she is miraculously transformed into a myrrh tree to avoid her father's punishment. When the tree blossoms, Adonis is born. Aphrodite is so enamored of the beautiful baby that she entrusts him to Persephone for safekeeping. But when Aphrodite returns to the Underworld to search for him, the equally enamored Persephone refuses to give him back. Zeus settles the dispute by decreeing that Adonis spend part of each year below the earth and part above.

When Adonis grows to magnificent manhood, he ignores Aphrodite's warning and hunts a wild boar, which gores him in the groin. The goddess cradles her dying lover and turns his drops of spilled blood—the color of the pomegranate—into anemones, which brighten the fields in spring. Barbara Walker reminds us in *The Woman's Encyclopedia of Myths and Secrets* that castration, a common fate of vegetation gods, is a metaphor for the reaping of the grain, personified by Adonis, who "died and rose again in periodic cycles, like all gods of vegetation and fertility." Only thus can the life of the whole continue.

The yearly death and resurrection of Adonis was celebrated in the summer in Alexandria and in spring in Syria. He was venerated four centuries into the Christian era.

Another god of vegetation—especially of trees and the vine—is Dionysus. After wooing and impregnating the earth goddess Semele in her incarnation as the princess of Thebes, Zeus reveals his godhead to her. The awesome sight reduces her to ashes—except for the fetal Dionysus, whom his father quickly snatches up and thrusts into his own thigh, whence the young god experiences a "second birth." The poet Nonnus reports another version of the myth, in which Zeus impregnates Persephone and she bears Dionysus. But when the infant ascends his father's throne, he is attacked by the Titans, giants seeking to rule heaven. Although he wards them off by assuming various animal forms, they finally cut him to pieces when he is in the form of a bull, and pomegranates spring from his blood. In yet another variation, Dionysus is the son of Zeus and Demeter, who pieces together his mangled limbs; in another it is Zeus who heals his mortal wounds.

Having survived (more or less) these childhood traumas, Dionysus is educated by nymphs and satyrs who accompany him on his journeys. He learns how to cultivate the vine and teaches the people this important skill. He descends into Hades and retrieves his mother Semele from the dead. He preaches the gospel of intoxication and ecstasy; his worshipers seek to promote fertility as well as to achieve mystical union with the creative divine through sexual coitus as well as through the transports of wine. He is the young god whom Plutarch believed stood for "the whole wet element" in nature: wine, blood, semen, sap.

The vegetation god Attis, worshiped from about 500 BCE to 400 CE, was the Anatolian counterpart of the Mesopotamian Dumuzi. This son/lover of the Great Mother Cybele is immaculately conceived by her earthly incarnation, the virgin Nana, when she eats a pomegranate (an almond in some versions). One day, Attis is pursued by a lustful monster while tending his sheep. To escape its advances and remain faithful to the Great Mother, he castrates himself and dies under an evergreen, where violets spring up, nourished by his blood. (In another version, he is gored by a wild boar with the same results.) When Cybele finds his body, she wraps it in mourning cloth and carries it, together with the tree under which he has died, to her mountain cave. She plants the tree and buries the body at the mouth of the cave. And every spring she performs her rituals of mourning.

For six centuries, beginning in 204 BCE, Romans carried a statue of Cybele—their *Magna Mater*—through the streets at the time of the Spring Equinox. They celebrated the passion and death of her son/lover Attis, as well as his conception, on March 25, nine months before the Winter Solstice celebration of his birth. At the annual commemoration of the god's death, they felled a sacred pine (a phallic fertility symbol), wrapped it in mourning cloth, hung an effigy of Attis on it, carried it in procession to Cybele's sacred cave or temple, and buried it on what was called Black Friday or the Day of Blood. There followed three days of lamentation, penance, and fasting, during which priests or initiates castrated or cut themselves in imitation of the self-sacrificing god and made their bloody offerings to the Great Mother. During this period, the god was believed to have descended into the Underworld. On the third day, Sunday, like the dawn light emanating from the temple-tomb, he rose from the dead. His followers, believing that his salvation from suffering assured theirs, celebrated with dancing and festivities, welcoming spring's new life.

Though a latecomer to the pantheon of vegetation gods, the Christian Jesus fits the mythological pattern. A solar god, born at Winter Solstice of a virgin mother made pregnant by a father god, he sacrifices himself for the benefit of humankind, endures suffering, dies, is buried, mourned by his mother and other women, descends to the Underworld, and on the third day rises from the dead at the time of Spring Equinox, when his conception is also celebrated. His resurrection—mirrored in the annual rising of spring flowers and the blossoming of fruit trees—assures the eternal life of his followers. After two millennia, his worship continues.

It may well be, however, that the solar god's connection to this theme came well after that of the moon goddess. The goddess's descent into the Underworld for three days represents the period between the disappearance (death) of the old moon and the appearance (birth) of the new, each month's "dark of the moon." This lunar female deity, Mother Nature, who makes all things new every spring, is the original Great Goddess, giver of all life. Archeological evidence suggests she was honored as far back as the Paleolithic Age, probably long before the male role in procreation was understood. It is possible that the discovery of this role precipitated the appearance of male deities. Baring and Cashford trace this development. The gods first appear in the form of sons of the goddess, then as son-lovers or consorts, then as equals— husbands or brother-lovers. In the next stage, the mother goddess is overshadowed by and subservient to the god. (The Iron-Age Babylonian Marduk actually murders and dismembers his mother Tiamat.) And finally, in the monotheistic religions, the goddess is excluded altogether and the male god creates the world alone. The myths related here reflect a period when the honor of creation and re-creation was still shared.

Our ancient ancestors had a deep respect for the role of their vegetation deities. Given their direct reliance on the fruits of the earth and their personal responsibility for planting and harvesting, they were probably even more appreciative of spring and eager to welcome it than we are.

No Ruz ("New Day"), a Zoroastrian feast older than Islam, has been celebrated at the Spring Equinox in what is now Iran, Iraq, and Afghanistan for more than twenty-five-hundred years. This New Year festival features prayers honoring the gods, the "preexistent souls," and the dead, as well as ritual drinking of a sacred liquor and ritual handshaking.

The ancient Romans welcomed spring by celebrating the resurrection of Attis, whose body—in the form of bread—was consumed by his worshipers.

In ancient Greece, the passion, death, and resurrection of Dionysus was celebrated annually. The Lydians believed he ushered in the spring. The Athenians held their Dionysia from March 24 to March 28 to welcome the spring. Greek drama was first introduced at this religious festival, growing out of the *dithyrambs*, hymns in honor of Dionysus. And at the Eleusinian Mysteries, celebrated by the Greeks up to the fourth-century CE, initiates ritually re-enacted the story of Demeter and Kore/Persephone and came to understand that all life is one, as mother and maiden are one, as life and death are one.

The ancient Germans celebrated the spring fertility goddess Ostara, the Radiant Dawn, who mated with the solar god to conceive a son who would be born at Yule. The Anglo-Saxons called her Eostre (from whose named *Easter* is derived) and celebrated her feast on the full moon following the Spring Equinox. Strictly speaking then, she was a lunar goddess, and her feast was a lunar rather than solar holiday. The association of this and other fertility goddesses with the Vernal Equinox explains why its traditional folk name is Lady Day.

In more recent times, natives of the Americas enacted seasonal fertility rites. The Iroquois welcomed the spring rains with their thunder ceremony. The eldest women of the Manda and Hidatsa Indians, who lived along the upper Missouri River, performed a corn dance ceremony each spring, according to E. Barrie Kavasch's and Karen Baar's *American Indian Healing Arts*. It was considered essential to a successful planting. The younger women fed a special meat preparation to the dancing elders, who gave them corn in return. Some of this ceremonial corn was mixed with the tribe's seed at planting time—a blessing on its growth.

Contemporary Celebrations Around the World

Even today, thousands converge on the ancient pyramids of Teotihuacan, according to Tim Gaynor's Reuters report, "Mexicans Trek to Pyramids to Mark Equinox," to take advantage of the site's special energy on the Vernal Equinox—a day that marked the start of the new agricultural cycle in the old calendar. They mount the steep steps of the Pyramids of the Sun and the Moon "in an annual rite marking the first day of spring, which is thought to date back to pre-Hispanic times." Although the pyramids, built some two thousand years ago, were abandoned in the sixth century, interest was revived in the twentieth century and "massive attendance . . . began in the late 1980s."

Modern-day Wiccans recognize the Vernal Equinox as one of their minor *sabbats* and often celebrate Ostara's Lady Day at the equinox sunrise or on its eve. Vestiges of pre-Christian goddess worship are reflected in the playful Spring Equinox custom, still popular in some Slovakian villages, of "burning winter." A straw figure is dressed in women's clothes to symbolize Morena, the goddess of winter in ancient Slavic mythology who is blamed for sickness and evil. Singing villagers carry the effigy in procession to the river, where they set it afire and throw it in. This enables Vesna, goddess of spring, to begin her reign. Feasting, games, and craft activities are part of the celebration.

Feasting is also the focus for contemporary Iranians, who gather with family and friends on the Equinox to exchange gifts and good wishes for the New Year. For the next twelve days they visit one another's homes, starting with the eldest. And on the thirteenth day, they eat together outdoors—in a green space—to welcome spring.

Jews around the world celebrate two feasts at this time: Purim and Passover. Purim, around March 24, is a feast commemorating the deliverance of the Persian Jews from massacre through the courageous intercession of Esther, whose name is a Hebrew cognate of Ishtar or Astarte. *Pesah*, or Passover, originally marked the beginning of the spring barley harvest. It celebrates the exodus of the Hebrews from slavery in Egypt, where the Angel of Death "passed over" their homes but slew the first-born son of every Egyptian household. Joseph Campbell points out in *The Masks of God: Occidental Mythology*, that the later festival of Passover was first celebrated in 621 BCE, on a date that coincided with that of the annual resurrection of Adonis, which became Easter in the Christian cult. But where the pagan and Christian myths celebrate the resurrection of a god, in the Hebrew myth the "chosen people" themselves descend into an underworld (Egypt), where they experience suffering and death (slavery) and are resurrected (into the Promised Land). For pagans and Christians both,

> the principle of divine life is symbolized as a divine individual (Dumuzi-Adonis-Attis-Dionysus-Christ), [but] in Judaism it is the People of Israel whose mythic history thus serves the function that in other cults belongs to an incarnation or manifestation of God.

The eight-day Passover celebration begins on the fourteenth day of Nison, the first month of the Hebrew calendar, around the time of the Spring Equinox.

Christians celebrate two feasts at this time of year. March 25, the day identified in the Julian calendar as Spring Equinox, exactly nine months before Christmas, was declared the Feast of the Annunciation, commemorating the Angel Gabriel's announcement to Mary that she was to conceive a divine son. (Its vigil, March 24, was named Gabriel's feast day.)

The Christian Easter, which celebrates the resurrection of Jesus, is tied to the Jewish Passover, since the gospels recount Jesus' eating a Passover meal with his disciples just before the events of his passion and death. In the liturgical calendar, Easter is a moveable feast, falling on the first Sunday after the first full moon after the Spring Equinox, thus occurring between March 22 and April 25. It is the most important feast of the Church, preceded by Lent, a forty-day period of penance that begins with Ash Wednesday, so named for the ashes that are smudged on the foreheads of the faithful as a reminder of their physical mortality. Holy Week, the week preceding Easter, includes many rituals commemorating the events leading up to the resurrection described in the gospels.

According to Venerable Bede, an eighth-century British scholar, Easter derived its name, as mentioned above, from the spring goddess of fertility Eostre/Ostara (a variant of Ishtar or Astarte). Despite this similarity in name, most Christians would not identify Easter as a fertility festival. There is not even anything in the liturgy that suggests a simple comparison of the resurrection of Jesus with the resurrection of new life in the plant and animal world at this time of year, let alone any reference to the mating of this sun god with an earth mother. And although the Easter Vigil service does include a reading of the Genesis account of creation, the emphasis is not on the present, natural world but on the future, supernatural one. The comparison drawn is between the resurrection of Jesus and that which will be enjoyed by his followers at their deaths if they are faithful to him and his teachings.

As a pledge of that fidelity, the worshipers renew their baptismal vows during the service and initiates are baptized. The water used is blessed with the large Paschal candle, a symbol of the risen Jesus, which bears the sign of the cross. Here, perhaps, we have the hint of fertility symbolism. In *Contributions to Analytical Psychology*, Carl Jung points out that the text of the *Benedictio fontis* recognizes the baptismal font as "the womb of the church." At the Easter vigil service,

> A *hierosgamos* or holy wedding is celebrated . . . and a burning candle as a phallic symbol is plunged three times into the font, in order to fertilize the baptismal water . . . to give a new birth to the . . . baptized.

Although the Easter liturgy doesn't acknowledge Jesus as a vegetation god, there are multiple references to his role as a solar deity. The prayer at the ceremonial blessing of the new fire, a symbol of new life, calls upon the God who bestowed light. In the darkened church, during the procession of the blessed Paschal candle, the celebrant raises the candle three times and chants, "Christ our light!" to which the people, lighting their own candles from it, respond, "Thanks be to God!" The deacon or cantor then sings the Exultet, a hymn of praise to the radiant brightness of Christ and of the Church, which is resplendent in his reflected light. The prayer that follows addresses him as the Morning Star, "which knows no setting, which came back from limbo and shed its serene light upon mankind." The nineteenth-century Jesuit poet Gerard Manley Hopkins valorizes this imagery of Christ-as-sun-god in his "Wreck of the Deutschland": "Let him easter in us, be a dayspring to the dimness of us, be a crimson-cresseted east."

Spring Customs

As with any feast whose roots are ancient, the stories and traditions associated with Spring Equinox filter down to us in transmuted forms. Not surprisingly, one of the chief symbols of the spring fertility goddess Ostara is the hare or rabbit, which reaches sexual maturity in only six months, has a life span of about ten years, breeds from February to October, and bears four to eight litters a year of three to eight offspring each, thus potentially producing as many as six hundred young. Ostara's feast was celebrated on the full moon following the Equinox, and believers often saw in this moon the image of the rabbit, a vision that may have been influenced by its nocturnal eating habits.

In some stories the goddess assumes the shape of a hare to traverse the land and renew it; in others, she is attended by hares. In her website article "Ostara," Christina Aubin claims that Eostre changes a bird into a hare in some stories, and this hare, in keeping with her old habits, builds nests and fills them with colored eggs: "It is believed that this tradition made its way into U.S. culture with the immigration of the Germans in the early 1700s—taking the form of the . . . lovable Easter Bunny, and her nests through time became baskets."

In *Wheel of the Year*, Pauline Campanelli offers a less fanciful explanation for the tradition of Easter baskets. After the deprivation of winter, early hunter-gatherers were happy to supplement their diet with clutches of eggs laid in the spring by many different kinds of birds. The hunt for these eggs may well be the origin of present-day egg hunts as well as of the custom of dyeing eggs "in imitation of the various pastel colors of the eggs of wild birds." It's also possible that people "first got the idea for weaving baskets from watching birds weave nests."

The egg—that miracle of life—is one of the oldest symbols of creation, associated with images of that primordial creator, the ancient Bird Goddess, whose Neolithic images archeologists discovered in Old Europe. She supplied both the water that fell from the sky and the water that came from below the ground. Because the fetus comes to life in the waters of the womb, "the egg and egg-shaped womb are both images of the beginning of life," according to Baring and Cashford.

> The single egg divides, becomes two, and from the separation
> of the two halves—female and male, heaven and earth—

creation comes. This motif, originating in the Paleolithic era, is clearly painted on Neolithic vessels several thousand years before it appears in the great Bronze Age civilizations of Sumer, Egypt, and Crete. The memory of this myth lingers in the custom of Easter eggs and also in the old wives' tale of the stork bringing the baby.

Thus the cosmic egg contains the universe in embryo. Walker tells us of a variation on this division theme in the Orphic tradition of sixth-century BCE Greece, according to which "the Great Goddess of darkness Mother Night first brought forth the World Egg, which was identified with the moon." Then the two halves of the eggshell became heaven and earth.

In some cultures, eggs were dyed red to mimic the red sky at dawn, which gives birth to the sun, which makes all life possible. The custom of putting eggs in or on graves—practiced by Egyptians as well as pagan Greeks and Anglo-Saxons—indicated their power to ensure rebirth into eternal life. Ancient Egyptians and Romans exchanged gifts of eggs at the Spring Equinox. Christians adopted the custom and saw the egg as a symbol of the risen Christ. Medieval British Christians gave their children red eggs at Easter to keep them healthy all year.

Drawing magical signs and symbols on the eggs was another pagan custom. Campanelli reminds us that "egg production of domestic fowl begins when the retina of a hen's eye is stimulated by more than twelve hours of light a day." And so drawing signs—especially sun symbols—on eggs was thought to ensure that the sun would gain strength and power over darkness at the Vernal Equinox. Egg-decorating reached its ornate zenith in the skill of Ukrainian Orthodox Christians, whose *pysanky* included elaborate geometric shapes incorporated into encircling or intersecting bands, as well as finely detailed drawings of sun symbols or the tree of life.

These symbols of Ostara (though not always understood as such) come together for children today when the Easter Bunny delivers decorated eggs (real and chocolate) in a basket/nest lined with "grass."

Like the cosmic egg, the seed is a source of new life. Depending on the region's climate, the Equinox may be sprouting time, planting time, or seeding time. In the temperate zone of the northern hemisphere, March can be a time to plant hearty vegetables like spinach, kale, leafy greens, cabbage, broccoli, cauliflower, and Brussels sprouts, as well as bulbs and tubers like onions, garlic, and potatoes. Some flowers that are tolerant of cool weather, such as pansies, violas, and anemones, can be planted as well.

For other plants, it may still be too early to brave the elements. But seeds of vegetables like squash, pumpkin, cucumber, and tomato, as well as herbs like basil and chives, can be planted in pots and nourished indoors until a later time. Flower seeds, like petunia, nasturtium, and marigold, can be planted in pots for later transplanting into the garden.

Whatever we plant, the urgency in spring to put hands to soil, to join in the creation of new life, must not be denied. Perhaps the impetus for that urgency comes from sensing—seeing, smelling, feeling—the new life around us. Depending on the weather in a given year, the spring flowers may still be in bud or starting to bloom at Equinox. In my neighborhood, snowdrops lead the way, followed by crocuses, tulips, forsythia, daffodils, and magnolias. And even though they are not in bloom yet, I know the cherry trees, azaleas, dogwood, and rhododendron will soon be bursting with pink and purple. The signs are appearing; the promise made by the Winter Solstice sun as it started its ascent will surely now be kept. The equinox flowers assure us that the sun will indeed rise to its zenith at Summer Solstice, providing nourishment for the crops that will grow and be harvested and give us food for another year.

Spring flowers are both a harbinger of things to come and a joy in their own right. Now the drab, gray winter is over. Now we can rejoice in bright colors, in sweet smells, in the surging life around us and inside us. We can walk among the spring flowers, decorate our homes with them, and feel in our own bodies and spirits the energy for renewed life.

No wonder Ostara is often portrayed as crowned with spring

flowers, holding the cosmic egg in her hand, mindful of the frol-
icking hares at her feet and the joyful birds flying above her head.
Ritual attention paid to fields and fowl at this time of year is doc-
umented by Ronald Hutton in *The Stations of the Sun*. He describes a nineteenth-century custom called "walking the wheat,"
which was practiced in parts of England. For example, paralleling
the wassailing of the orchards at midwinter, Monmouthshire
farmers would go round their fields on Easter Day "carrying
plum-cakes and cider and eating and drinking to the good fortune
of the sprouting cereals." They then buried some pieces of the cake
and scattered other bits for the birds, saying,

> A bit for God, a bit for man,
> and a bit for the fow's of the air.

As with all celebrations of the seasons, Spring Equinox is the
occasion for major feasts in which families and friends gather to
share a meal and renew their ties to one another. Often at such
meals, the food has symbolic as well as sustaining value.

Ham is a popular seasonal tradition, possibly because the pig
has been a symbol of prosperity in many cultures (consider our
children's piggy banks) and so a fit dish for a special feast. A reason dating back to classical times is that pigs were the animals sacrificed to Demeter, the grain goddess, and sacred to the Norse
Freya. And as recounted in the myths above, it was a wild boar that
gored Adonis and Attis.

Lamb may be even more common as it is associated with this
season in several traditions. An old folk belief has it that sheep
bow three times to the east to welcome the rising sun. The Jews in
Egypt sacrificed a lamb to make the blood markings on their door
that would signal the Angel of Death to pass over them. Christians
hail Jesus as the Lamb of God, sacrificed for their sins. On Easter,
early Christians placed lamb meat under the altar and feasted on
it after it was blessed. Lamb is a traditional favorite for the
Equinox/Passover/Easter meal.

For the Jews, the Passover meal, or *Seder*, is itself the celebration, consisting of a series of smaller rituals related to the symbolic food. For example, horseradish represents the bitterness of slavery; the mixture of nuts, apples, and wine stands for the mortar the Hebrews used for building; and the *matzoth* calls to mind the unleavened bread they ate in their hurry to escape the pursuing army of the Pharaoh.

Eggs in any form, but especially hard-boiled and dyed, often play a large role in the holiday menu. The baking of special breads is another widespread custom. The devotees of Inanna made "cakes for the Queen of Heaven," which were sweetened with honey. At the Eleusinian Mysteries, which celebrated the return of Kore to her mother, the grain goddess Demeter, the climax of the ceremony was the holding up of a single sheaf of wheat in profound silence. Contemplating this would enable the initiates to understand that Kore the maiden had become one with her mother, that the grain of wheat that went below the earth returned as the mature sheaf, from which would come the seed that would go below the earth only to rise again, ensuring the cycle of renewal.

At their celebration of Easter Mass, Christians eat bread believed to be transformed into the body of Jesus. In the gospel story, Jesus declares, "Unless a grain of wheat fall into the ground and die, it remains alone; but if it dies, it brings forth much fruit." The mystery celebrated at Easter is that the "fruit" of Jesus' resurrection is salvation for his followers.

A common custom is baking breads that feature eggs. Some, like the Polish *Paska* bread and the Russian and Italian versions of Easter bread, are characterized by the inclusion of many eggs in the recipe. A popular style of loaf at this season is one in which the dough is braided and shaped into a circle and a number of dyed boiled eggs pressed into the dough, which rises around them.

Perhaps the most famous of this season's breads are hot cross buns, round yeasted wheat cakes containing spices and raisins or currants. They are marked with a cross on the top, symbolizing the four phases of the moon, the four directions, the four seasons, or possibly the balanced light-and-dark of the equinox itself. So popular were the buns that the Christian Church had difficulty dissuading its converts from eating them and so adopted their marking as a symbol of the cross of Christ. Today hot cross buns are often eaten on Good Friday and sometimes Ash Wednesday.

The rituals that welcome spring are celebrations of life, the renewal of life in the earth after the dormancy of winter and the renewal of life in our own spirits. Perhaps we can learn from the earth how best to appreciate that renewal.

WAYS TO CELEBRATE

Appreciate nature's coming to life.

⑥   Lean against a tree and envision the sap rising with your blood.

⑥   Sit facing a daffodil and watch it grow. Draw what you see with chalk or crayons.

⑥   Take a walk in a forest or park and notice the buds on the different trees.

⑥   Visit an arboretum or conservatory.

⑥   Take a walk in your neighborhood and share tips with fellow gardeners at work.

⑥   Make mud pies with children.

Give your home a good spring cleaning.

⑥   Put away the snow shovel and clear the yard, porch, and deck of debris.

⑥   Clean the winter salt off the car.

⑥   Wash all the windows in the house. Then leave them open and invite the spring air in.

⑥   Brighten the house by cleaning all the light fixtures.

☉   Take a mop to cobwebs, polish furniture, wax floors, dust, vacuum, indulge in a paroxysm of purification!

Welcome spring into your home.

☉   Put away your winter table cloth or place mats, the bed and bath linens, and/or the sofa-throw and bring out floral or pastel replacements.

☉   Exchange comforters and quilts for lighter bedding.

☉   Bring fresh daffodils into the house.

☉   Create a Japanese *ikebana* arrangement with three budding twigs or sprays of forsythia.

☉   Make a trip to the local nursery for potted pansies, violas, anemones, artemisia, or boxwood. Arrange them in a painted shallow crate or a child's wagon for a moveable indoor garden.

Nurture new life.

☉   Offer your babysitting services to new parents.

☉   Take in a stray puppy or kitten.

☉   Celebrate all the newborns (babies, pets, projects) in your family or neighborhood with a welcome party.

☉   Begin work on a new project that has been "germinating" during the winter.

☉   Learn a new song.

☉   Memorize a new poem.

☉   Take the first concrete steps toward "growing" a good habit or quality you've been wanting to develop, such as exercising, meditating, playing a musical instrument, or being more tolerant, patient, or courageous.

◐ Make a change in your life for the better by applying for a job that is more spiritually rewarding, befriending someone who needs it, letting go of an old grudge, or spending more time with children.

Honor the earth.

◐ Watch the sun rise on the Vernal Equinox.

◐ Make plans to celebrate Earth Day.

◐ Organize a litter-lifting brigade.

◐ Take canvas bags to the grocery store (or reuse paper ones).

◐ Make a wind sock and decorate it with symbols of the season. Hang it on your porch and honor the power of the wind.

◐ Hang wind chimes in the yard or on the porch so that their music can welcome the spring breeze.

Celebrate with your body and spirit.

◐ Dance to mime new shoots springing from the earth, or the sun climbing higher in the sky, or butterflies emerging from their cocoons.

◐ Act out the stories of Inanna, Attis, Isis, or Persephone.

◐ Audition for a local passion play.

◐ Sing songs celebrating the season.

◐ Listen (and maybe dance) to Igor Stravinsky's *Le Sacre du Printemps* (*The Rite of Spring*).

◐ Create and wear a spring bonnet or head wreath.

◐ Join with friends outdoors to read aloud poems celebrating spring. Then write one!

Celebrate community.

☙ On this day, when everyone on earth experiences the same number of hours of light and darkness, honor this common experience by singing songs that celebrate our kinship.

☙ Organize an egg hunt for children.

☙ Prepare baskets of food or clothing for poor families.

☙ Dress like the ancient Bird Goddess and distribute colorful eggs to children or help the children decorate the eggs and distribute them to the adults.

☙ Visit a house-bound relative, neighbor, or friend and take a newly planted seed.

☙ Invite friends to a potluck of egg dishes and leafy green vegetables—or prepare them for your family.

Bring spring into your kitchen.

☙ Grow bean sprouts or alfalfa spouts—both wonderful symbols of the season's new life—and enjoy them in sandwiches or salads.

☙ Make a cake in the shape of an egg or a bunny.

☙ Update an old tradition by using your bread machine to make hot cross buns. Here's my method:

HOT CROSS BUNS

Put in the bread machine in this order:

½ cup milk
¼ cup water
1 egg
3 cups bread flour
⅓ cup sugar
1 teaspoon salt

½ to 1 teaspoon (total) of spices of choice (cinnamon, nutmeg, cloves, allspice, cardamom)
¼ cup (½ stick) butter, softened
3½ teaspoons yeast

Set bread machine for "Dough" cycle and for "Add extras" and start. Then mix together:

½ cup raisins
⅓ cup (total) of chopped nuts of choice (pecans, walnuts, almonds)
1 tablespoon lemon zest (optional)

Put this mix in the "Extras" compartment of the bread machine. If yours doesn't have one, listen for the beep and add manually. When dough is finished, remove from pan onto floured board and with floured hands divide into 12 or 15 pieces, depending on size desired for buns. Roll these pieces into balls and place on greased cookie sheets, 2 inches apart. Cover and let rise in warm place for about an hour. Heat oven to 375°. If "shiny" appearance is desired, lightly brush tops with melted margarine or with an egg white mixed with 1 tablespoon of water. When oven is hot, bake for 12 to 15 minutes. When buns are cooled, use your favorite recipe to make an icing, or simply combine ½ cup of confectioners' sugar with enough hot milk (about 2 teaspoons) to get the desired consistency. Add ¼ teaspoon vanilla or lemon or orange extract or rum for flavoring. Make an equilateral cross on each bun.

Think green!

⚜ Collect the ashes of winter from the fireplace, mix them with potting soil, and spread them in the garden.

⚜ Begin planting cool-weather-tolerant flowers like pansies, violas, anemones, flowering cherry and pear trees, azaleas, viburnums, and rhododendron; leafy greens like spinach and kale; or hearty bulbs and tubers like onions, garlic, potatoes, cabbage, broccoli, cauliflower, and Brussels sprouts.

✹ Plant seeds of herbs or flowers in a window box, seeds of a new project in your subconscious, or seeds of spiritual growth in your heart.

CELEBRATE NEW LIFE

A SPRING EQUINOX RITUAL

Twelve candles in spring colors have been set up in the front of the gathering space.

Narrator   The sun has come halfway from its lowest path in the sky to its highest. The earth is warming. Animals are coming out of hibernation. Plants are sprouting. On this day of the Vernal Equinox, everyone on earth experiences the same number of hours of light and darkness. Let us think about our sisters and brothers in other countries and hemispheres, our human kin in other time zones and climate zones. No matter what our differences of culture, race, government, and religion; no matter what our differences in clothing, diet, or lifestyle, on this day we have an important common experience. On this day nature reminds us we are the same. We depend on the same sun for warmth and light. We rely on the same earth for food, the same sky for rainwater. We breathe the same air. Our differences are superficial compared to this most basic, most vital commonality: this dazzling and dangerous natural world. May this sharing unite us. We now light twelve candles in honor of the twelve hours of light we share with all humankind on this day.

Twelve participants who have volunteered or been recruited come forward. Each lights a candle while speaking.

Lighter 1   In the name of everyone here, I light this candle for all those who live in Asia.

Lighter 2   In the name of everyone here, I light this candle for all those who live in Europe.

Lighter 3   In the name of everyone here, I light this candle for all those who live in Africa.

Lighter 4   In the name of everyone here, I light this candle for all those who live in Australia.

Lighter 5   In the name of everyone here, I light this candle for all those who live in Antarctica.

Lighter 6   In the name of everyone here, I light this candle for all those who live in South America.

Lighter 7   In the name of everyone here, I light this candle for all those who live in North America.

Lighter 8   In the name of everyone here, I light this candle for blessings on our planet Earth.

Lighter 9   In the name of everyone here, I light this candle for blessings on our solar system.

Lighter 10   In the name of everyone here, I light this candle for blessings on our universe.

Lighter 11   In the name of everyone here, I light this candle as pledge of our promise to work for peace among all peoples.

Lighter 12   In the name of everyone here, I light this candle for all those who have gone before us, calling upon their spirits —who live within us—to bear witness to this promise.

Narrator   Let us celebrate our oneness in song and send this song to every corner of the universe.

Choir sings "Gather the Spirit" by Jim Scott.

Choir   Gather the spirit, harvest the power.
              Our sep'rate fires will kindle one flame.
              Witness the mystery of this hour.

Our trials in this light appear all the same.

Gather in peace, gather in thanks.
Gather in sympathy now and then.
Gather in hope, compassion, and strength.
Gather to celebrate once again.

Gather the spirit growing in all,
drawn by the moon and fed by the sun.
Winter to spring, and summer to fall,
the chorus of life resounding as one.

Gather in peace, gather in thanks.
Gather in sympathy now and then.
Gather in hope, compassion, and strength.
Gather to celebrate once again.

Welcoming the Spring

Leader   At Spring Equinox, we rejoice in the rebirth of the vegetation gods, whose myths and rituals have been celebrated for millennia—the deities who die or journey beneath the earth in autumn and winter only to rise up again in the spring. Let us listen to one of the many stories that explain the origin of the changing seasons, the story of Demeter and Persephone.

Dancers enact the following story as it is read. A short musical interlude follows the story.

Reader 1   In the ancient time of eternal spring, Demeter, mother goddess of grain, makes all things grow. Her daughter Kore is much beloved of her mother. One day when Kore is gathering flowers with her friends, the earth trembles and from a great gaping hole bursts the chariot of Hades, ruler of the Underworld. Kore screams with fright, but Hades thrusts her into his chariot and urges the immortal horses back to his Underworld domain. The distraught Kore shouts to her father Zeus for help, but he turns a deaf ear to her cries.

Mad with grief, Demeter tears the veil from her hair and the cloak from her shoulders, and like a wild, lonely bird, searches over land and sea for her lost daughter. When she discovers that Zeus has granted Kore to the Lord of the Underworld, the raging, grieving mother withdraws from Olympus, the home of the gods. In her absence, nothing grows on the earth, not the grain in the fields, not the fruit in the orchard, not the flowers in the meadows, not the young in the wombs of animals or humans. Snow covers the earth and famine haunts the people.

Finally Zeus sends a messenger to Demeter, bearing gifts and promises of honors to come if only she will return to Olympus. But the goddess is a rock of resistance. Nothing can move her save the recovery of her daughter. Zeus relents.

Kore returns from the Underworld and is restored to her mother, whose joy knows no bounds. At their reunion, the flowers bloom, the grain grows, the trees bear fruit.

But Kore has eaten the seeds of the pomegranate that Hades gave her in the Underworld. She has gone from innocent to knowing. Having eaten food from the land of the dead, she is destined to return there for part of each year and fulfill her role as Persephone, Comforter of the Dead.

So every fall Kore descends deep into the earth, and in her absence, her mourning mother weeps the world into winter. But every spring, Persephone rises up again. Overcome with delight at the return of her beloved daughter, Demeter fills the world with green and growing things.

Narrator   Perhaps of all those who welcome spring, it is our poets who best appreciate it. In sharing their thoughts and images with us they enlarge our own appreciation. Thank Goddess for William Wordsworth!

Reader 2   I wandered lonely as a cloud
That floats on high o'er vales and hills,
When all at once I saw a crowd,
A host of golden daffodils;
Beside the lake, beneath the trees,
Fluttering and dancing in the breeze.

Continuous as the stars that shine
And twinkle on the milky way,
They stretched in never-ending line
Along the margin of a bay:
Ten thousand saw I at a glance,
Tossing their heads in spritely dance.

The waves beside them danced; but they
Outdid the sparkling waves in glee:
A poet could not but be gay
In such a jocund company:
I gazed and gazed but little thought
What wealth the show to me had brought.

For oft, when on my couch I lie
In vacant or in pensive mood,
They flash upon that inward eye
Which is the bliss of solitude;
And then my heart with pleasure fills,
And dances with the daffodils.

—"Daffodils"

Leader   Let us celebrate Kore's return and the dancing of the daffodils with song and flowers.

One or more of the following rituals can be enacted while all sing "Lo, the Day of Days Is Here," words by Frederick

Lucian Hosmer. Children and/or adults bearing baskets or vases or garlands of spring flowers might formally process to the front of the gathering space and place them there. Or Servers carrying baskets of cut flowers might circulate around the space, distributing individual blooms to all the participants. These flowers might have been donated in advance by those who have gardens in bloom. Or each participant might have been asked in advance to bring a single flower to the service and put it in a basket at the door. In any case, the flowers should include daffodils.

All sing   Lo, the day of days is here, Alleluia!
            Festival of hope and cheer, Alleluia!
            At the south wind's genial breath, Alleluia!
            Nature wakes from seeming death, Alleluia!

            Fields are smiling in the sun, Alleluia!
            Loosened streamlets seaward run, Alleluia!
            Tender blade and leaf appear, Alleluia!
            'Tis the springtide of the year, Alleluia!

            Lo, the Eastertide is here, Alleluia!
            Music thrills the atmosphere, Alleluia!
            Join, you people all and sing, Alleluia!
            Love and praise and thanksgiving, Alleluia!

Honoring the Fertility Deities

Narrator   Persephone is not the only deity associated with fertility. Mythologies from around the ancient world tell us of gods and goddesses who suffer and die and journey beneath the earth, only to be reborn as a source of hope of new life for their followers. In remembering them, we honor our ancestors, whose lives were made the richer for their faith in the Spirit of Life, which is eternal. As we call upon them now, we invite you to respond with the words "Teach us your lesson!"

Leader   Inanna of Sumer, you who abandoned your royal trappings to descend into the Underworld and face your sister, your darkest self, you who died and after three days, came back to life,

All   Teach us your lesson!

Leader   Ishtar of Babylonia, you who went below the earth to awaken your sleeping son-lover Tammuz so that the earth might once again bear fruit,

All   Teach us your lesson!

Leader   Isis of Egypt, you whose tears of mourning made the Nile rise, you who searched the world for your brother-lover Osiris and breathed life back into him so that the crops might grow again,

All   Teach us your lesson!

Leader   Adonis, beloved of Aphrodite, you whose shedding of blood makes the flowers grow, you whose yearly dying and rising brings new life to the earth,

All   Teach us your lesson!

Leader   Dionysus, god of ecstasy and the vine, god of all in nature that is wet and wonderful—of wine and blood and semen and sap, you whose shedding of blood makes the pomegranates grow, whose yearly dying and rising brings new life to the earth,

All   Teach us your lesson!

Leader   Attis, beloved of Mother Cybele, you whose sacrificial blood makes the flowers grow, you whose suffering and dying and rising promises salvation from suffering,

All   Teach us your lesson!

Leader   Jesus of Nazareth, beloved son of Yahweh and the

Virgin Mary, you who suffered and died and rose again
that we might all be reborn in the spirit,

All   Teach us your lesson!

*For suggestions on a spontaneous litany rather than a
scripted one, see page xvii.*

Narrator   The lesson of the fertility deities is clear: All that lives
must die, but the life well spent nourishes the life that
comes after. The Gospel of John tells us, "Unless a grain
of wheat fall into the ground and die, it remains alone;
but if it dies, it brings forth much fruit." The seeds of
last year's harvest produce this year's food. The very
bodies of our ancestors—phallus and womb, seed and
egg—give us physical life, which we pass on to our descendants. The seeds of wisdom of our ancestors give us
understanding, which we pass on to our descendants.

In our own individual lives, too, there is a time to
lose and a time to find. Our losses—of health, of
dreams, of loved ones—take us, as Demeter's loss takes
her, into the winter of despair. But if we let our mourning transform into making, the wheel will turn, the
seasons will change, and we will find a new—though
different—way of living and loving.

There is a time to die and a time to be born. May
we welcome the dying—however painful—of our old
selves paralyzed by the bonds of fear and greed and in-
tolerance and rise to a new life of courage and generosity and love. Let us spend a quiet time looking into
our hearts for the new life trying to push through the
hardened wintry soil of lethargy or pettiness, anxiety
or anger, loss or despair. Let us find a way to soften that
soil, to nurture the seeds, to let the spirit rise and grow.

All read   Out of the dusk a shadow,
Then, a spark.

Out of the cloud a silence,
Then, a lark.
Out of the heart a rapture,
Then, a pain.
Out of the dead, cold ashes,
Life again.

　　　　　　　　　—John Bannister Tabb, "Evolution"

Silence

Turning the Wheel of the Year

A large cart wheel decorated with seasonal flowers has been set flat on a small lazy Susan on a table. Four large candles are set in it, symbolizing the four seasons.

Narrator　The circle of the spring wreath here symbolizes the wheel of the year, the complete cycle of the four seasons, represented by four candles. It is decorated with the flowers we hope the spring will bring us—signs of nature's renewal and thus the promise of our own.

　　　　　Lighter and Turners cross to wheel. Lighter, with a taper, stands behind the spring wreath. Turners stand on either side of the wreath.

Leader　　We invite you to join in turning the wheel, reading responsively.

Leader　　As candle wick and flame now meet,

　　　　　Lighter lights the first candle.

All　　　　From the core of earth, we call up heat.

　　　　　Turners turn the wheel clockwise one quarter.

Leader　　We turn the wheel; the winter's done.

　　　　　Lighter ignites second candle.

All   Closer now we bring the sun!

Turners turn the wheel one quarter.

Leader   We turn the wheel of death and birth.

Lighter ignites third candle.

All   We change the seasons of the earth!

Turners turn the wheel one quarter.

Leader   We turn the wheel to beckon spring.

Lighter ignites fourth candle.

All   May new life rise in everything!

All sing "Now the Green Blade Riseth," words by John Campbell Crum.

All sing   Now the green blade riseth from the buried grain,
             wheat that in the dark earth many days has lain;
             Love lives again, that with the dead has been:
             Love is come again like wheat that springeth green.

             When our hearts are wintry, grieving or in pain,
             Love's touch can call us back to life again,
             fields of our hearts that dead and bare have been:
             Love is come again like wheat that springeth green.

Blessing and Planting the Seeds of Community

Leader   We invite the women present who are pregnant with new life to come forward to bless these seeds, the symbol of our community.

Pregnant women come forward. (If there are none present, the youngest mothers can be invited to come forward.) Leader holds up tray with a number of small glass bowls. Each bowl is labeled and full of a different kind of seed.

In these bowls are seeds of garden vegetables and flowers: squash, pumpkin, cucumber, tomatoes, petunias,
nasturtiums, marigolds. . . . We ask you to bless them.

Women   (*extending their hands over the seeds*) Even as new life
grows in us, may it grow in you. When you are planted,
may the good earth nurture you, and the sky rainwater
on your roots until you sprout and reach for the sun.
May you be a source of pleasure for eye and tongue, a
nourishment for animals and humans. And may those
who plant you honor their ties to the earth and to one
another.

*The women step aside. One woman takes up the tray of
seeds. Another fetches a tray of tiny pots or eggshells with
soil in each.*

Leader   We invite the children to come forward to plant the
seeds.

The Leader addresses the Children, who respond in unison.

Leader   Who are you?

Children   We are the reason for your joyful shouts.
We are the water for your spirit's droughts.
We are the hope that hushes all your doubts.
We are your sprouts!

Leader   Will you plant these seeds for us?

Children   We will!

*Each child takes a seed and plants it in a pot or eggshell.
When they are finished, the trays are set down. Children
and Women hold hands, circle the trays, and sing the following three times as a round, to the melody of "Go Now
in Peace."*

Children   Grow now in sun

and	Grow now in rain
Women	May the loving earth surround you
sing	every night
	every day
	you may live.

Each child takes away one pot or eggshell. The Pregnant Women process to the back of the gathering space and deposit the remaining seeds on a table next to some baggies or containers for participants to take them home in. As the Women process, the Leader continues.

Leader   As we leave this place today, let us take these blessed seeds for our gardens or flower boxes. And as we plant them in the earth, let us remember to plant in our hearts the seeds of love, to be at peace with all in this community, to work for justice in the world around us.

All sing the following words, as a round, to the melody of "Go Now in Peace."

All sing   Grow we in hope.
Grow we in love.
May we work for peace and justice
every night
every day
we may live.

Sharing the Pomegranate Juice

Servers come forward with trays of pomegranate juice in small cups.

Narrator   For many of the fertility deities, the pomegranate—that beautiful red, many-seeded fruit—was a sacred symbol of life and death. Eating the pomegranate enabled Cybele to conceive Attis. The blood shed by the dying Adonis was the color of pomegranates. At the death of Dionysus, pomegranates sprang from his blood. Because Kore ate of the pomegranate of Hades while under the earth, she was destined to return there for part of each year as Persephone, Comforter of the Dead.

Leader   Let us drink the juice of the pomegranate that we may remember those who have gone before us, and in remembering, give them life again.

Narrator Let us drink the juice of the pomegranate that we may remember—in the winters of our doubting, in the frozen paralysis of our pain—that the seasons of our lives, like the seasons of our earth, have their reassuring cycle: Winter gives way to spring, despair to hope, sadness to joy.

Leader   We invite you to come forward for a cup of juice. Please return to your place with it, and when all have been served, we'll enjoy it together.

          Instrumental music plays as all return to their places. The Narrator holds up a cup as he or she speaks. All hold up their own cups as they respond. Then All drink.

Narrator The pomegranate, sweet and red,
          is food for living and for dead.

All   Now after time of wintering,
          may we who drink its juice find spring.

Narrator As spring returns to the earth and to our hearts, we have much to be grateful for. Please join now in a litany of seasonal blessings. We invite you to respond to each blessing with "Alleluia!"

Leader   We give thanks for the sun that warms and lights our planet and nourishes all who live on it.

All   Alleluia!

Leader   We give thanks for spring breezes and spring showers—

All	Alleluia!
Leader	And a host of vivid flowers—
All	Alleluia!
Leader	And the earth that nurtures them.
All	Alleluia!
Leader	We give thanks for mud and the worms that wiggle in it.
All	Alleluia!
Leader	We give thanks for the seeds of leafy green vegetables we plant in spring—
All	Alleluia!
Leader	And for our mothers who made us eat them.
All	Alleluia!
Leader	We give thanks for spring cleaning and the urge to do it.
All	Alleluia!
Leader	We give thanks for the birds, their bright colors and sweet singing.
All	Alleluia!
Leader	We give thanks for chipmunks and rabbits and bears and all animals leaving their winter homes.
All	Alleluia!
Leader	We give thanks for butterflies emerging from their cocoons.
All	Alleluia!
Leader	We give thanks for poets and composers who write songs about spring—

All	Alleluia!
Leader	And for all those who sing them.
All	Alleluia!
Leader	We give thanks for skates and scooters and bicycles—
All	Alleluia!
Leader	For lacrosse and tennis and baseball.
All	Alleluia!
Leader	We give thanks for colored eggs, jelly beans, and marshmallow chicks—
All	Alleluia!
Leader	And chocolate!
All	Alleluia!
Leader	We give thanks for egg hunts and Easter Bunnies.
All	Alleluia!
Leader	We give thanks for the spring sap rising in the trees that makes them leaf—
All	Alleluia!
Leader	And for the spring juice rising in us that makes us love.
All	Alleluia!
Leader	We give thanks for infants and puppies and kittens and newborns of every species—
All	Alleluia!
Leader	May we build a peaceful world for them to grow up in.
All	Alleluia!

For suggestions on a spontaneous litany rather than the

following scripted one, see page xvii.

During the following, Servers circulate with baskets of hard-boiled, dyed, and/or decorated eggs for the participants. These eggs may have been prepared in advance by volunteers or by the children. Or each participant might have been asked in advance to bring an egg to the gathering and put it in a basket at the door.

Narrator   The ancient Germans celebrated the spring fertility goddess Ostara. The Anglo-Saxons called her Eostre, from whom Easter gets its name. One of her chief symbols is the hare or rabbit, famous for its fertility. In some stories the goddess brought renewal to the land by traversing it disguised as a hare. In others, Eostre changed a bird into a hare, but this hare, remembering her customary ways, built nests and filled them with colored eggs. Our tradition of an Easter Bunny delivering a basket—or nest—of eggs may be traced back to this.

Leader   Another explanation is that after the long winter, ancient hunter-gatherers were eager to enjoy the tasty and beautiful pastel bird eggs laid in the spring. Perhaps the search for these eggs is the origin of our egg hunts, as well as of the tradition of dyeing them.

Narrator   The egg is a miracle of life and thus one of the oldest symbols of creation. Neolithic peoples of Old Europe looked to a primordial creator, the Bird Goddess, to provide both the water that fell from the sky and the water that swelled up from the ground. The fetus thrives in the waters of the womb, and so both the egg and the egg-shaped womb are images of the beginning of life. The cosmic egg contains the universe in embryo.

Leader   Some ancient peoples—the Egyptians, Greeks, and Anglo-Saxons—put eggs on the graves of their dead to ensure that they would be reborn. The living also exchanged gifts of eggs at the Spring Equinox. For Christians, the egg became a symbol of their risen savior.

Narrator Let us accept this egg as a gift and be reminded of the cosmic egg, symbol of all creation; symbol of Ostara, the goddess of fertility; symbol of Jesus and the promise of new life; and symbol of creativity. May its taste nourish our bodies and its symbolism feed our spirits as we welcome, with the earth, a new beginning and celebrate in song the never-ending cycle of life.

All sing the following to the melody of "Christ the Lord Is Risen Today." The words are from "Lo, the Earth Awakes Again" by Samuel Longfellow.

All sing Lo, the earth awakes again—Alleluia!
from the winter's bond and pain. Alleluia!
Bring we leaf and flower and spray—Alleluia!
to adorn this happy day. Alleluia!

Once again the word comes true, Alleluia!
All the earth shall be made new. Alleluia!
Now the dark, cold days are o'er, Alleluia!
Spring and gladness are before. Alleluia!

Change, then, mourning into praise, Alleluia!
And, for dirges, anthems raise. Alleluia!
How our spirits soar and sing, Alleluia!
How our hearts leap with the spring! Alleluia!

Beltane and May Day

May 1

Juice will out. It rises in the dazzling rainbow of tulips, in the gentle pink of magnolia and dogwood, in the wild-hussy magenta of azalea, in the luscious scent of lilac. It surges in the eager frenzy of puppies greeting parks, in the bright song of birds greeting dawn, in the tireless energy of teenagers flinging Frisbees and planning proms. It's a time to rejoice in flora and fertility, a time for feasting and fun and falling in love. It's May Day!

The Seasonal Calendar

The astronomical seasons—the ones identified in our calendar—more closely represent the *thermal* seasons than they do the *solar* seasons. Solar winter is the quarter of the year with the shortest days and least potential for solar energy, beginning in early November and reaching its midpoint around December 21. Its opposite, solar summer, has the longest days and the greatest potential for solar energy and begins in early May and reaches its midpoint around June 21. For the old agrarian communities of Europe, which would have used the solar cycle, May 1 was the beginning of summer since it marks the start of that quarter of the year with the most sunlight.

This beginning of the warm, light half of the year, the approximate midpoint between Spring Equinox and Summer Solstice, was celebrated by the Celts as Beltane.

Mythology and History

Bel means bright or fortunate and *tene* means fire, though some scholars suggest that *Bel* is derived from Belenus, a pastoral god of light and healing who shares many of Apollo's characteristics, or even from Baal, the Hebrew Testament's most prominent pagan god.

At Beltane the Celts lit huge bonfires to honor the sun and welcome the summer. At the end of the cold, dark half of the year, when food supplies had dwindled, they were eager for the growing season, ready to celebrate the return of life and fertility and to implore the sun god for blessing on the crops and pastures and animals. On Beltane, the people extinguished the fires in their hearths and took their livestock, which had been penned in home fields, to the highpoint of a nearby hill. Here they kindled ceremonial bonfires and—to assure the fertility, purification, and protection from disease of the flocks and herds—drove them between the fires (or rows of fires) out into the high summer pastures, where the new grass was so plentiful that cows reportedly had to be milked three times a day.

The fire itself was believed to have curative, protective, and even magical powers, and rituals related to it survived well into the nineteenth century. One witness, Sir William Wilde, recounts in *Irish Popular Superstitions* that when the flames were low enough, a man about to embark on a dangerous enterprise might steel himself for it by leaping over the fire. Young women might jump the flames, wishing for a good mate. Barren women hoping for conception and pregnant women hoping for a safe delivery might follow. Even children were carried across the smoldering ashes of the "lucky fire."

The earliest written description of a Beltane ritual was rendered in 1769, by Thomas Pennant, who reports in *A Tour in*

Scotland that *bannocks,* ceremonial cakes of oatmeal, were baked in the fire. Bannocks were made with nine raised knobs, each of which was "dedicated to some particular being, the supposed preserver of . . . flocks and herds, or to some particular animal, the real destroyer of them." Participants faced the fire, broke off a knob of cake, and threw it over their shoulders while calling upon the preserver to guard the sheep, the horses, etc. Then using the same gesture, they offered knobs of cake to the fox, the crow, etc., with an invocation to spare their lambs or calves. According to Ronald Hutton, author of *The Stations of the Sun,* by the late nineteenth century the *Bannoch Bealltainn* had lost its knobs and instead bore a cross. These hot cross buns were—like eggs at Easter—rolled down hills; superstition had it that if they landed cross-side down, bad luck would befall the owners.

An early British ritual involving bannocks required that the cakes be quartered and put in a bag. Participants each drew a piece, and those whose pieces were burnt had to leap three times over the fire to assure a good harvest. Hutton suggests that the widespread rites involving a symbolic scapegoat "may embody a memory of actual human sacrifice." In *The Woman's Encyclopedia of Myths and Secrets,* Barbara Walker reports that the god Balder was burned in effigy on May Eve in rural Scandinavia, and a man representing him leaped through "Balder's balefires." She believes this custom dated back to the "real burning of the man who represented the god in his love-death." Whether it was a human or an animal who was originally fed to the fire to propitiate the sun god and guarantee fertile fields and flocks, it seems reasonable to suppose that at some propitious point, leaping over the fire became a sane substitute for dying in it.

After the ritual came the feast: dancing around the bonfires, enjoying the food cooked in them, and no doubt taking advantage of their warmth to get a head start on invoking the blessing of human fertility. Following the celebration, villagers lighted brands from the bonfires and carried them home to relight their own hearths, further sharing the communal sacred fire.

Hutton concludes that Beltane rituals were performed for protection against the powers of evil, "because those malign powers were supposed to be particularly active at this turning point of the year" and the most obvious means of protection was the symbolic use of fire, "the archaic weapon against darkness and large predators." He reports that the perceived danger of May Eve and the use of fire rituals to ward it off were found not just in Ireland and western and northern Britain but (acknowledging James Frazer's observation) also in Denmark, Sweden, Norway, Saxony, Silesia, Moravia, Bohemia, and Austria—all countries with a pastoral economy involving the seasonal movement of livestock. Yet in other places on the Continent—as well as in most of England in historic times—"the opening of summer was less fraught, and its rituals far more celebratory and less defensive."

Given the invasion and occupation of Britain by the Romans in the first and second centuries, it is not surprising that May Day festivities there shared characteristics of the ancient Floralia. Flora was the Roman goddess of spring who gave her protection (and her name) to flowers and whose festival was celebrated from April 28 through May 2 with the planting of seeds—both vegetable and human. The Romans decked themselves and their animals with garlands of flowers and enjoyed singing and dancing, games, pantomimes, and (sometimes lewd) theatrical performances. As symbols of fertility, goats and hares were freed. Humans too enjoyed sexual freedom at this time.

The Greek Maia, another classical deity, gave her name to the month whose first day marked her festival. A minor consort of Zeus, she gave birth to Hermes, whose symbol was a phallic pillar or post.

In Welsh mythology, Beltane is the time of the yearly battle between Gwyn ap Nudd and Gwythur ap Greidawl for the most beautiful maiden of the land. This represents the struggle between the god of summer, light, and life and the god of winter, darkness, and death for the possession of the fertility goddess or the land itself. A more familiar version of this struggle is that of the old King Mark and his young nephew Tristan for the favor of Isolde or that of the old King Arthur and the young Sir Lancelot for the favor of Guinevere. (In Welsh mythology, Gwenhwyfar is the name of the goddess of childbirth and fertility.)

In Thomas Mallory's *Morte D'Arthur*, Guinevere commands that ten knights and ten ladies—all dressed in green silk—ride with her a-Maying into the woods. They return "bedashed with herbs, mosses and flowers." Walker, citing *Chariot of the Sun* by Peter Gelling and Hilda Ellis Davidson, sees

> traces of a divine marriage ritual in the "May-riding," when knights and ladies rode in pairs into the wood, led by the Queen of the May on a white horse and her male companion on a dark one. They impersonated Frey and Freya [major divinities of northern Europe], "the Lord" and "the Lady" whose union made fertility magic each spring.

But not all who went into the woods did so dressed in silk and riding fine horses. The common folk also enjoyed "bringing in the May" or "gathering the May." In the early morning of May Day, young people collected flowers and green or flowering branches—especially hawthorn, whose blooming signals planting weather—and returned to share these symbols of the arrival of summer. This sharing took many forms. They might make wreaths or garlands and exchange them with sweethearts or friends. They might use them to decorate homes, barns, or other buildings. They might fill May baskets with flowers and other goodies and leave them at the door of infirm or elderly neighbors (knocking on the door, then running away—the reverse of "trick-or-treating," at the opposite point on the seasonal calendar). Or a young man might decorate the window or door of a young woman's home as a sign of his romantic interest, a custom known as May boughing.

Since Beltane marks a transition between two seasons, between the two halves of the year, some of the customs associated with it involve marking boundaries. These included repairing fences, barriers, and other markers, as well as "beating the bounds," or walking the perimeter of one's property. I like to think this last custom was also intended to cast a protective circle on which to call down blessings rather than merely ensuring that no encroachment had taken place during the year.

A custom popular with young women was washing in May Day dew, which was believed to bring beauty, health, good luck, and even a husband. As the traditional verse advises,

> The fair maid who, the First of May,
> goes to the field at break of day
> and washes in the dew from the hawthorn tree,
> will ever after handsome be.

But not all May Day rites were so innocent. The young men and maids gathering greenery in the woods may indeed have spent the night there performing their own private fertility rites—an activity immortalized by Rudyard Kipling in his "Tree Song":

> Oh, do not tell the Priest our plight,
> or he would call it a sin;
> but we have been out in the woods all night,
> a-conjuring Summer in!

The sometimes transitory nature of these couplings is perhaps suggested in the old English rhyme:

> Married in May and kirked [churched] in green,
> Both bride and bridegroom won't long be seen.

Children resulting from these "greenwood marriages" were often given names that reflected their "divine" conception (Godkin) or their forest origin (Robinson, for Robin Hood; Johnson, for Little John; Jackson, for Jack in the Green, etc.).

One Puritan writer complained that of a hundred maids who went into the woods, scarcely a third returned undefiled. Another claimed that nine out of ten came home with child. Yet Hutton assures us that contemporary demographic historians have failed to discover an increase in the number of pregnancies during this season. Still, the cries of disapproval attest to the practice, which was not limited to young, single folk—since marriage vows were temporarily suspended for the occasion. Indeed, Sir Walter Scott postulates that the common belief that "only bad women" married in May suggested there was a taboo on all weddings during this licentious month. (Perhaps this is one reason for a traditionally disproportionate number of June weddings?) The sexual freedom of this time is both eulogized and satirized by Allan Jay Lerner in *Camelot*:

> Tra la, it's May, the lusty month of May,
> that lovely month when everyone goes blissfully astray.

By far the most spectacular of May Day rites was the maypole dance. Although it is not clear how old the custom is, records indicate that by the late Middle Ages, it was well established in southern Britain, as well as on the Continent from the Pyrenees to Scandinavia and Russia.

> Come all ye lads and lassies,
> join in the festive scene.
> Come dance around the maypole
> that will stand upon the green.

Sixteenth-century Londoner Philip Stubbes provides a description: The maypole, covered with flowers, is drawn by oxen whose horns are tipped with nosegays. Men, women, and children follow with great devotion. They set up the maypole (typically a birch or fir tree stripped of its branches and bark) in the town square, decorate it with green boughs, and dance around it.

The dance usually involved young people playfully kissing at each turning. A seventeenth-century balladeer describes their choreography:

> Dance about both in and out,
> Turn and kiss, and then for greeting.

By the nineteenth century, the round dance had become a spiral dance in which each dancer holds one end of a long ribbon, the other end of which is attached to the top of the pole. Starting as far away from the pole as the ribbons will allow, men dance in one direction, women in the other. As they weave in and out, the ribbons are braided, bringing the dancers closer to the pole and (conveniently) to one another. Some large towns had permanent maypoles in the town square.

The origin and symbolism of the maypole are disputed. Throughout the Roman Empire, pillarlike figures called *herms*, for the god Hermes, were placed at crossroads and decorated with greenery in May. Some had erect penises protruding from them, which made their symbolism clear. In *Faith and Folklore of the British Isles*, Carew Hazlitt claims the maypole near Horn Castle, Lincolnshire, stands on what was probably the site of a *herm* in Roman times. This association with *herms*, combined with its shape, has led many scholars to see the maypole as a phallic symbol, planted in the womb of the earth, a fitting focus for the fertility dance. But Hutton insists there is "no historical basis for this claim, and no sign that the people who used maypoles thought that they were phallic."

One possibility, neither proved nor disproved by evidence, is that the maypole was a remnant of much earlier tree-worshiping cults. The Canaanite goddess Asherah, nurturer of gods and kings, was worshiped as a tree. As we saw in the previous chapter, the tree figured importantly in the rites of Attis. The oak was sacred to the druids. In primitive religions, the spirit of the shaman is believed to ride along the trunk of the sacred tree to the spirit world. The Norse god Odin sacrificed himself on the World Tree (Yggdrasil) to obtain the sacred runes, as did the Christian Jesus to obtain salvation for believers. Indeed, tradition has it that the cross on which he died was the Tree of Life from the Garden of Eden, the World Tree with roots in the underworld and branches reaching into the heavens, the very axis of the universe, which we also celebrate in the sacred tree of Yuletide.

Pauline Campanelli ties the symbols together in *Wheel of the Year*:

> The Maypole is at once the venerated phallus and the World
> Tree. The connecting idea is that the spirit leaves the body
> and travels among the spirit realms via the World Tree dur-
> ing the shamanistic experience, the near-death experience,
> or that experienced through spiritual initiation and death.
> The spirit reenters a physical body after death and prior to
> rebirth via the phallus. So the phallus and the World Tree are
> two sides of the same coin or two aspects of the God in his
> relationship to the Goddess in the endless cycle of birth,
> death, and rebirth.

The *hieros gamos*, the sacred marriage of the goddess and the
god, reenacted in so many archaic fertility rites, may be reflected in
the choosing of a May queen and a May king (or Green Man, representing the vegetation god or the return of summer) to accompany the procession of the maypole to its place of honor and to
rule over the festivities. Just as in ancient times the ritual mating of
the royal couple honored, through imitation, the mating of the divine procreators and assured the health of the kingdom and the
fertility of its fields and flocks and folk, so the "mock" marriage of
the young May queen and king, as well as the maypole dance, assured the fertility necessary to the health of the village. (Are prom
queens and kings the modern version of this vestigial royalty?)

The May bride, dressed in white and wreathed and garlanded
with flowers, was a symbol of both the earth itself and the fertility
goddess. Her role was a coveted one, as suggested by Alfred Lord
Tennyson's poem "The May Queen":

> You must wake and call me early, call me early, mother dear;
> To-morrow 'ill be the happiest time of all the glad New-year;
> Of all the glad New-year, mother, the maddest merriest day,
> For I'm to be Queen o' the May, mother, I'm to be Queen o'
> the May.

As might be expected, the Church took a dim view of these proceedings. The seventh-century bishop of Noyons pleaded with his converts to abandon the sexual rites of May—to no avail. Perhaps not coincidentally, in the same century, the Church established the Feast of the Holy Cross, or Holy Rood, celebrated as Roodmass in the liturgical calendar on May 3, thus providing Christians with an alternate event whose solemnity might have the desired sobering effect.

In the Catholic Church May is dedicated to Mary, the virgin mother of Jesus, Queen of Heaven and Earth. Even in modern times, it is the month when parochial school children bring flowers from their home gardens to place on the May altars in their classrooms. It is the month of May processions, when a long line of youngsters singing hymns snakes through the parish streets to a place where the statue of Mary has been enshrined on a pedestal decorated with greenery. At the end of the line, behind her attendants and the priests, comes the teen-age May queen, dressed in a bridal gown, who places a wreath of flowers on the statue of Mary at the ritual's climax.

The connection between Mary (venerated by Catholics as the mother of God) and the Great Mother Goddess (venerated by ancient peoples as the creator of all)—both honored by May queens in this month of nature's rebirth—is made clear in Gerard Manley Hopkins's "May Magnificat":

> May is Mary's month. And I
> Muse at that and wonder why: . . .
> Why fasten that upon her,
> With a feasting in her honour? . . .
> Ask of her, the mighty mother:
> Her reply puts this other
> Question: What is Spring?—
> Growth in every thing—
> Flesh and fleece, fur and feather,
> Grass and greenworld all together;
> Star-eyed strawberry-breasted

Throstle above her nested
Cluster of bugle blue eggs thin
Forms and warms the life within;
    And bird and blossom swell
    In sod or sheath or shell.
All things rising, all things sizing
Mary sees, sympathizing
    With that world of good,
    Nature's motherhood.

Contemporary Celebrations Around the World

Many Britains still celebrate the arrival of solar summer. In Edinburgh, for example, the Beltane Fire Festival is an exuberant, spectacular event staged on top of Calton Hill, where a chorus of drummers beat winter into retreat. Perhaps the most famous English festivals are the procession of the Obby Oss (hobby horse) in Padstow on the north coast of Cornwall, where dancers, singers, and musicians welcome spring, and the Furry Dance in Helston, West Cornwall, a May 8 event for which the town is decorated with flowers and greens and its inhabitants parade in their finery through the streets, shops, and houses, celebrating their solidarity as a community.

May Day retains its hold on the European imagination even today, as evidenced in the festive dancing beneath the maypole still popular in so many communities, both rural and urban. The Church, after centuries of ascendancy, seems no longer threatened by these (now much tamed and no longer "religious") festivities. A striking example of this peaceful coexistence is the seventeenth-century Church of Mariahilf in bustling Vienna, whose front paving stones support a huge, brightly beribboned maypole some ten yards from the church door.

The nine-day festival of Walpurgis commemorates, in Nordic and Germanic countries, Odin's self-sacrifice upon the World Tree. On the last day, at the moment of his ritual death, the world goes dark and chaos reigns. But then the light returns as the great bonfires are lit. The Faust legend has immortalized Walpurgis as a night of licentious behavior. Ironically, it takes its name from an eighth-century English abbess of a German monastery, whose earliest feast day may have been set on May 1 to replace the pagan festival; her purview was protection against magic. *Butler's Lives of the Saints* suggests that the iconography depicting St. Walpurga with ears of corn reflects her connection to "the old heathen goddess Walborg or Mother Earth." Her association with fertility is evident also in her role as patron of pregnant women.

May 1 is called Valborgsmässa (Walborg's mass) in Sweden, and on its eve, people gather round the bonfires, visible all over the countryside, and sing spring songs. Modern German traditions include ceremonial plantings, the drinking of May wine, a maypole dance presided over by a May queen, and a maypole climbing contest (for which the tree trunk is shaved and polished). A Bavarian custom also practiced in England was the mischievous stealing of a rival village's maypole.

In Greece, children sing spring songs on the morning of May Day after locating the first swallow of the season. They bring the good news back to their neighbors, who reward them with special treats of food. As the children reach puberty, they develop and celebrate other interests. Adolescent boys in Switzerland and the Czech and Slovak Republics place May trees, or maypoles, in front of their sweethearts' windows. In Italy they serenade their sweethearts and show off for them by climbing greased maypoles to win the prizes at the top.

In Bulgaria, the national feast of *Gergyovden* (St. George) is celebrated on May 6 (April 23 on the liturgical calendar). Although all we know for sure of St. George is that he was an early Christian martyr, legend has made him a dragon-slayer and patron saint of armies as well as of several countries, including England, Russia, and Bulgaria. In "Background to Bulgarian Myth and Folklore," Moni Sheehan suggests that St. George was a reincarnation of the Thracian Horseman, probably a god of nature and vegetation who, as the dispenser of life and death, was believed to bring in summer, the season of fertility. The Plovdiv City Guide tells us that since *Georgius* is the Greek word for farmer, Bulgarians honor him as guardian of shepherds and herds. It suggests that originally his festival was an ancient pagan one, celebrating the first milking of sheep and goats. On the eve of the feast, young unmarried women and girls gather flowers and herbs in the field, ritually feeding the sheep and the cattle with them, and they make three wreaths from those flowers and herbs. The first wreath is for the sheep that will be milked first; the second one is for the lamb that will be offered to the saint; and the third one is for the vessel with the milk. Then they dance in a chain around the houses, barns, and granaries; bathe in the morning dew; decorate their homes, as well as the cattle-sheds and sheep pens; and finally light candles and drink three sips of "silent water" (water drawn in silence) to ensure health and prosperity.

There is no official celebration of May Day in the United States, possibly because the founding English Puritans brought their disapproval across the Atlantic. However, a good number of maypole dances are held in parks and playgrounds. While not official May Day events, proms and flower marts certainly qualify as festivals celebrating love and new life. And of course, Mother's Day, declared an American national holiday in 1914 and observed on the second Sunday in May, is a joyful, albeit sedate, celebration of fertility.

Long before the English arrived in the New World, Native Americans were using the cycles of the sun and stars as guides to planting. At the beginning of May, the Pleiades are no longer visible in the night sky. According to Von Del Chamberlain, author of "May Day Announces the Onset of Summer," the Navajo people referred to the Pleiades as "Dilyehe" and had a saying: "Never let the Dilyehe see you plant." They began planting only when the Pleiades were not visible and finished before they returned to the sky.

Since 1928 Hawaiians have celebrated May 1 as Lei Day. People give leis to one another with a traditional kiss. Festivities include lei-making contests, music and hula dancing, and the crowning of Lei Day royalty with accompanying pageantry.

Wiccans celebrate Beltane, one of their eight *sabbats*, as a time of rebirth, renewal, passion and sexual love, and fertility and creativity. They light bonfires, dance around the maypole, and honor the appearance of the Horned One (the solar/vegetation god) and his impregnation of the earth goddess, which marks the start of summer.

Asian religious and secular festivals mark the new season. In India, *Buddha Jayanti* (Buddha's Birthday) is observed as a national holiday the first week of May. *Maia*, origin of the month's name, is also the name of the mother of the Buddha, Enlightened One of the Hindus, as it is of the mother of Hermes, Enlightened One of the Greeks. Clearly the association of May with mothering and fertility crosses cultures and continents.

In Sri Lanka, the Vesak Festival, observed on the day of the full moon in May, commemorates Buddha's birth, enlightenment, and death. It is a day of prayer, devotional singing, almsgiving, processions, temple visits, and flower offerings, but it also features exchanging greeting cards, decorating with paper lanterns, and enjoying street theater performances.

Dating from the sixth century, the Aoi Matsuri, or Hollyhock Festival, takes place on May 15 in Kyoto, the ancient capital of Japan. People use the dark, shiny leaves of the hollyhock to decorate for the event and believe its leaves protect them from natural disasters. The solemn procession of ox carts, cows, horses, and hundreds of people dressed in imperial-court costumes wends its way to the Shimogamo and Kamigamo shrines, where sacred rites are performed. Michel Friang, in "Rites of Heritage: Spring Festivals in Kyoto, Japan," claims that the original Shinto Matsuri is traceable to 300 BCE, when rice farmers performed rites to ask the gods for good health and good harvests.

People around the globe—whatever their culture—find a way to welcome the warm, growing season.

WAYS TO CELEBRATE

Welcome the warm season with your body.

◉   Lie in the grass under a flowering tree and look up at the sky through the blossoms.

◉   Dress all in green.

◉   Braid your hair, weaving flowers into it, or make a wreath of flowers for your head.

◉   Make a lei to wear around your neck. Then make another to give away.

◉   Dampen your face with early morning dew.

◉   Collect the dew (be inventive!) and add it your bathwater—together with petals of flowering trees.

◉   Dance with friends around a maypole. You may want to practice. Invite friends or family members who play instruments to accompany your dance with lively music. If none is available, provide recorded music or ask the onlookers waiting for their turn at the pole to clap and sing.

◉   Mime (perhaps to musical accompaniment) the struggle between Summer and Winter for the favor of Mother Earth.

Welcome the season with words and music (alone or with others).

◉   Read aloud poems celebrating spring.

◉   Sing songs reveling in the flowering time of the year.

Enjoy the outdoors.

◉   Take a walk in a park or garden and admire the blooms.

⑥ Have lunch *al fresco*.

⑥ Make offerings to the garden animals: birds, rabbits, squirrels, chipmunks. Then enjoy watching their responses.

Interact with animals.

⑥ Take your pet for a run in the park.

⑥ Take children to visit a farm or a petting zoo.

⑥ Take a trail ride. (Remember to take along an apple for the horse.)

In honor of the fertility rites of Beltane/May Day, celebrate sexuality.

⑥ Read love poems. Or write one.

⑥ Welcome spring fever, celebrate vitality, be open to love, new or renewed. Whatever our age, we are young at Beltane.

⑥ Write in your journal about the loves of your life.

⑥ Make love with your partner or spouse outdoors, or if it's still too cold, inside by a blazing fire in the hearth, or in the bedroom ablaze with candles, or all three! Scatter petals of flowering bushes or trees on the bed.

⑥ Donate to Planned Parenthood.

⑥ Volunteer for a Rape Crisis Hotline.

⑥ Encourage the young people in your family to cherish their sexuality and behave responsibly by providing them with accurate sex education and urging them to respect themselves and others.

Let your creative juices flow.

⑥ Make music or art, Napoleons or nightshirts . . . whatever you're good at or just want to try.

⑥ Design a greeting card, website, garden, or whatever strikes your creative fancy.

⑥ Play with children; think of ways to keep them engaged and having fun.

Honor your mother.

⑥ If she's alive, fix her a special meal, give her flowers, tell her how grateful you are for the gift of life and her lessons, spoken and unspoken, on how to live it.

⑥ If she's no longer alive, honor her memory by making something she taught you how to make and sharing it with others, or telling your favorite memories of her to your children or friends.

Complete "spring cleaning" and "summerize" your home.

⑥ Clean the porch, deck, and/or patio, get out the summer furniture, and pot the geraniums.

⑥ Put the screens in the doors.

⑥ Wash windows.

⑥ Open up the house.

⑥ Change the filter in the furnace.

⑥ Clean out the refrigerator and change the baking soda.

⑥ Clean out the medicine cabinet and throw away expired medications.

⑥ Turn the mattress and wash the cover.

⑥ Store boots and heavy jackets; put away flannels and wools; break out the cottons, linens, and sandals.

⑥ Donate clothing to the poor.

"Beat the bounds" of your property (whether rented, owned, or mortgaged).

⑥ Walk a circle around the perimeter and determine to be a good steward of all that is within.

⑥ Give thanks for your yard, your trees, or just your tiny patch of grass.

⑥ Understand that no piece of earth can really belong to you. You belong to the earth. Give back to it the physical and spiritual nourishment it gives you.

⑥ Feed the trees and plants. Weed. Mulch. Mow. Admire.

⑥ If you live in a townhouse or apartment, invite your neighbors to join you in "beating the bounds" of the whole building or block or neighborhood.

Be a midwife to growing things.

⑥ Plant perennials in your garden.

⑥ Plant a hawthorn (maybush) to use for Beltane rituals in years to come.

⑥ "Bring in the May" to your home. Decorate with branches of hawthorn, dogwood, azalea, or flowering fruit trees, or a simple vase of tulips or lilacs.

⑥ Create a wreath of greenery for the door.

⑥ Plant flowers in a window box for someone who can't get outside to enjoy them.

⑥ Prepare a May basket for an elderly relative or friend. Fill it with flowers and special treats. Hang it on the doorknob, ring the bell, then run away! Better still, deliver it in person and stay for a visit.

⑥ Press flowers onto cards and send them to friends.

Celebrate with a Beltane bonfire.

⑥ Create a fire in your backyard hibachi. Leap over it and make a wish!

⑥ Create two small hibachi fires and run between them with your children and pets, appreciating the walls of warmth and offering thanks for the arrival of the warm season. If you don't have an outside area to do this, use candles indoors.

Make a Beltane sacrifice.

Early celebrants of Beltane offered a sacrifice in the fire to assure a fruitful growing season. What are you willing to sacrifice in order to grow—in spirit, in mind, in physical health? What are you willing to give up in order to contribute to the growth and well-being of the world community? Write it on a piece of paper, offer it to the Beltane fire, and then act on it. Here are some examples:

⑥ Sacrifice smoking or excessive drinking or recreational drugs for your physical health.

⑥ Sacrifice an hour a day of television to read a book for your mental health.

⑥ Sacrifice fifteen minutes of sleep each morning to meditate for your spiritual health.

⑥ Sacrifice an hour on e-mail each week to call an elderly relative or lonely friend.

⑥ Give up your gas-guzzler for an economy car, or give up driving one day a week and ride public transportation or your bicycle.

⑥ Give up meat one day a week. According to the Center for a New American Dream, this will save seventy pounds of grain, seventy pounds of topsoil, and forty thousand gallons of water a year.

⑥ Protect wildlife and ground water by giving up pesticides.

Celebrate with seasonal foods.

☽   Prepare an outdoor wedding feast for the earth goddess and the vegetation god and invite friends and neighbors. Have a contest for who will be May queen and king. (Who can sing the most songs or recite the most poems with "May" in them? Who can leap the highest?) Or draw lots among the young people. The menu for the feast might include: grilled lamb or beef, representing the animal sacrificed to the Beltane fire; grilled vegetables of the season to honor the vegetation god and the earth goddess; bannocks or oatmeal cakes/cookies; fruits that are in season in your region; dairy products galore in memory of the triple-milking made possible by the plentiful new grass; milk, strawberry punch, and May wine.

☽   In memory of bannock, the ceremonial oatcakes eaten at Beltane, make your favorite oatmeal bread or oatmeal cookies.

☽   Enjoy a bottle of May wine along with seasonal vegetables such as asparagus.

☽   In *Witch in the Kitchen*, Cait Johnson reminds us that asparagus has been considered an aphrodisiac for centuries because of its phallic shape. (Revelers of Dionysus carried a thyrsus, a staff tipped with a pine cone that had a shape resembling an asparagus.) Her recipe playfully mates asparagus with almonds, long recognized as having vulva-like shapes.

BELTANE ASPARAGUS WITH TOASTED TAMARI ALMONDS

Ingredients:

1 pound fresh asparagus spears
2 tablespoons butter for sautéing (optional)
toasted tamari almonds (below)

Wash asparagus and prepare by snapping off the bottom of each spear with your hands: It will break off with a satisfying crack just at the point where the stem is beginning to turn rough and woody. (Very young, tender asparagus won't need this treatment.) Steam over boiling water in a steamer basket, or sauté in butter over medium-high heat for just a few minutes. Asparagus should be bright green and crisp-tender. Place asparagus spears decoratively on plates, tying each "bundle" with a chive, if you like. Top each bundle with the almonds as prepared below:

½ cup sliced almonds
tamari or shoyu
butter or olive oil

Preheat oven to 300°F. Spread sliced almonds in a shallow layer on a baking sheet and sprinkle with tamari or shoyu and stir to moisten. Dot with butter or a little olive oil. Bake the almonds, stirring often, for 10 minutes or so, keeping an eye on them, as nuts burn easily. They will smell toasty and delicious when they're done, and they will have turned a rich and delicious golden brown.

WELCOME THE WARM HALF OF THE YEAR

A BELTANE/MAY DAY RITUAL

All gather outdoors and sit on chairs, benches, blankets, or grass. The makings of two bonfires, about ten feet apart, have been set up. (Go to the library or look on the Internet for instructions on how to build a bonfire. If necessary, hibachis or other heavy containers can hold the wood for the fires.) Open by singing the following words to the melody of "Be Thou My Vision."

All sing   Come thou, O Summer, and lengthen our days.
              Warm thou our spirits with thy fiery rays.
              Cold was the winter with long, dreary nights.
              Open our senses to all your delights.

              Green grow the woodlands, the hawthorn's in bloom.
              Lilacs amaze us with luscious perfume.

Apple and pear tree and cherry have all
flaunted their blossoms, then let them fall.

Young loves and old ones are coming alive.
Sap in the greenwood upwardly strives.
Juices rejoice in both human and beast.
Praise to all Nature on this May Day Feast!

Narrator Now is the time to rejoice in flowers and fertility. Now
is the time for feasting and fun and falling in love. It's
May Day! This day marks the beginning of solar summer, the three months of the year when the light is
strongest and the days are longest.

Litany of Seasonal Blessings

Leader There are so many good things to appreciate at this time
of year. Please join now in a litany of seasonal blessings.
We invite you to respond with "Let us rejoice!"

For warm weather and long days and the energy to
enjoy them,

All Let us rejoice!

Leader For all the flowers and bushes in bloom, for tulips and
magnolias and lilies of the valley, for dogwood and
azalea for [*whatever is blooming locally*],

All Let us rejoice!

Leader For the feathery leaves sprouting on trees,

All Let us rejoice!

Leader For the greenness of growing things,

All Let us rejoice!

Leader For the bright song of birds greeting dawn,

All	Let us rejoice!
Leader	For the frenzy of puppies greeting parks,
All	Let us rejoice!
Leader	For proms and graduations and the special beauty of all young people,
All	Let us rejoice!
Leader	For spring fever and falling in love,
All	Let us rejoice!
Leader	For romance and passion,
All	Let us rejoice!
Leader	For baseball and Frisbee,
All	Let us rejoice!
Leader	For gardeners who weed and clear and plant and feed and mulch and mow,
All	Let us rejoice!
Leader	For asparagus and strawberries [*name local vegetables and fruits in season*],
All	Let us rejoice!
Leader	For Mother's Day and the women it honors,
All	Let us rejoice!
Leader	For the fertility of mind and spirit that makes us creative.
All	Let us rejoice!
Leader	For the miraculous fertility of the earth and all its plants and animals and people,

All   Let us rejoice!

Leader   For our determination to take good care of it,

All   Let us rejoice!

           *For suggestions on a spontaneous litany rather than a
           scripted one, see page xvii.*

Narrator   Perhaps nothing has been celebrated in song and po-
           etry more than love, especially at this time of year.
           Poets have sung its praises in texts both sacred and sec-
           ular. May our spirits be lifted by listening to this one
           from the Song of Songs.

Reader 1   (*a young man*)
           Come then, my love,
           my lovely one, come.
           For see, the winter is past,
           the rains are over and gone.
           The flowers appear on the earth.
           The season of glad songs has come,
           the cooing of the turtledove is heard in our land.
           The fig tree is forming its first figs
           and the blossoming vines give out their fragrance.
           Come then, my love,
           my lovely one, come.

Lighting the Beltane Fire

*Servers distribute small wooden pencils and small pieces of paper to
everyone. The Narrator crosses to where the makings of two bonfires
have been set up.*

Narrator   This beginning of the warm, light half of the year, the
           midpoint between Spring Equinox and Summer Solstice,
           was celebrated by the Celts as Beltane, which means "for-
           tunate fire" or fire of the sun god Bel. They lit huge bon-

fires to honor the sun and welcome the summer. At the end of the cold, dark half of the year, when food supplies had dwindled, they were eager for the growing season, ready to celebrate the return of life, to ask for blessing on the crops and pastures and animals. Even today, on top of Calton Hill in Edinburgh, at the spectacular Beltane Fire Festival, a chorus of drummers beats winter into retreat.

Drummers play. If live drumming is unavailable, you might use a recorded version of "Huron 'Beltane' Fire Dance" by Loreena McKennitt.

Leader   We light these fires to turn the wheel of the seasons, to welcome the warm, light half of the year, to give thanks for the renewal of life.

Lighter lights the two bonfires.

Narrator   At Beltane, the people extinguished the fires in their hearths and climbed to the high point of a nearby hill, taking their livestock with them. Here they kindled the ceremonial fires, from which they would light brands to take back to their homes. To assure the fertility, purification, and protection of the flocks and herds, they drove them between the fires on their way to the high summer pastures. They believed the fire itself had curative, protective, even magical powers. And when the flames were low enough, they leapt over the fires, even carrying the children, hoping for the blessing of health and fertility.

Leader   Early celebrants of Beltane offered a sacrifice of a ceremonial oatcake called bannock, to assure a fruitful growing season. Perhaps it is always thus: Growth requires sacrifice. What are we willing to sacrifice in order to grow—in spirit, in mind, in physical health? What are we willing to give up for the well-being of the world community? What did those who have gone before us sacrifice for *our* growth? Let us meditate for a moment and then write on a piece of paper what we are willing to sacrifice for growth and fold up the papers. When the music begins, we'll offer these to the Beltane fires as we slowly and carefully pass through them.

After a time of silent meditation, Servers usher partici-pants between the fires as a guitarist sings "Cup of Wonder" by Ian Anderson.

Celebrating the Taste of Life

Narrator In the high summer pastures where the Celts took their herds and flocks, the new grass was so plentiful at this time of year that cows reportedly had to be milked three times a day. For this reason dairy products were a favorite treat at this festival. But the ceremonial food was the oatcake. The people faced the fire and offered bits of their bannock, invoking in turn the respective protectors of the sheep, the horses, and the cattle. Then they broke off more pieces and offered these in the name of the fox, the crow, and other predators, that these might spare the flocks and herds. Ironically, this symbolic giving away of the bannock to guardian spir-its and animals assured that the people would have enough for themselves. Before we moderns mock what we might consider their superstitious beliefs, we might consider the wisdom of this practice. Perhaps it is only in sharing that we ever have enough for ourselves.

Leader We invite you to come forward and take an oatcake, and when all have been served, we'll bless the cakes to-gether and then share and enjoy them.

Servers come forward with trays of small oatmeal rolls or oatmeal cookies and distribute to all.

Narrator   Behold the food of ancient Beltane:
            the product of butter, milk, and grain.

All   This piece we offer to birds of the air,
            whose songs delight us everywhere.

            All offer a piece to the birds.

Leader   Behold the food of ancient Beltane,
            the product of butter, milk, and grain.

All   This piece I give my neighbor here,
            whose life and health I reckon dear.

            All offer a piece to a neighbor.

Narrator   Behold the food of ancient Beltane,
and   the product of butter, milk, and grain.
Leader

All   Upon the Spirit of Life we call.
            May we, by sharing, have enough for all.

            *All eat, then sing the following words to the melody of
            "'Tis a Gift to Be Simple."*

All sing   'Tis a joy to be sharing, 'tis a joy to be one,
            'Tis a joy to sing here in the Beltane sun.
            For when we welcome summer in with fire bright,
            We celebrate all the buds that delight.
            May Day! And all the world is green.
            The blossoms, the birds, and the lovers are seen.
            It's time now to honor Mother Earth
            As with great elation she gives all birth.

Celebrating the Victory of Summer Over Winter

Narrator   According to the Welsh, at Beltane two mighty mytho-
            logical figures, Gwyn ap Nudd and Gwythur ap
            Greidawl, engage in mortal combat for the loveliest

maiden of the land. This represents the yearly struggle between the god of summer, light, and life and the god of winter, darkness, and death. The maiden symbolizes the fertility goddess or the earth itself. A more familiar version of this conflict is that of the old King Arthur and the young Sir Lancelot for the love of Guinevere, who is the goddess of childbirth and fertility in Welsh mythology.

To instrumental musical accompaniment, performers playing Winter, Earth, and Summer ritually mime the yearly battle. The scenario might look like this:

Winter, dressed in white and gray and black, with a white beard and hair, struts before the audience, proud of his power.

Winter dances sedately with Earth, who is dressed in a brown cloak. At the end of the dance, Earth lies down and falls asleep. Winter lovingly keeps guard over her.

Summer, a young man dressed in green clothes and decorated with greenery, appears and admires the sleeping Earth.

Winter becomes jealous. They play out their rivalry with sticks (bamboo poles or stripped tree branches) or with choreographed martial arts or dance movements. They alternate in having the upper hand. Eventually, Winter's experience seems to be getting the better of Summer. But finally Summer's youth and strength enable him to win. Defeated, Winter leaves.

Summer approaches Earth, kisses her gently. Earth wakes slowly, smiles at him. He offers his hand, by which she pulls herself up. Earth throws off her brown cape to reveal green clothing underneath. She dances with exuberance.

Finally Earth invites Summer to join her and they dance together. If possible, they finish by dancing and holding hands around a maybush (or a maypole or tree). Hanging there is a basket containing the petals of whatever trees or bushes are flowering in the area.

Earth and Summer take down the basket and scatter the petals among the audience while singing "The Lusty Month of May" from Camelot, *and encourage participants who know the song to join in.*

Dancing Around the Maypole

A maypole has been prepared and decorated.

Narrator   On May Day in England, young men and women of the village enjoyed "bringing in the May." They went early to the woods (or sometimes even spent the night there!) and gathered greenery, especially boughs of the may-bush, the flowering hawthorn. They decorated houses with it and made May baskets of flowers for loved ones.

Leader   But the most spectacular May Day rite was the maypole dance, widely popular in Europe by the late Middle Ages. The maypole, usually a stripped birch or fir tree, was covered with flowers and drawn by decorated oxen—with all the townsfolk following—to the village square. Here they set it up, decorated it with green boughs, and danced around it. The May Queen, dressed in white, presided over the festivities. Wearing a wreath of flowers, she represented the fertility goddess and the earth itself. Her role was a coveted one, as suggested by this excerpt from Alfred Lord Tennyson's poem, "The May Queen."

Reader 2   (*a young woman*)
You must wake and call me early, call me early, mother dear;
To-morrow 'ill be the happiest time of all the glad New-year;
Of all the glad New-year, mother, the maddest merriest day,
For I'm to be Queen o' the May, mother, I'm to be Queen o' the May. . . .

Little Effie shall go with me to-morrow to the green,
And you'll be there, too, mother, to see me made the
  Queen;
For the shepherd lads on every side'll come from far
  away,
And I'm to be Queen o' the May, mother, I'm to be
  Queen o' the May.

The honeysuckle round the porch has woven its wavy
  bowers,
And by the meadow-trenches blow the faint sweet
  cuckoo-flowers;
And the wild marsh-marigold shines like fire in
  swamps and hollows gray,
And I'm to be Queen o' the May, mother, I'm to be
  Queen o' the May. . . .

All the valley, mother, 'ill be fresh and green and still,
And the cowslip and the crowfoot are over all the hill,
And the rivulet in the flowery dale 'ill merrily glance
  and play,
For I'm to be Queen o' the May, mother, I'm to be
  Queen o' the May.

*Choir sings "Now Is the Month of Maying," a madrigal
by Thomas Morley.*

Choir   Now is the month of Maying,
    When merry lads are playing,
    Fa la la la la la la la la, fa la la la la la la.

    Each with his bonny lass,
    Upon the greeny grass,
    Fa la la la, fa la, la, la la la la la, fa la, la, la.

    The Spring clad all in gladness
    Doth laugh at Winter's sadness.
    Fa la la la la la la la la, fa la la la la la la.

And to the bagpipe's sound,
the nymphs tread out their ground,
Fa la la la la la la la la la la, fa la la la la.

Fie then! Why sit we musing,
Youth's sweet delight refusing?
Fa la la la la la la la la la, fa la la la la la.

Say dainty nymphs and speak,
Shall we play barley break?
Fa la la la la, fa la la la la la la la, fa la la la.

Narrator   In some places, the May queen was joined by a May king or Green Man, believed by some scholars to represent the vegetation god. They accompanied the maypole in procession and presided over the festival. The "mock" marriage of these young people may have been a remnant of an archaic fertility rite, in which the royal couple of the kingdom enacted a ritual mating that imitated the *hieros gamos*, the sacred marriage of the goddess and the god. By imitating the divine creators, they assured the health and fertility of all in the kingdom.

Leader   Come all ye lads and lassies,
Join in the festive scene.
Come dance around the maypole
That stands upon the green!

A group of young people who have volunteered or been recruited and who have rehearsed the dance now come forward and dance around the maypole. Ideally, this dance would be accompanied by sprightly music provided by live musicians. Fiddle, flute, and/or drum would be lovely. If this is not possible, recorded music can be used or the onlookers can clap and sing.

All dancers hold the end of a long wide ribbon whose other end is attached to the top of the pole and start by standing as far away from the pole as the ribbons will allow. Half move in one direction, half in the other. Each person moves to the right of the dancer coming toward them, then to the left of the next dancer. Those on the inside duck; those on the outside hold their ribbons high. When the ribbons are tightly woven around the pole and the dancers are so close together they can no longer move, all release the ribbons and clap, then return to their places.

Around the World

Narrator   There are May Day celebrations around the world. In Teutonic countries, the festival of Walpurgis commemorates the god Odin's self-sacrifice upon the World Tree. His death throws the world into darkness and chaos. But when the great bonfires are set ablaze, light and order return to the world.

Leader   In Sweden people light bonfires and sing spring songs on the eve of May 1. In Germany there are ceremonial tree plantings, maypole dances, and maypole climbing contests.

Narrator   In Greece the children sing spring songs on the morning of May Day, after locating the first swallow of the season. They bring the good news back to their neighbors, who reward them with sweet treats.

Leader   Teenage boys in Switzerland and the Czech and Slovak Republics court their Sweethearts with May trees or maypoles outside their windows.

Narrator   Italians boys serenade their girlfriends and compete for prizes by climbing greased maypoles.

Leader   Bulgarians celebrate the Feast of St. George, who may be a legendary reincarnation of a god of nature and vegetation, who was believed to bring in summer.

Narrator   In the United States, while there is no formal observation of May Day, proms and flower marts celebrate love and new life. And of course, Mother's Day is a joyful, if dignified, celebration of fertility.

Leader   For Hawaiians,

> May Day is Lei Day.
> Colorful blossoms abound.
> They dance the hula, sing and play
> and cheer the royalty crowned!

Narrator   For Wiccans, Beltane is the beginning of summer, a festival of renewal, creativity, and sexual passion, when the Horned God impregnates the Earth Goddess.

Leader   In India Buddha's birthday is celebrated the first week of May—a month named for his mother, Maia.

Narrator   In Sri Lanka Buddha's birthday is celebrated on the day of the full moon in May. There are prayers and processions, singing, and offerings of flowers at temples, as well as secular entertainments.

Leader   The Japanese celebrate the *Aoi Matsuri*, or Hollyhock Festival, in mid-May. People dressed in period costumes —together with their farm animals—process to shrines for the performance of sacred rituals that are over two thousand years old.

Narrator   Isn't it amazing—and yet reassuring—that people around the globe, whatever their culture, find a way to welcome the warm, growing season? Let us end our ritual by celebrating its arrival in song.

            All sing the following words to the melody of "De Colores."

All sing   Welcome summer! Greet the blue skies above
                and the weather we love and the flowers!
            Welcome summer! Say "Hello" to the robins

and finches and jays in their bowers!
Happy May Day! May we live, may we love,
 may we care, may we share and be glad
for the sights and the sounds, for the smells that
 abound when the earth in her blossoms is clad!

Welcome summer! Greet the tulips and dogwoods,
 azaleas, and lilacs convening!
Welcome summer! Say "Hello" to the pinks and the yel-
 lows and everything greening!
Happy May Day! When the warm days are calling
 and everyone's falling in love—
Yes, rejoice in the nurturing earth 'neath our feet
 and the sun that sustains from above!

You may want to extend the May Day celebration with some of the following activities:

🜨 Follow the ritual with communal gardening—plantings on the grounds of the church, community center, or park where the event has taken place.

🜨 Provide brown bag lunches so participants can extend their fellowship while eating *al fresco*.

🜨 Encourage others to dance around the maypole.

🜨 Have a May Fair, setting up booths or tables for various activities related to the season, such as making leis, braiding or weaving flowers into hair, making wreaths of flowers, pressing flowers, making Mother's Day cards, making May baskets, and making bird feeders with pine cones and peanut butter.

Summer Solstice and Midsummer

June 21-22

If Winter Solstice is the birthday of the sun deities, Summer Solstice is the celebration of their peak of power. The reluctant Amaterasu, who had to be coaxed from her cave in December, now dances at her zenith. The strong rays of the sun have brought foliage to maturity and transformed stark tree limbs into shimmering canopies. My neighborhood is abloom with daisies and lilies, hosta bells and butterfly bushes, magenta impatiens, and red balsam. Purple clematis and pink roses climb their trellises. Hiding among their large, shiny clusters of leaves, white magnolias open like giving hands. Strawberries and blueberries sweeten breakfast cereal. Finches and chickadees flutter with their young at the thistle feeder. What's blossoming in your world?

This is a magical time. School bells are silenced. Wedding bells are ringing. It's time for trips to the beach, the pool, the campgrounds. It's time for fireworks and Ferris wheels and Father's Day. It's time to make hay while the sun shines. It's time to wake up and smell the honeysuckle. It's Summer Solstice!

The Seasonal Calendar

Once again, as at the Winter Solstice, the sun seems to stand still, rising at the same point on the horizon for a few days. But this time, because of the North Pole's tilt toward the sun, that point will be as far north as sunrises get in the northern hemisphere, whereas at Winter Solstice, the point of sunrises and the point of sunsets are at their most southern extremes. In the modern calendar the usual date of Summer Solstice is June 21 for the northern hemisphere and December 21 for the southern hemisphere.

Now the sun, which has been waxing since the Winter Solstice, is so high in the sky at noon that it seems directly overhead. (Although we speak of the sun as "waxing," it is, of course, the earth's relative proximity to it rather than a change in the sun's power that allows us to receive its energy in a more direct and focused way.) Now we enjoy the longest period of daylight. Indeed, north of the Arctic Circle, "land of the midnight sun," the sun doesn't set at all on Summer Solstice.

This day marks the official beginning of astronomical summer, though it has been traditionally celebrated as "midsummer." As noted previously, thermal seasons—associated with the astronomical markers reflected in our calendars—lag behind solar seasons. While June 21 is rarely, if ever, the hottest peak of summer or even the average in terms of temperature, it is the indisputable pinnacle of light. The weeks on either side of it contain the longest days; it is thus mid-solar summer.

In much of the northern hemisphere's temperate zone, Summer Solstice is the midpoint in the growing season of the agricultural cycle—about halfway between the beginning of planting in early spring and the harvesting in early fall. This "breathing time" in the labor of farmers has traditionally provided both the occasion and the opportunity for celebrating the relationship between earth and sun.

Richard Heinberg, author of *Celebrate the Solstice*, provides detailed descriptions of structural calendars around the world that mark the Summer Solstice. The structures are also pictured and described on their respective websites. Perhaps the most famous of these is Stonehenge on Salisbury Plain in southwestern England. The ruins of this prehistoric monument, originally built over a period of centuries, consist of a circular arrangement of gigantic standing stones—bluestones and sarsen sandstones. Some pairs of these pillars are connected by a third, lintel stone, thus creating giant arches, or *trilithons*. Outside the circle, near the entrance to the monument, is the heel stone. At Summer Solstice, the sun rises over the heel stone, framed by three of the great trilithons. Further north, on the Kintyre Peninsula of Scotland, three standing stones at Ballochroy align with both the Summer and Winter Solstices.

Predating Stonehenge is the observatory built at Nabta Playa in the Sahara Desert. Here a twelve-foot calendar circle of flat standing stones includes four pairs of larger megaliths, two of which are aligned with the Summer Solstice sunrise. Another Egyptian monument marking the Solstice is the Great Temple of the sun god Amen-Ra at Karnak. Archaeoastronomer J. Norman Lockyer believes its main hall aligned with the sunset at Summer Solstice, during which time a shaft of light momentarily brightened the sanctuary.

Minna and Kenneth Lönnqvist, authors of *Archeology of the Hidden Qumran*, claim that based on the angle at which the Summer Solstice sunset enters it, the largest room of the ruins at Qumran, Palestine, where the Dead Sea Scrolls were discovered in 1947, may well be a sun temple. The room in the complex used by the Essenes, an ascetic Jewish sect that flourished from the second century BCE to the second century CE, was formerly thought to be a dining area although it contains two altars. It is situated at exactly the same angle as the Egyptian shrines of the sun god.

In Asia stone structures provided calendars. Angkor Wat, a temple complex in Cambodia honoring one of the Hindu creator gods, Vishnu, served as an observatory, marking both solstices and Spring Equinox. In the Polynesian settlement of Tonga, a gigantic rectangular coral megalithic arch, the Ha'amonga'a Maui, marks the Summer Solstice sunrise.

Natives of both Americas celebrated the Summer Solstice. At the full moon nearest it, most of the Plains tribes of North

America held their ceremonial sun dance to purify themselves and renew the earth. For the sun dance the tribe created a circular lodge of twenty-eight vertical poles, each supporting one end of a roof pole whose other end rested in the crotch of a tall sun pole at the center of the lodge. This sun pole, believed to connect heaven and earth, was carefully chosen and ritually cut down to serve its sacred function. Also associated with male puberty rites, the Sun Dance Ceremony lasted one to four days.

Native Americans created stone structures as well. The Bighorn Medicine Wheel is a stone circle in Wyoming that marks the Summer Solstice sunrise and sunset. On top of Fajada Butte, a mountain in the Anasazi ruins of Chaco Canyon in New Mexico, at midday on Summer Solstice a thin shaft of light that archeologists have dubbed "sun dagger" intersects a delicate spiral petroglyph engraved on a cliff behind large slabs of rock, which shadow the carving at all other times.

And in Central America, the two-hundred-foot-high Pyramid of the Sun at Teotihuacán, Mexico, constructed two millennia ago to honor the sun god Huitzilopochtli, is aligned with the Summer Solstice sunrise and sunset. The Mayans built three temples at Uaxactun to mark both solstices and the equinoxes.

Astronomy was more than a pastime to the ancients. For the desert people of the Nabta Playa, predicting the timing of the solstice was of paramount importance since this event heralded the monsoon season. The people of Karnak could use the Great Temple there to predict the time of—and thus prepare for—the flooding of the Nile, whose first signs appeared at Syene (modern Aswan) by the end of June. In Native American and other cultures, such structures served as agricultural calendars, indicating the time for planting and harvesting various crops.

Where there were not such structures, other parts of the topography were used as markers. These functions were so important that tribes often assigned sun watchers or sun priests for what was considered a sacred duty. Heinberg reports that among the Pomo Indians of northern California,

Each valley was watched by a special sun priest who noted the position of sunrise each day in relation to a particular hill on the horizon, and thereby kept track of the Sun's progress toward a Solstice. When sunrise occurred in the same spot for four consecutive days, the sunwatcher proclaimed the Solstice.

The sun priest of the Zuni prayed and fasted for eight days before the expected solstice. The Hopi sun chief announced the solstices and the timing of agricultural cycles and also used the sun to keep track of the ceremonial calendar. According to Anthony Aveni, author of *The Book of the Year*, the Mayan calendar specialist was called a *hmeen* or "daykeeper," and he observed the sunrises over the Uaxactun temples from a platform built into the large pyramid opposite them.

Given that it has always been possible to identify the time of the solstices using natural markers on the horizon and that it is possible to have a ceremony in a simple setting, we have to ask why would Neolithic peoples go to all the trouble of building—at unimaginable cost in human energy—such great megalithic structures? Since we have no recorded accounts of their motivation, it's unlikely we will ever know. But when we ask why medieval Europeans, who could much more easily have built simple wooden structures in which to attend services, raised up instead majestic, towering, labor-intensive, lifetime-consuming cathedrals, the answer is frequently "to honor their deity." Perhaps the same was true for our earliest ancestors.

Aveni contends that the great stone structures were built not just as observatories but as convening places for seminomadic people to conduct religious rituals, share stories, and create community. The megalithic structures were a visual version of medieval church bells. They called the people to worship when the time was right. Aveni invites us to "imagine how impressive the rites to the sun god would have appeared" to viewers of a sunrise streaming down the accessway at Stonehenge or "framed by massive Inca pillars on a mountainside in the Peruvian Andes or perched in the doorway of a sculpture-adorned Maya temple in Yucatan."

Mythology and History

For Chinese Taoists, the Summer Solstice marks the birth of the *yin*, or divine female principle—especially manifest in Mother Earth and her fertility—which is then in ascendancy until Winter Solstice, when the *yang*, or divine male principle, is (re)born.

Mythology from around the world makes it clear that the sun and its worship played a vital role in the life of ancient peoples. In his *Encyclopedia of Gods*, Michael Jordan identifies more than seventy solar deities. Patricia Monaghan, in *The New Book of Goddesses and Heroines*, describes fifty-five sun figures. Other sources record solar myths from many cultures. While these stories of the origin, purpose, and powers of the sun—personified in local and national deities—differ in their specifics, they reveal a remarkable similarity of themes and patterns. Although the following provides a far-from-exhaustive sampling, it brings home the point: Reverence for the sun was widespread among our ancestors for millennia. Celebrating the sun filled a fundamental need in their lives.

Typically the parentage of sun deities is illustrious, revealing high status in their respective pantheons. Apollo is the son of Zeus; Daksa is the son of Brahma and the Hindu goddess Aditi, "Woman Clothed With the Sun." The Norse Freyr is son of the sea god Njord. Helios (immortalized in the Colossus of Rhodes) is son of Hyperion, god of primordial light. Liza, sun god of the Fon people of West Africa, is born from Nana Buluku, creator of the world. The primordial Greek sun god Phanes is the first to hatch from the cosmic egg, fertilized by Cronos. The Egyptian Ra (or Re) emerged from a cosmic egg rising out of primeval waters. The Hindu Surya is another son of Aditi and himself the father of a sun goddess, also named Surya. Huitzilopochtli is magically conceived by the Aztec mother goddess Coatlicue when a feather falls from the sky and lands on her breast. These and more sun deities come to their position through a kind of divine bloodline.

Other deities, especially female ones, often have their greatness thrust upon them, sometimes as a result of trauma. In ancient Scandinavia, the young girl Sunna was so lovely that her father named her for the most brilliant star of heaven, the sun. Offended by this insolence, the gods of Asgard took the girl away and made her ride the chariot of day ever after. Another victim of kidnapping is Tahc-I, a girl of the Louisiana Tunica who was wooed by the kingfisher disguised as a human. One dark night he took her home to his "upstairs room." But upon waking, she was unhappy to discover that she was in a nest in a hackberry tree. She grew even more miserable when the kingfisher brought her a school of fish for breakfast. She began to sing her misery, and her singing made her give off light and rise up to the sky, where she became the sun goddess. Another young woman wandered into the sky on her own. Gnowee lived among the Wotjabaluk of southeast Australia in the time of perpetual night, until one day her child strayed from the camp. Taking a large torch, she set out to find him but never did. She still searches the sky every day, looking for her son.

Several myths feature a sun goddess who is a victim of rape. Akycha is raped by her brother. She tries to escape but he pursues her—right up into the sky, where she is transformed into the sun and he into the moon, shining on the people of Greenland, Canada, and Alaska. A variation on this is the story of Kn Sgni, whose brother moon is as bright as the sun until his passion for her is aroused. Angry, she scorches his face, thus taking off some of his sheen; in his shame, he wanders the skies. The Inuit people of Greenland tell a similar story—of Malina who is raped by her brother and escapes into the sky, where she becomes the sun. Her unrepentant brother Anningan pursues her and becomes the moon. The chase goes on every day and night, until he rapes her again at each solar eclipse. So obsessed is Anningan with his passion that he neglects to eat and grows thinner and thinner, then disappears for three days to feed himself, which accounts for the waning and dark of the moon.

In a gentler Cherokee variation, the sun goddess Unelanuhi is visited once a month by a lover who pleasures her without revealing his identity. When she discovers it is her brother, his shame makes him keep as much distance as possible between them, though once a month, at the dark of the moon, he continues to visit her bed. Even gentler is the version in which the East African sun god Liza and his partner the moon goddess Mawu are said to be making love when there is an eclipse. A harsher variation is the story of Saule and her moon-husband Meness. While Saule is busy with her sunly duties each day, the fickle Meness sometimes stays home. One evening Saule returns home and cannot not find their beloved daughter, the morning star. When she discovers Meness has raped the daughter, she slashes his face, leaving deep marks, and banishes him from her sight so that they can never be together in the sky. (In another version the changeable moon-husband courts an unrelated morning star.)

An example of a male traumatized into the role of sun god is Tayau, father sun of the Huichol Indians of Mexico. According to legend, this young son of the grain mother is thrust into the oven by shamans. From there he travels beneath the ground until he rises in the east as the sun.

When the sun deity is male, he often has a sister moon goddess (Apollo and Artemis) or a consort or wife moon goddess (the Mayan Ah Kin and Acna, the Incan Inti and Mama-Kilya, and Liza and Mawu of the West African Fon people), but he is generally not the victim of her violence. An exception is Huitzilopochtli, whose sister Coyolxauhqui—one of four hundred star children of Coatlicue—believing their pregnant mother has disgraced them, incites her siblings to commit matricide. But the sun god springs from his mother's womb, fully armed, and slays the would-be murderers. He cuts off his sister's head and tosses it into the heavens, where it becomes the moon.

Whether they took on the role willingly or were forced into it, some sun deities temporarily abandon it. A number of myths explain the "disappearance" (waning) of the sun as Winter Solstice approaches. Some of these were discussed in the first chapter: The Japanese Amaterasu, disgusted with her brother's bad behavior, hides herself in a cave. The Cherokee Unelanuhi locks herself in her house when her daughter is killed. The Indian Bomong hides under a rock when her sister is killed. In the case of the Finnish Paivatar, rather than choosing confinement herself, the goddess is kidnapped by witches. The Australian aboriginals of the Flinders Range tell of the sun goddess Bila, who lights the world with a fire fed by human bodies. But when Kudnu the lizardman attacks her with his boomerang, she blows up and disappears, leaving the world dark and cold. In all cases, the sun deity must be rescued or coaxed out of hiding to save the earth from perpetual darkness and its inhabitants from famine.

On the other hand, one myth probably intended to explain the longer summer days is that of the Polynesian trickster Maui, who in order to provide his mother with more daylight hours to make bark cloth, cuts off a length of the hair of his wife Hina (the moon goddess), and makes a rope from it to catch the rising sun. Weakened by Maui's beating, the sun slows down in his course.

Another similarity among the sun deities is the imagery used to describe their daily journey across the sky (the very name of the Hindu Dhanvantari means "traveling through an arc"), though differences in topography sometimes dictate variations in entry and exit points.

The Hungarian sun goddess Xatel-Ekwa traverses the sky mounted simultaneously on three horses. The Hindu Surya rides in a one-wheeled chariot drawn by seven mares. When Surya's wife cannot bear his intense heat and light, she escapes to a forest and disguises herself as a mare. But he pursues her in the form of a horse and mates with her there. The horses that pull the chariot of Saule never tire or perspire. Still she washes them in the sea each evening before retiring to her silver-gated castle. In the case of the ancient Irish Ainé, the goddess herself takes on the form of a red mare who cannot be outrun.

In Lapland, the Saami goddess Beiwe and her daughter ride in an enclosure of reindeer antlers. The Navajo Tsohanoai has no such luxury. By day he carries the sun on his back across the sky, and at night he hangs it on a peg on the west wall of his house. Garuda, in Vedi mythology originally a sun god born from an egg, came to be depicted as a human-bird hybrid who provides transportation for the divine couple Vishnu and Lakshmi.

Like many other sun deities, the Norse Freyr, the Bright One, journeys into the Underworld when he is not in the sky. The Sumerian Shamash rides the sky in a chariot, then descends into the Underworld through the West Mountain. The Mayan Ah Kin relies on the god Sucunyum to carry him through the Underworld at night.

The Etruscan Cautha is portrayed rising from the sea. The Greek Helios rides his sun chariot in the sky by day and travels under the sea by night. The Australian Wuriupranili carries a bark torch across the sky, extinguishes it in the western sea, and uses its glowing embers to navigate the subterranean journey to her eastern rising point. The Japanese Chup-Kamui rises from the mouth of a devil, having escaped being devoured each night. Because the Mesopotamian Utu rises in the mountains of the east and sets in the mountains of the west, he carries a saw-like weapon to cut through the mountains.

In some pantheons, the sun's duties are divided. Aurora is the Roman goddess of dawn. The Hindu dawn or morning star Aruna drives the chariot of the sun god Surya. In Egypt the sun rises as Ra and sets as Osiris. On the other hand, some sun deities' duties are doubled. As mentioned above, some rule the sky by day and the Underworld by night. The Egyptian Re is not only the sun but the father of all creation including humans, who come from his tears, as well as god of the Underworld. The Aztec Tonatiuh also oversees the afterlife of men who die in war and women who die in childbirth. In the Nandi religion, the East African sun god Asis becomes the supreme creator god. The Cherokee bow their heads to each dawn and pray to Unelanuhi, "Hail, sun, my creator." The Navajo Tsohanoai is credited with creating the big game animals. Wai protects the forest animals in Zaire. In some versions of the West African myth, the solar god Liza is also a creator, sharing this role with his moon-goddess partner Mawu (who in Dahomey is acknowledged as Mother of All). The Hittite solar deity Arinna is also a *chthonic*, or earth, goddess. The Baltic Saule is a fertility goddess as well. Beiwe is credited with bringing green plants in the Arctic spring.

In addition to serving as creators of the natural world and its various components and to parenting other divine beings in their respective pantheons, some solar deities are believed to have founded dynasties ruled by human offspring; others are tutelary deities for a given people.

Huitzilopochtli was the patron god of the Aztecs. Kazyoba was the creator and guardian of the Nyamwezi tribe of Tanzania. Inti was believed to be the progenitor of the Inca rulers at Cuzco, just as the Irish sun goddess Mor was considered the progenitor of the royal line of kings of Munster. Aryaman, one of the children of the Hindu goddess Aditi, is acknowledged as the ancestral god of all Aryans. Perhaps the most striking example is Amaterasu, believed well into the twentieth century to be the ancestral deity of the imperial house of Japan. It wasn't until 1946, with Japan's defeat in World War II, that Emperor Hirohito publicly repudiated his descent from the sun goddess and renounced his claim to the title Son of Heaven.

While the ancient sun deities, like the sun itself in modern times, are appreciated as a source of light and warmth and sustenance in the natural world, they are not without their dark side. The Mayans feared Ah Kin as the bringer of drought. A Chinese myth explains that three millennia ago there were ten suns that were supposed to take turns in the sky. But one day they decided to join together, and their combined heat had such disastrous effects on the earth that the heavenly archer Yi was sent to shoot them. The only survivor is the one we see.

Egyptians of the Nile delta worshiped a separate god, Mahes, as the destructive power of the sun's heat. But even their creator sun god Ra was sometimes depicted wearing on his head a sun disk bearing a cobra, suggesting his role as bringer of death. The Australian Bila cooked her victims over a great open fire. The Aztec gods Huitzilopochtli and Tonatiuh both required blood to cool their heat and maintain their strength and so fed on sacrificial human hearts, which were ritually torn from their owners.

As might be expected, with the arrival of Christianity, sun gods made an appealing target for demonization. It should not be surprising that a sun god would be cast as a devil, given that in the Judeo-Christian tradition, Lucifer himself was an angel of light before his fall from heaven.

Our modern sensibilities are horrified by stories of divine rape and incest and human sacrifice. However, a closer look at the myths involving rape reveals that the perpetrator is usually shamed and punished (scorched, scarred, alienated, etc.). Could these stories have provided object lessons reinforcing the incest taboo? The rituals involving human sacrifice also affront our contemporary notions of morality. And yet, this was merely an *extreme* practice of the more general notion of sacrifice to please a deity. Lesser versions of sacrifice (meaning "to make holy") are still practiced in various religions today—from such simple customs as fasting to more demanding practices such as vowed celibacy. While human sacrifice may have been widespread millennia ago, this eventually gave way to animal sacrifice (as reflected in the Genesis account of Abraham and Isaac) or to ritualized enactments in which an actor pretended to be "sacrificed" (as in the case of the fires in which the Norse Balder's cremation was reenacted to please his father Odin).

Despite what we might consider negative features of some of the harsher stories, the myths and legends generally put more emphasis on the positive aspects of the sun deities. In addition to providing the physical benefits of light and warmth, the sun is a symbol for a much broader kind of light—a clarity in intellectual and civic pursuits. Thus Apollo is the god of logic and reason, Surya is the personification of cosmic order and the wellspring of all knowledge, and Inti is credited with teaching his people the arts of civilization.

The Sumerians reasoned that since the sun was in a position to see everything on earth, their sun deity Shamash should also be the god of justice. His two children represented justice and law. The Sumerian Utu was a god of justice and law as well and his Babylonian counterpart, Samas, was attended by deities who included justice and righteousness. The Siberian Yeloje personifies justice and morality. Likewise the Siberian Pu'gu is associated with justice and honorable living and punishes evildoers. The Hittites viewed Istanu as a god of judgment. The cobra element in Ra's iconography implies his power to deliver quick retribution.

If the light of the sun is clarifying, the heat of the sun is healing. This is another pattern of perception reflected in the attributes of solar deities. Apollo and the Celtic Belenus were invoked as healers. Mayans prayed to Ah Kin to cure illness. Hindus turn to Garuda to cure snakebites. They pronounced Daksa the guardian deity of hospitals and honor Dhanvantari for bringing medical science to humankind. The sick of Bihar and Tamilnad turn to Surya for healing. Soldiers occupying Britain in the first century chose the site of natural hot springs to build their healing and reinvigorating Roman baths and the town of Aquae Sulis, named for Sul, the sun goddess whose name means the underground sun that heats the waters. It is likely that the nearby hill of Solsbury, or Sulisbury, was a seat of her worship.

Many sun deities were honored with rituals or festivals, which sometimes included sacrifices. The ancient Roman Vestalia, honoring the goddess of the hearth/fire, was celebrated in June. Her priestesses cleansed the temple and offered up the first fruits of grain. The Tunica of Louisiana performed a yearly dance in honor of Tahc-I. Up until the nineteenth century, at midsummer, farmers of Knockainy (Cnoc Ainé) in Limerick, Ireland, implored Ainé for their cattle's protection and fertility by waving fiery torches over them. The Bella Coola tribe of British Columbia toss pieces of seal or goat meat into a sacrificial fire, calling on their sun god Senx as "Our Father." In late May the Huichol of Mexico sacrifice a sheep and a turkey to Tayau's fire, then sing till dawn. At the festival of Helios on Rhodes, the ancient Greeks drove a chariot with four horses off a cliff to symbolize the sun's setting into the sea. The Cheremis of Russia also sacrificed horses at the annual festival honoring their mother sun, Keca Aba, selecting the ones whose shuddering at a particular point in the ceremony was believed to indicate their willingness. At both solstices, the Saami of Lapland sacrificed white female animals to Beiwe, threading the meat on a stick and then bending the stick into a circle and decorating it with ribbons. They said special prayers for the insane since the absence of the sun goddess in winter was believed to cause madness. At dawn, they smeared their doors with butter to be "eaten" (melted) by the sun, while they themselves ate a sacramental sun porridge.

While sun worship was prevalent in the ancient world, Judeo-Christian mythology offers relatively little sun imagery. In *Dictionary of the Bible*, John L. McKenzie notes far fewer references to sun than to light, which is the preferred metaphor for divinity and its effects associated with both Yahweh and Jesus:

> As a natural body the sun was a creature of Yahweh; it was created after light, which was conceived as a distinct being, indeed the primary being associated with deity. The sun is merely a bearer of light (Gn 1:16). It moves in obedience to the command of Yahweh (Jb 9:7; Mt 5:45).

Perhaps the authors of these scriptures sought to avoid identification of—or mere equality of—their god with the pagan sun gods. The Book of Revelations promises that there will be no need of sun in the heavenly Jerusalem, which will be lit by the glory of the Christian god.

Due to various calendrical changes, by the late Middle Ages Europe was celebrating the Summer Solstice on June 23-24, the festivities beginning on the eve and carried over into the day. The church had established June 24 as the feast of St. John the Baptist, whom the gospels describe as a prophet, cousin, precursor, and baptizer of Jesus, born six months before him (an arbitrary date, of course, since scholars cannot agree on the actual birth date of Jesus). Although it was standard liturgical practice to assign a saint's feast to the date of *death*, an exception was made in the case of John, thus setting his birthday festival directly opposite that of Jesus in the cycle of both the astronomical and liturgical calendars. *The Catholic Encyclopedia* acknowledges a "resemblance of the feast of St. John with that of Christmas," since both days were marked by the celebration of three masses—at midnight, at dawn, and at 9 a.m. Anthony Aveni calls the timing of John's feast a

> brilliant example of religious syncretism. Baptism is the principal rite of admission into the Christian Church. It offers both the washing away of sins and a rebirth, and it grew out of an older Jewish practice. Who better to incorporate the idea of purification once associated with cleansing by fire to bathing at sunrise than he who consecrated the rite of purification upon Christ himself.

The myths of many pre-Christian peoples feature a struggle between rival gods or kings—often two sides of the same figure—who represent light (born at Winter Solstice, when the light begins to wax) and darkness (born at Summer Solstice, when the light begins to wane). The Holly King and Oak King, who contend ritually at the solstices, are a prime example. Some scholars have viewed Jesus and John as part of this pattern. When questioned about his "rival," the Baptist concedes, "He must increase; I must decrease." Thus does one season give way to another. John's feast was so important that it was preceded by a fasting vigil with its own mass, which would have neatly coincided with—and likely competed with—the beginning of Summer Solstice festivities. In some places, these festivities were celebrated in two installments, perhaps allowing for an extension if the weather permitted or a rain date if it didn't. This practice would have the possibly weeklong celebration culminating on June 29, the feast of Saints Peter and Paul, which also had its vigil, or "eve."

In *The Stations of the Sun* Ronald Hutton documents the importance and prevalence of a pre-Christian midsummer ritual celebrated on and around the British Isles for perhaps as long as fifteen centuries. The earliest recorded accounts, dating at least as far back as the fourteenth and possibly the fourth century, describe the rolling of a flaming wheel downhill into a river on June 23, Midsummer Eve. Later folklorists provide more detail: The wheel, which had been padded and stuffed with straw, was sometimes guided by men prodding it with sticks or holding either end of a long pole passed through its center. Loud cheering encouraged its progress, for if it stayed afire all the way down, it would bring good luck and a good harvest. In 1954, the villagers of Widdecombe revived this tradition, which "has a recorded history of almost two millennia, stretching back into the pagan past."

The lighting of festive fires, though first recorded in the twelfth century, is believed to be of much older origin. By the nineteenth century, the custom was widespread throughout Europe and even in parts of Africa. A fourteenth-century English monk describes the fires as made with bones (bonfires) or clean wood (wakefires), or bones and wood (St. John's fires). Other possible etymologies of the word suggest its association with beacon (*baun*-fire), with gifts provided by nature or generous humans (*boon*-fire), or with protection against evil (*bane*-fire).

In North Africa, reports James Frazer in *The Golden Bough*, people burned sweet-smelling herbs in the fires, fumigated their houses with torches lit from them, and hoped that leaping over the fires and rubbing their bodies with the cooled ashes would bring good luck and good health. The fact that the Islamic calendar is a lunar one, not admitting of solar festivals, suggests that the Midsummer fires here were a remnant of pre-Islamic culture.

Practices connected with the fires on the British Isles included throwing fragrant flowers and herbs into them, hanging out lamps, decorating the doors of homes and churches with greenery and herbs, garlanding children, leaping the flames for blessings or good fortune, the parading of medieval guildsmen through the towns, and of course, playing music, singing, dancing, making merry, and engaging in activities designed to encourage fertility. A Cornish midsummer bonfire song—handed down through oral tradition and still sung in the Penzance area today—reflects this practice:

> The bonny month of June is crowned
>> with the sweet scarlet rose;
> The groves and meadows all around
>> with lovely pleasure flows.
>
> As I walked out to yonder green,
>> one evening so fair;
> All where the fair maids may be seen
>> playing at the bonfire.
>
> Hail! lovely nymphs, be not too coy,
>> but freely yield your charms;
> Let love inspire with mirth and joy
>> in Cupid's lovely arms.
>
> Bright Luna spreads its light around,
>> the gallants for to cheer;
> As they lay sporting on the ground,
>> at the fair June bonfire.
>
> All on the pleasant dewy mead,
>> they shared each other's charms;
> Till Phoebus' beams began to spread,
>> and coming day alarms.
>
> Whilst larks and linnets sing so sweet,
> To cheer each lovely swain;
> Let each prove true unto their love,
>> and so farewell the plain.

The more raucous forms of merriment sometimes reached the point of requiring a special police force to discourage mayhem. In a gentler custom, the wealthiest townsfolk set out tables laden with bread and meat and ale and invited their neighbors and

passersby to join them in giving thanks. It was a time to be generous with one's bounty, to be reconciled to enemies, and to be
purged of bitter feelings.

Indeed purging was one of the main purposes of the festival.
In some places, the bonfires were lit—often to the accompaniment
of prayers—on the windward side of fields so their smoke would
waft over the crops growing there. Torches ignited from the bonfires were carried around the fields and cattle pens for blessing and
protection. The very air itself was thought to be in need of purification. And why not? Hutton reminds us that June ushered in the
season during which "crops would be most vulnerable to weather
or blight, and livestock to their diseases." It also heralded the
months "in which insects multiplied most widely and in which,
therefore, humans were most likely to contract bubonic plague,
typhus, and malaria." It was against these very real dangers that
the protection of the St. John's fires was invoked.

The gradual withering over the years of this belief in the purging
power of the Midsummer fires accounts, in part, for the disappearance of the tradition. The other reason was the disapproval of the
Protestant clergy. Since the Roman Catholic Church had "baptized"
the pagan Summer Solstice event, making its possibly week-long
festival a celebration of vigils and feasts of three major saints—in
whose honor the fires could be lit and to whom the invocations
might be addressed—and since in any case these feasts did not share
the importance of Christmas, the Church's objection to the summer
festival probably would not have been as strong as its objection to
the Saturnalian Winter Solstice celebration. In the heat of the
Reformation, however, the Protestant clergy, critical of saints' days
and already determined to get rid of such magical props as holy
water, ashes, and candles, condemned the bonfires as yet another
display of superstitious popery. The combination of disbelief and
disapproval finally took its toll. Gradually, the Midsummer fire festivals were reduced to a secular "entertainment"; by the end of the
nineteenth century they were, in most places, history.

But at their height, according to Frazer, the fire festivals ranged from Ireland in the west to Russia in the east and from Norway and Sweden in the north to Spain and Greece in the south. He contends that the original Midsummer fires were both ceremonies of sun worship and rituals of protection. Although there doesn't seem to be as much evidence for the first as for the second, Hutton admits to seeing in the fiery wheels of Midsummer a reflection of the spoked wheel, one of the most popular symbols of the sun in prehistoric Europe, and further concedes that the two explanations "are wholly compatible," for after all, "it would have made perfect sense to use the flames when the greatest fire in the traditional cosmos, the sun, was putting out most strength."

Contemporary Celebrations Around the World

While there are few places left where the sun is still worshiped, Midsummer is celebrated around the world.

For most of us living in the United States, the rituals are secular. Summer Solstice is the latest possible date for Father's Day, established in 1910 as the third Sunday in June. Is the timing of this "creator-honoring" coincidental? The major summer ritual here commemorates the founding of the country. July 4 is celebrated with fireworks and parades, family picnics, cookouts (the twentieth-century version of fire festivals?), baseball games, concerts, boat races, trips to the beach, and in the best capitalist tradition, major sales in every merchandising enterprise. Ironically, Hutton's research of British festivals reveals that "Old Midsummer's Eve . . . has fallen on 4 July after the calendar change of 1752," twenty-four years before the signing of the Declaration of Independence from English rule and conveniently in time to make the original Fourth-of-July event a true Midsummer celebration.

On the other hand, for many Native Americans of the United States, the old religious customs are still practiced. Richard Heinberg reports,

Just after the summer Solstice, the Hopi celebrate a festival they call *Niman Kachina*. It is the time when the *kachinas*—the spirits of the invisible forces of life—return home to the spirit world. When it is summer Solstice in this Earth, it is winter Solstice in the lower world, and in this way balance is maintained in the universe. The Niman Kachina celebration is focused on a ceremony of the four energies—the germination of plants, the heat of the Sun, the life-giving qualities of water, and the magnetic forces in the Earth and atmosphere.

Canadians celebrate National Aboriginal Day on the Solstice, honoring the unique heritage, cultures, and contributions of the First Nations, the Inuit and the Métis people. French Canadians across the country demonstrate pride in their cultural heritage with parades and parties on June 23, combining ancient Summer Solstice and Christian observances in honor of St. John the Baptist, declared their patron saint by Pope Pius X in 1908.

Across the Pacific, the Chinese mark the Solstice with a Dragon Boat Festival, which has been a commemoration of the esteemed poet and patriot Qu Yuan since the third century BCE, but the actual boat races are thought to have started several centuries earlier and the impulse behind the races to be of even older origin. In the river valleys of ancient China, people believed the river god-dragon determined the distribution of rainwater and therefore controlled agriculture and their own lives. To propitiate him, they offered sacrifices at Summer Solstice. The boats shaped in his image not only pleased the dragon god but also provided spectacle to amuse the emperors.

Well into modern times, many Chinese, especially in the south, celebrated the festival, which lasted several days, culminating in the dragon boat races, and included customs designed to exterminate insects and expel the gods of plague. This is not surprising given the season of steamy weather, which facilitates the growth of disease-producing insects. (We are reminded of the purging fires used for the same purpose in the countries of western Europe.) These customs included hanging strips of yellow paper bearing incantations and images of poisonous creatures, burning *realgar* (a kind of disinfectant), wearing fragrant pouches, and hanging mugwort leaves, calamus, or garlic in doorways. Before 1949 the festival was a general holiday in some parts of the country, marked by the closing of businesses, schools, government, and financial offices. Today this is not the case. But the festival still celebrates Qu Yuan with dragon boat races, which are especially popular in the south, and although many of the old customs are now thought of as superstitions, some families still hang mugwort and calamus leaves.

In Europe where the fire festivals have a long history, the tradition has been resurrected in many places in recent years, though frequently as a tourist attraction more than as a religious service. In Barcelona, for example, according to a *Time-Life* report in 1998, six thousand tourists gathered in a cave near Zugarramurdi to welcome the Solstice with bonfires and dancing. Nearly 34,000 people viewed the sunrise at Stonehenge in 2003.

Farther north and east, in the Scandinavian and Baltic countries where the climate is colder, Midsummer celebrations are even more widespread. In Denmark, natives and tourists alike enjoy bonfires on the beach, sometimes preceded by torchlight processions and accompanied by patriotic songs. But the oldest fires were probably in Norway, where they were ritual reenactments of the cremation of the tree-spirit Balder, son of Odin. The original human sacrifice included in this rite eventually gave way to "play-acting" sacrifice, which was finally replaced by jumping over the fire to bring good luck.

In Finland and Sweden, Midsummer is a public holiday fixed on the third weekend in June and it is as popular as Christmas. Since Christianization, the Finns have known it as *Juhannus*, but in pre-Christian times it honored Ukko, their god of thunder, who supplied the rain necessary for the crops. The traditional bonfires were built close to the water and the honor of igniting them fell to the oldest man in the village. In the coastal areas of Finland and Sweden, Midsummer poles (comparable to maypoles) replace the bonfires. Traditional customs associated with the festival include decorating houses and doorways with flowers and birch branches, eating dairy products, and dancing. Young women wear wreaths of flowers and put midsummer flowers under their pillows so their dreams might reveal their future husbands. Immigrants to the United States brought these traditions with them. Even today, there are Scandinavian Midsummer festivals in New York, Minneapolis, and Astoria, Oregon, featuring traditional music and food and folk dancing around the garlanded pole.

The Magic of Fire, Plants and Water

The Baltic states of Lithuania and Latvia resisted Christianity longer than other northern countries, in some places retaining their native religions even into modern times. Here the solstice feast, called Ligo, once honored Saule, the sun goddess of growth and fertility, with fires and flowers. With the transformation into St. John's Day, Saule's fires became Jani-fires but still served the same "magical" purposes: to purify, protect, and promote fertility. This last was also reflected in the custom of young women making wreaths of flowers. Although Scandinavian maidens slept on their wreaths to dream of future husbands, young women in Baltic countries tossed the wreaths up onto trees, equating the number of branches they caught with the number of years until the maidens would marry.

Marriage is the theme of Shakespeare's *Midsummer Night's Dream*, believed by many scholars to have been written for performance at the Festival of St. John, just as *Twelfth Night* was written for the winter festival. In *Dream*, the fairy king Oberon makes mischief at Midsummer with a love potion. He sends his minion, the forest spirit Puck, to fetch a magical flower with which he can play a trick on his queen Titania:

> Fetch me that flower; the herb I shew'd thee once;
> The juice of it on sleeping eyelids laid,
> Will make a man or woman madly dote
> Upon the next live creature that it sees.

I'll watch Titania when she is asleep,
And drop the liquor of it in her eyes.
The next thing then she waking looks upon,
Be it on lion, bear, or wolf, or bull,
On meddling monkey, or on busy ape,
She shall pursue it with the soul of love.

While the alleged power of some flowers may indeed be "fantastical," many herbs do have time-tested medicinal powers. In Latvia, Midsummer Eve is known as Herb Day, when the herbs and roots collected are believed to have power to heal the sick—both human and animal. Some herbs are used as well in wreaths for wearing or for decorating homes, wells, or byres. Before the Inquisition and the burning of witch-healers, herbal medicine was widely practiced. Hildegard of Bingen wrote a manual on the subject in the twelfth century. Herb gathering at Summer Solstice was a common practice in Europe.

It stands to reason that some herbs would be at their most powerful at the time when the sun is strongest. Saint-John's-wort, for example, which blooms around the Baptist's feast, has bright yellow flowers that have been used for centuries to heal skin wounds and treat depression, anxiety, and insomnia. Other midsummer herbs include vervain (used for liver diseases, fatigue, fever, insomnia, asthma, postnatal depression, and menstrual cramps) and mugwort (for nervousness, shaking, insomnia, indigestion, and poison ivy). We who have benefited from the "miracle" of modern medicine can well appreciate the "magic" of medieval herbs.

Flowers and herbs aren't the only magical elements at Midsummer. According to folklorist Guntis Smidchens, interviewed in the *Seattle-Post Intelligencer*, at this time "the world is most alive, so everything is particularly powerful—the water coming out of the earth, the springs, dew, all the medicinal plants." The Swedes like to bathe in a river on Midsummer—as do the Finns and Lithuanians—in the hope of staying young. They also collect dew, believed to have healing properties. In Russia, people pour water over one another. The Portuguese bathe their children and cattle in rivers; the Latvians take their horses swimming. It is possible that this ancient belief in the power of water at Summer Solstice influenced the church's choice of the Baptist to "christen" this feast.

Mara Mellena of the Latvian Institute claims that though her country's seasonal traditions originated in the countryside and "reflect the values and lifestyle of people who worked and loved the land," they have adapted, over time, to city life and remain popular today:

> The traditional Latvian worldview develops in dialogue with nature, God (deities), and other people. Dialogue is necessary to attune, but additionally, harmonious living is one of our ancestors' most fundamental insights—to be in harmony with nature, God, other people, and oneself.

Surely this is so for all of us.

WAYS TO CELEBRATE

Enjoy the warmth of the sun at the height of its power.

๖ Lather yourself in sun-screening lotion and lie in the sun. Close your eyes, relax your muscles one by one, and *feel* the healing rays of the sun.

๖ Sleep outdoors.

๖ Eat outdoors.

๖ Go to a baseball game.

๖ Go to an outdoor theater performance.

๖ Go to an ethnic festival or arts fair.

๖ Take a walk in a park or your neighborhood before breakfast, stopping to study the plants and flowers in bloom. Notice the shapes, colors, and textures.

⑥ Take a walk after dinner, stopping to chat with neighbors and admire the sun's effect on their gardens or flower boxes.

⑥ Open the window in the bathroom, and take a long, lazy bath when the room is brightest. Sprinkle rose petals in your bathwater.

⑥ Walk on the beach and watch the play of sun on water.

⑥ Enjoy playing in the sun-lit water. Swim, surf, or water ski.

⑥ Go camping. Build a bonfire at sunset and dance around it all night to welcome the sun at dawn.

Take a summer vacation.

⑥ From TV, e-mail, or using the car when you can walk.

⑥ From whining, criticizing, or demanding.

⑥ Pretend you're a tourist on summer vacation where you live. Look at your own town in a "new light" and take in the sites you would recommend to visitors.

Invite Earth's creatures to join you in celebrating the summer.

⑥ Fill all the bird feeders.

⑥ Scrub out the birdbath and keep it filled with fresh water.

⑥ Bring cut flowers from your garden into the house. Or if you don't have a yard, plant flowers in a window box. (It's not too late!)

⑥ On St. John's Eve (June 23), gather herbs and seasonal flowers that are believed to possess healing, magical powers: Saint-John's-wort, mugwort, chamomile, vervain, rue, trefoil. Decorate your door with them.

Use the sun to protect the earth and air.

⑥ Install solar heating for your home.

⚭   Trade in your SUV for a (partly) solar-powered car.

Play in the sun.

⚭   Teach children outdoor games you played as a child.

⚭   Learn a new one from them.

⚭   Draw pictures of the sun or people enjoying the sun. Use chalk on sidewalks, finger paint on paper, or create mandalas with crayons on paper plates.

⚭   Read poems about summer. Memorize your favorite and recite it to the sun. Write one of your own.

⚭   Find songs about summer and sing them to the sun. Make up one of your own.

Celebrate the sun's power.

⚭   Sing and/or dance the sun up on Solstice dawn or sing it to sleep at sunset. Or just watch the show and applaud!

⚭   Do the yoga "salute to the sun."

⚭   Burn candles.

⚭   Shoot off fireworks.

⚭   Play marbles with red, orange, yellow, and gold ones.

⚭   Make sun catchers with colored cellophane.

⚭   Eat round golden fruit like peaches, apricots, oranges, and golden delicious apples. (For the decadent, try doughnut holes with lemon or orange glaze!)

⚭   Create a fire in your backyard hibachi. When the flames are low, leap over it as high as you can and wish for crops to grow that high or for high hopes to be realized.

☉ Make sun symbols like wreaths, spheres, disks, medallions, or mandalas, using readily available materials such as gold foil, yellow, orange, white, and gold ribbons, flowers, herbs, fabric, paper, pipe cleaners, and/or costume jewelry.

Celebrate your own power.

☉ Write in your journal about your strengths and assets, your personal and professional accomplishments, and your social, physical, and mental skills.

☉ Update your resume.

☉ Write a serious or humorous song, poem, or monologue in praise of your talents. Share these with your friends around the bonfire. Have a "Boasting," followed by a "Roasting."

☉ Cook your special dish and give it to an overworked mother with young children.

☉ Volunteer to cook for a soup kitchen.

☉ Mow the lawn for someone who can't do it.

☉ Drive someone who doesn't have a car to the grocery store.

☉ Play music for someone in need of it.

☉ Rescue someone whose computer has crashed.

☉ Warm a stranger with a compliment. Praise a salesperson, receptionist, toll booth operator, any worker you see doing a good job.

☉ Give thought to the effects your power has—on family, friends, and coworkers; on members of your local, national, and global community; and on the environment and its plant, animal, and human inhabitants. Resolve to use that power for good, to follow the sun's example: Warm, light, and heal one day at a time. Make a specific resolution for tomorrow: to smile at your most cantankerous coworker, eat lunch at the table with the least popular group, write to your Congressional representatives asking them to support legislation that will reduce violence or protect the environment, do a favor for a family member with whom you've recently had a disagreement.

Develop *new* powers. Try something you've never done before.

֎   Try an outdoor sport that's new to you, like tennis, golf, hiking, running, cycling, sky diving, wind surfing, or mountain climbing.

֎   Master new skills. Learn how to use hand tools or power tools and build a bird house or a bookcase. Learn how to use a sewing machine and make an apron for the "griller" in your household.

֎   Take on a new intellectual challenge. Study a foreign language, learn the different birds in your locale and how to recognize them, take a summer course in ecology or geology or something with lots of outdoor field trips.

֎   Try a form of meditation you haven't tried before. Mow a labyrinth in your backyard or chalk it on the driveway or street. Learn to drum or play a musical instrument you've never played. Read a new book of prayerful poems and then write one.

Honor sun-reverencing peoples around the world by joining in their prayer.

֎   With the Japanese, go outside in the morning, face the east, bow, and clap your hands to welcome Amaterasu.

֎   With the Cherokee, bow and greet the dawn with "Hail, Unelanuhi, the apportioner, who divides the year into seasons!"

֎   With Tantric Buddhists, welcome the dawn: "I salute you, O Marici, glorious one, sun of happiness!"

֎   With the Duala of Cameroon, pray after sunset to ensure Loba will return the next morning.

Enjoy summer foods.

◌   Host a Solstice cookout. Invite family, friends, and neighbors to bring fruits and vegetables that are in season or dishes that are the color or shape of the sun.

◌   Try a new Solstice recipe. Here's one from Cait Johnson's *Witch in the Kitchen*:

FLOWERING SALAD

Ingredients:

lettuce leaves for salad base
cucumber
sprigs of fresh-picked wood sorrel (or 1 small tomato)
a sprinkle of edible flower heads (try nasturtium—peppery
    and vivid; cucumber-like borage; or calendula)
salt and pepper to taste

For each serving, you'll need a few tender lettuce leaves to use as the base for your salad. Experiment with unusual varieties—many supermarkets now carry organic mesclun or field greens mixtures that are flavorful and rich in nutrients, or you could use curly or red lettuces mixed with the darker green of young spinach. Arrange the greens artfully on a plate. Take the cucumber and peel it if it's not organic, and cut it into either chunks, 1/4-inch rounds, half-moons, or long quarters. Place cucumber pieces on top of the bed of lettuce, along with several sprigs of fresh-picked wood sorrel. (This plentiful wild green is available in most yards at this time of year: just be sure to avoid sprayed or contaminated areas. Look for their cloverlike leaves and tiny white or yellow flowers.) If wood sorrel is unavailable, substitute one small ripe tomato, cored and cut into quarters or chunks. Decorate each salad with the flower heads. Dust the salad with salt and pepper to taste, and drizzle with Simple Summer Dressing.

Ingredients:

⅓ cup extra-virgin olive oil
2 tablespoons red wine vinegar or freshly squeezed lemon juice
1 garlic clove, crushed
sea salt to taste
freshly ground black pepper to taste

Combine ingredients and whisk until smooth.

CELEBRATE THE MIDSUMMER SUN

A SUMMER SOLSTICE RITUAL

Gather outdoors in a semicircle.

Narrator   The strong summer sun has nurtured foliage to its peak. No longer a feathery yellow-green, the leaves are now dark rich canopies providing cool shelter. Our world is abloom with daisies and lilies, hosta bells and butterfly bushes, impatiens and balsam (*substitute what is blooming in the area*). Roses and clematis slither up trellises. Finches and chickadees flutter to their feeders (*substitute other birds of the area if different*). Now we are held close in the embrace of the sun, in the very middle of solar summer when days are longest. It's a bright time, a warming time, a healing time, a magical time. It's Summer Solstice!

All sing the following words to the melody of "You Are My Sunshine."

All sing   We love your sunshine, O dearest daystar,
How sweet to feel you up in the sky.
You hold the planets in all their orbits,

Rule the Universe from on high.

You are the source of, the solar source of
All life on earth, all energy.
To you we owe the rain that washes,
The wind that blows, the plants that feed.

At Summer Solstice, you shine the brightest,
When days are longest and life is sweet.
O Star of Heaven, thank you for shining,
Thank you for light and thank you for heat.

Litany of Seasonal Blessings

Leader   Let us give thanks for all the good things we enjoy at this time of year. We invite you to respond with "We give thanks to the sun!"

For weather that beckons us outdoors, and long-lasting days to spend there,

All   We give thanks to the sun!

Leader   For the regal rose and the lowly daisy and all the flowers that bloom in summer,

All   We give thanks to the sun!

Leader   For all the magical healing herbs that flower at Midsummer,

All   We give thanks to the sun!

Leader   For vitamin D,

All   We give thanks to the sun!

Leader   For sandals and shorts and T-shirts,

All   We give thanks to the sun!

Leader   For strawberries and blueberries and raspberries and blackberries,

All	We give thanks to the sun!
Leader	For vegetable gardens and the energy to work in them,
All	We give thanks to the sun!
Leader	For the cooling power of perspiration,
All	We give thanks to the sun!
Leader	For the cooling power of air-conditioning,
All	We give thanks to the sun!
Leader	For summer vacation,
All	We give thanks to the sun!
Leader	For trips to the beach, the pool, the campgrounds, and the fuel to get there,
All	We give thanks to the sun!
Leader	For swimming and surfing and sailing,
All	We give thanks to the sun!
Leader	For hiking and biking and fishing and sunbathing,
All	We give thanks to the sun!
Leader	For fireworks and Ferris wheels,
All	We give thanks to the sun!
Leader	For Father's Day and the men it honors,
All	We give thanks to the sun!
Leader	For graduations and weddings and all the new lives beginning,
All	We give thanks to the sun!

Leader	For picnics and cook-outs and gatherings of family and friends,
All	We give thanks to the sun!
Leader	For outdoor concerts, games, and tournaments,
All	We give thanks to the sun!
Leader	For ethnic celebrations, street fairs, and arts festivals,
All	We give thanks to the sun!
Leader	For sitting out on porches, stoops, and decks,
All	We give thanks to the sun!
Leader	For warm rays that heal our bodies and renew our spirits,
All	We give thanks to the sun!

For suggestions on a spontaneous litany rather than a scripted one, see page xvii.

Reader 1 (*a young child*)
I told the Sun that I was glad,
I'm sure I don't know why;
Somehow the pleasant way he had
Of shining in the sky,
Just put a notion in my head
That wouldn't it be fun
If, walking on the hill, I said
"I'm happy" to the Sun.
—John Drinkwater, "The Sun"

Turning the Wheel of the Year

Narrator The earliest Summer Solstice rituals in Europe—some of which were continued into Christian times—involved lighting festive fires and rolling a flaming wheel downhill into a river to assure a good harvest.

People threw fragrant flowers and herbs into the fires, hung out lamps, and decorated their doors with greenery and herbs and their children with garlands of flowers. Some folks leapt over the flames for blessings or good fortune. They also played music, sang songs, danced and made merry, and engaged in activities designed to encourage fertility.

Leader   Sometimes the wealthiest townsfolk set out tables laden with bread, meat, and ale and invited neighbors and passersby to join them in giving thanks. It was a time to be generous with one's bounty, reconciled to enemies, and purged of bitter feelings.

Narrator   Indeed, purging was one of the main purposes of the festival. In some places, the bonfires were lit on the windward side of fields so that their smoke would waft over the crops growing there. Torches ignited from the bonfires were carried around the fields and cattle pens for blessing and protection. The air itself was thought to be in need of purification. And why not? June ushered in the season when crops, animals, and people were most vulnerable to diseases caused by insects. Thus the Midsummer fires were ceremonies honoring the sun and rituals of protection as well as occasions for celebration.

Let us sing out our celebration of the sun!

All sing the following words to the melody of "Morning Has Broken."

All sing   Hail to the sunrise, hail to the sunset,
Hail to the noon prize, high overhead.
Welcome the sun's rays, warming our spirits.
Treasure the long days; darkness has fled.

Joy in the bright blooms, joy in the green leaves,
Bless the new bridegroom, bless the June bride.

Cherish the bee's buzz, cherish the bird's song,
Cherish the peach fuzz, all our life wide.

Sing to our Mother, Praise to the Great Earth!
Sing to our Father, Praise to the Sun!
Sing to our life here—here in this garden.
Give thanks that our dear parents are one.

Narrator   Now that our sun is high in the sky, it is time for us to
light our festive fire and turn the Wheel of the Year, to
celebrate the changing of the seasons. I invite you to
gather around the wheel. Those who wish may make
an offering of herb or flower.

*A wheel from a large cart, painted gold or yellow and dec-
orated with seasonal blooms and herbs, has been set flat on
a table, on a small lazy Susan. Four large candles are set in
it, symbolizing the four seasons. Participants come forward,
forming a circle or concentric circles around the wheel.
Those who have brought additional seasonal flowers,
petals, or herbs scatter them on the ground at the base of the
platform. Or a basket of these may be set out in advance
from which participants might take bits for offering. Two
Turners and a Lighter have been designated in advance.*

Narrator   The circle of the floral wreath here symbolizes the Wheel
of the Year, the complete cycle of the four seasons, represented by four candles. Our ancient ancestors believed
they played an important role in turning of the Wheel of
the Year. They understood that their ritual celebrations
helped the seasons change and encouraged the sun on
its journey. Some erected great monuments to mark that
journey: at Stonehenge in England, Karnak in Egypt,
Angkor Wat in Cambodia, Ha'amonga'a Maui in
Polynesia, and Teotihuacán in Mexico. Early peoples
revered the elements that ruled their lives. Their beliefs
may seem unscientific and quaint to us. And yet perhaps

if we shared their reverence for nature, our lives would be healthier and happier. Perhaps if we respected the earth as they did, we would take better care of it. Let us return to reverence for the natural world. Let us acknowledge our role as stewards of the earth and play our part in changing the seasons.

Leader   We invite you to join in turning the wheel of the year, responding as indicated in your programs.

       Lighter with a lit taper stands behind the wheel. Turners stand on either side of it.

Leader   As the brilliant sun rises higher and higher,

       Lighter lights the first candle.

All   So may the flame of this festive fire.

       Turners turn the wheel clockwise one quarter.

Leader   We turn the wheel, we urge the sun,

       Lighter ignites second candle.

All   To stay the course that's now begun.

       Turners turn the wheel one quarter.

Leader   We turn the wheel of death and birth.

       Lighter ignites third candle.

All   We change the seasons of the earth!

       Turners turn the wheel one quarter.

Leader   We bring the summer, coming 'round.

       Lighter ignites fourth candle.

All   May earth with nourishing fruit abound!

       Choir sings "Chant for the Seasons" words by Mark L.

Belletini. All repeat chant as they return to their places.

Choir   Vernal clouds have turned the star-wheel,
                     summer is upon us.
             Vernal clouds have turned the star-wheel,
                     summer is upon us.
             Gliding are the hawks,
                     hovering above the hot and yellow hillside.
             Vernal clouds have turned the star-wheel,
                     summer is upon us.
             Crickets in the night
                     chirping in our ears the sound of moonlit music.
             Vernal clouds have turned the star-wheel,
                     summer is upon us.

Honoring the Sun Deities

Narrator   Myths from around the world make it clear that rever-
            ence for the sun played a vital role in the life of many
            ancient peoples. The sun was personified in a myriad
            of deities, and their stories reveal notable similarities.
            Often the parentage of sun deities is illustrious. Some
            are hatched from the primordial cosmic egg. Others
            are offspring of great mother goddesses or creator
            gods—or are themselves creators of the earth. A num-
            ber of myths explain the "disappearance" or waning of
            the sun at Winter Solstice as the hiding of the deities,
            who must then be rescued or coaxed back into the sky.

Leader   The imagery used to describe the daily journey of sun
            deities across the sky is similar: They often ride horses
            or a chariot drawn by horses. Some rise or set in the
            sea, others in the mountains. Some travel under the sea
            or earth by night and are thus seen as rulers of the
            Underworld.

Narrator   Some solar deities are believed to have founded dynasties ruled by human offspring; others are patrons of a given people.

Leader While the ancient sun deities are appreciated as a source of light and warmth and sustenance in the natural world, they are not without their dark side, for they can bring killing fires or drought and famine. Some were thought to require blood to cool their heat and maintain their strength and so were fed on human or animal sacrifices.

Narrator But the myths primarily emphasize the sun's positive aspects. Perhaps no people revered the sun more than the ancient Egyptians. Over three thousand years ago, Pharaoh Akhenaten offered a heartfelt "Hymn to the Sun." Here is an excerpt.

Reader 2 O living Aton, beginning of life,
how lovely is your dawning!
When you rise in the East,
you fill every land with your beauty,
for you are great and glittering, high over the earth.

Bright is the earth when you rise.
Darkness is banished when you send forth your rays.
The people of the land awake and stand;
they bathe and dress and lift their arms in adoration,
then go about their work.

All creatures thrive in your warming light:
the cattle grazing, the sheep dancing,
the birds fluttering, the fish leaping.
You create the seed in man and the child in woman;
you nurse the unborn in the womb, giving the breath
 of life.

How manifold are your works!
No other is like you.

You created the earth—
all the humans and beasts that walk upon it,
even the birds that fly above it.

You set each of us in our place
and supply all our needs.
You make the Nile on earth to preserve the life of
     the people.
You set the Nile in the heavens
that floods the mountains and waters the fields.
Your rays nourish every garden;
when you rise, they live and grow.
You make the seasons, bringing coolness and heat.
By you, all people live.

When you set in the West,
the earth is in darkness like the dead.
All creatures sleep; the world is silent,
for he who made all has gone to rest.

How excellent are your designs, O Lord of eternity!
The world is in your hand
And you are in my heart.
          —adapted from translation by James Henry Breasted

Narrator   To the ancients, the sun did more than provide the physical benefits of light and warmth. It was also a symbol for a much broader kind of light—a clarity in intellectual and civic pursuits as well as a source of healing. Let us honor our ancestors and the sun gods they revered in this litany of remembrance. Responses to the litany are in your program.

Leader   Apollo of Greece was god of logic and reason.

All   May we be clear in our thinking, discerning in our daily works.

Leader   Surya of India was order in the cosmos and wellspring of all knowledge.

All   May we be informed with wisdom.

Leader   Inti of the Incas taught his people the arts of civilization.

All   May we be civilized in our national policies toward all people on whom the sun shines.

Leader   Shamash of Sumeria, Utu of Mesopotamia, and Yeloje of Siberia were gods of justice.

All   May we shine the light of justice where the hopes of people grow dim.

Leader   Belenus of the Celts and Ah Kin of the Mayans were believed to cure illness.

All   May we be inflamed with desire to heal the earth and the spirits of those who are oppressed.

Leader   The hot springs of the goddess Sul healed the ancient Britains.

All   May we bring the waters of comfort to those in need.

Leader   The Hindus credit Dhanvantari with bringing medical science to humankind.

All   May we use that science for the good of all.

Narrator Many sun deities were honored with rituals or festivals, which sometimes included sacrifices. Our ancestors appreciated the gifts of the sun and made these sacrifices for what they believed was the good of the earth and its people. Let us take a moment to ponder the many good things the sun provides for *us*, and to consider how we might best use the energy from the sun and the resources of the earth. Let us reflect on what sacrifices we could make for the good of the earth and its people.

Silence. Then guitar soloist sings "Sunshine on My Shoulders."

Celebrating the Taste of Life

Narrator   Sunshine makes us happy. But happiness is complete only if it is shared. We invite you to come forward for a taste of the sun—in the form of sunflower seeds and the juice of the orange, that perennial symbol of the golden orb. Please return to your place with them, and when all have been served, we'll toast the sun and enjoy these treats together.

Instrumental music. Depending on the setting, participants come forward or Servers circulate with trays containing small cups of orange juice and small cups of sunflower seeds and offer these to participants. When all have been served, the Narrator holds up a large sunflower.

Narrator   The flower of the sun behold,
Its giant stem, its leaves of gold!
(*gesturing to sky*) No matter where the Great Eye
    shines,
(*gesturing to flower*) Its face adoringly aligns.

All   A generous plant is this fair friend,
One on whom we can depend.
It gives us oil, it gives us seed,
That folk and feathered birds may feed.

Following the Narrator's lead, all eat some of the seeds and toss the rest to the birds. The Narrator holds up two halves of an orange together so that it looks whole.

Narrator   Behold the orange that grows in the sun,
A tasty treat for everyone.

Opens orange, holding up half in each hand, with cut side facing out.

And if you slice it into two,
It shows rays of the sun to you.

All   Now before our rite is done,
All join in drink to toast the sun!

All toast and drink, then sing the following words to the melody of "Morning Has Broken."

All sing   Sing to our Mother, Praise to the Great Earth!
Sing to our Father, Praise to the Sun!
Sing to our life here—here in this garden.
Give thanks that our dear parents are one.

Learning from the Sun

Audience sits in semicircle for a short play.

Narrator   The sun is the source of all life in our ecosystem, the origin of the power that runs our planet. And yet we have much to learn from the sun about the use of power. Here is one lesson.

Traveler enters.

Traveler   "The Wind and the Sun," by Aesop. Sort of.

Traveler exits. Sun, a child or youth who wears around the face a large golden circle of cardboard or wired fabric suggesting rays and around the wrists ribbons of yellow fabric, enters. Sun smiles, and dances in and around the audience, perhaps touching individuals lightly on the head with the wrist-rays. After a moment, Wind, a child or youth who wears around the face a large gray/white circle of cardboard or wired fabric with ribbons suggesting currents of air, enters. Wind carries a battery-operated fan and dances in and around the audience, blowing on people. After a few moments, they meet at center stage.

Sun   Good afternoon, my dear Wind. Isn't it a beautiful day?

Wind   Oh, yes, yes, yes, my dear Sun! A lovely breezy day.

             Wind blows heartily at Sun and dances so that ribbons flutter.

Sun   A magnificent sunny day.

             Sun dances, thrusting his or her head at Wind.

Wind   The day couldn't be better, cleaner, more refreshing, thanks to my power.

Sun   Ah, but it couldn't be brighter, clearer, more pleasant, thanks to my power.

Wind   Are you suggesting my power is weaker than your power?

Sun   Heavens, no! I'm suggesting my power is stronger than your power.

Wind   Oh. (*realizes*) What? Are we in a power-play here?

Sun   Only if you insist.

Wind   I do. I do insist (*puffs up cheeks, expels air*) on a contest!

Sun   Very well. How shall we determine the winner?

Wind   (*striking boxing pose*) Put up your dukes. I'll *blow* you out of the ring!

Sun   Something more subtle perhaps?

Wind   (*striking a wrestling pose*) I'll throw you to the mat.

Sun   I'm afraid direct contact would result in . . . well, con-flagration. Possibly even incineration. Of you.

Wind	Hmm . . . . In that case, let's try our powers . . . on somebody else!
Sun	Very noble of you.

Traveler enters, then does a "mime walk" in place.

Sun	Shall we try them on that Traveler?
Wind	How?
Sun	(*indicating audience*) Let's ask them. (*to audience*) Which of you children has an idea of what we could do to test our power on this Traveler?

Traveler sits. Sun takes suggestions from children in the audience. If someone comes up with the "right" idea . . .

Sun	That's it!

If no one does, Sun appears to be considering all the options, then . . .

Sun	Hmm. So many good ideas, I don't know which one to . . . . Look!
Wind	What?
Sun	The Traveler is wearing a cape.
Wind	Yeah, so?
Sun	We could see which of us can persuade him/her to take off the cape. That one will prove the stronger.
Wind	(*casually confident*) Piece o' cape.
Sun	You go first.
Wind	But when I succeed, how will we know that you would have failed?
Sun	You won't succeed.

Wind   Will too!

Sun   Will not!

Wind   Will too!

Sun   Okay, okay. We'll ask the Traveler to put the cape back on for my turn.

Wind   (*to Traveler*) Would you do that?

          Traveler shrugs a "why not?"

Wind   (*to Sun*) It's a deal.

          Wind extends hand, palm up, to be slapped. Sun slaps it. Wind registers burning sensation.

Wind   Oooo, aahhh, ugh, ugh, ugh, ouch! (*blows on hand, waves it for cooling*)

Sun   I'll just wait behind that cloud.

          Sun crosses upstage. Traveler gets up, circles edge of stage, walking at normal pace. After a moment, Wind, center stage, blows on Traveler. Traveler pulls cape a little tighter. Wind gets closer but never touches, blows harder; Traveler pulls cape tighter. This goes on until Wind is exhausted from blowing and collapses, defeated. Traveler goes a bit farther. Noticing the wind has died down, Traveler stops, releases grip on cape, sits down, takes a peach or apricot from pocket, admires it, and eats it. Sun crosses to where Wind is sitting.

Sun   My turn.

          Traveler starts circling stage again while Sun crosses to center, faces Traveler, smiles and rotates in place as Traveler loosens cape at neck fastening. Sun moves closer; Traveler opens cape. Sun moves closer; Traveler extends arms, holding edges of cape, testing the air. Sun moves closer; Traveler stops, enjoys the warmth of Sun, removes cape, drapes it over arm. Sun turns to audience and holds out arms.

Sun   However cold or dark your world may be,
               take heart, have faith, and turn to me.
               And if you would another's will to sway,
               do it not harshly but in a warming way.

               Wind and Traveler come forward on either side of Sun. All bow, then exit.

Narrator   Until recently in human history, people all over the earth responded to the power of the sun with awe and gratitude, with a reverence demonstrated in both spontaneous and ritualized celebration. Today this sun-worshiping spirit is left to poets and sunbathers who, thanks to our breaking down of the ozone layer in the upper atmosphere, must screen themselves against the warming rays of the sun.

Leader   Even so, who of us can lie on the grass or the beach in summer, feel the tensions of work and winter drain away, and not understand in our very bones why our ancestors revered this source of healing warmth and power? Who of us finding welcome relief from ailments on warm, sunny days, does not share that reverence?

Narrator   The myths of the sun deities are, like all myths, the secrets of our psyches, the telling tales of our collective unconscious. The festivals honoring the sun connect us to our deepest need to celebrate the source of life and energy and to share that life-giving energy with others. May our hearts be on fire with desire to warm and heal the world.

               All sing "This Little Light of Mine."

All sing   This little light of mine, I'm gonna let it shine.
               This little light of mine, I'm gonna let it shine.

This little light of mine, I'm gonna let it shine.
Let it shine, let it shine, let it shine.

Everywhere I go, I'm gonna let it shine.
Everywhere I go, I'm gonna let it shine.
Everywhere I go, I'm gonna let it shine.
Let it shine, let it shine, let it shine.

Building up a world, I'm gonna let it shine.
Building up a world, I'm gonna let it shine.
Building up a world, I'm gonna let it shine.
Let it shine, let it shine, let it shine.

While this ends the formal ritual, the solstice celebration may continue with less formal activities like the following:

๑ Invite a professional storyteller to present Native American or other myths and legends about the sun.

๑ Invite a gardener to give a demonstration on growing and harvesting herbs.

๑ Invite an herbalist to speak on the medicinal use of herbs.

๑ Invite a cook to give a demonstration on cooking with herbs.

๑ Have a solar fashion show (children and adult categories) and award prizes in each category for the "brightest," "sunniest," "most original," "roundest," etc.

๑ Have a talent show in which individuals or groups recite poems or sing (or play on instruments) songs about the sun, sunshine, sunrise, sunbeams, etc. Encourage original entries.

๑ Make miniature dragon boats from balsa wood and float them in a washtub. (The Chinese celebrate solstice with dragon boat races.)

๑ Have a "Leaping for Life" event with age or height categories.

When the ancient Celts, British, and Scandinavians built their Midsummer bonfires, they often jumped over the flames to bring blessing on the crops, some believing that the crops would grow as high as they could jump. Set a gymnastic mat or an old mattress on the ground. Just at the edge of its head, set up two vertical poles with notches at different heights. Set a horizontal pole across the lowest pair of notches for the youngest and shortest jumpers, and work up the vertical poles to the highest notches for the strongest and tallest. The jumpers approach the horizontal marker in a run (or walk) and leap over it onto the mat. If they trip, the mat cushions their fall. (For the youngest children, the pole might be hand-held by two spotters who can adjust it to assure success or lend a hand if needed.) All can try as many times as they like at whatever level is comfortable until they succeed so that everyone gets a prize. Prizes can be based on the height attained by the jumpers, perhaps a strawberry for the little ones who jump as high as a strawberry plant, a cherry tomato for those who jump higher, and a small bag of popcorn for the highest leapers.

☙ Have a Summer Solstice potluck dinner or lunch that features seasonal fruits and vegetables and dishes that are the color or shape of the sun.

☙ If the ritual is scheduled for late afternoon or early evening, have a time of silence to appreciate the setting sun. Then end the solstice celebration by applauding the sun's performance. (Or schedule the ritual for dawn and let sunrise be the opening event.)

Lughnasa and Lammas

August 1

In my neighborhood at this time of year, the butterfly bushes are sending out their purple spikes and the day lilies their orange trumpets. The spindly black-eyed susans lean over the driveway. The crepe myrtles are awash in pink. The hollyhocks are ringing their bells. The magnolias are setting their seeds and the dogwoods their berries. The morning glories announce it's time for breakfast, on most days the only meal that can comfortably be eaten *alfresco* because it's August-hot. It's vacation time, lazy time, time for sitting on the dock with a fishing pole, time for sprawling on the sunny beach with a good mystery, time for languishing in a shaded hammock with a lemonade. Summertime, and the livin' is easy. Yet in older agrarian cultures, this was a busy time, a tiring time—the beginning of the harvest, the first cut of grain. Among the early peoples who marked this time with a festival were the Celts of Ireland.

The Seasonal Calendar

The ancient Celtic festival of the first harvest was Lughnasadh (pronounced "LOO-nah-sah"), a commemoration of the god Lugh. Variations on this Irish name for the month of August include Lughnasa, Lugnasa, and the modern Irish Lúnasa. In

Scotland it was Lunasda or Lunasdal; Laa Luanys in the Isle of Man; Gwl Awst, the August Feast, in Wales. Another name for the festival was Bron Trogain, "earth's sorrowing in autumn," and indeed it marked the start of that season in the British Isles of the Middle Ages. Although the festivities lasted from July 15 to August 15, the highpoint was August 1, which marked the midpoint of the warm half of the year that had begun at Beltane (May 1) and would end at Samhain (November 1). Unlike the other quarter days, which were pastoral in character (Imbolc marking the ewes' coming to lactation; Beltane, the driving of herds and sheep into the summer pastures; and Samhain, their return), Lughnasa was an agrarian feast, celebrating the harvest and the baking of bread from the new grain. Prudence Jones and Nigel Pennick, authors of *A History of Pagan Europe*, see this as an indication that it might have been "imported into Ireland at a later date, perhaps by continental devotees of Lugh," who was a latecomer in the Irish pantheon and more modern in character than the other deities.

Mythology and History

Also called Lug or Lugus, Lugh was one of the most powerful of Celtic gods. His popularity, according to some scholars, is attested to by the original names of a host of cities that imply his patronage. These include Lyons, Leon, Laon, and Loudon in France; Leiden in Holland; Liegnitz in Silesia, Carlisle (formerly Luguvallium); and London (formerly Lugdunum) in England. However, Ronald Hutton disputes this connection in *The Stations of the Sun*, raising the possibility that the prefix *Lug* did not necessarily refer to the god but was simply of more general significance.

Lugh is a young, handsome, athletic god, and his exploits are the subject of many legends. Although in Wales he is Lleu Llaw Gyffes (Llue of the Dexterous Hand) and born of the virgin goddess Aranrhod, in Irish myth he is Lug Lámfota (Lug of the Long Arm), the offspring (some versions say the only survivor of triplets) produced by Cian of the Tuatha Dé Danann tribe and

Eithne, daughter of Balor, the one-eyed giant of their enemy tribe, the Fomorians. In fulfillment of a prophecy that precedes his birth, Lugh kills Balor in battle, becomes the acclaimed hero of his people, and fathers Cú Chulainn, the greatest of Ulster champions.

Lugh's reputation as a warrior is matched by his role as patron of the arts, crafts, and magic. No god is more skilled. This is reflected in the story of his arrival at the gates of Tara, where he must win acceptance by the Tuatha Dé Danann. In *Celtic Mythology A to Z*, Gienna Matson provides one version. Asked by the scoffing guards what he has to offer, Lugh boasts of his ability to forge powerful tools and accurate weapons. But the guards dismiss him, saying they already have a smith. Then Lugh claims to be a master carpenter, but the guards tell him they have one of those too. Do they need someone who can make superior armor? No, they have a metal worker. Lugh assures them he is a mighty warrior, a talented harpist, and an eloquent poet, as well as a sorcerer and a physician. Do they have any *one* man with all these skills? The guards report this to the king, who becomes intrigued and challenges Lugh to a game of *fidchell* (a variant of chess), but since Lugh *invented* the game, naturally he wins. Finally the three great gods of craft set challenging tests for him. When he accomplishes these seemingly impossible tasks, he is welcomed to Tara and becomes known as the god of all skills.

The Romans saw Lugh as the equivalent of Mercury, and according to Barbara Walker, author of *The Woman's Encyclopedia of Myths and Secrets*, "Lug was Christianized as several saints: St. Lugad, St. Luan, St. Eluan, and St. Lugidus, depending on local dialects."

Scholars disagree about the connection between Lugh and the August festival. Some, like Matson and Peter Berresford Ellis in *A Dictionary of Irish Mythology*, associate him with light or call him a sun god. If indeed he was worshipped as such, a case might be made for seeing the athletic games of Lughnasa as funeral games honoring the waning light, though it is more common to observe the ritual dying of sun deities at Fall Equinox, when the balance observably shifts to darkness. In her *Standard Dictionary of*

Folklore, Mythology, and Legend, Maria Leach suggests the possibility that the festival celebrates sexual awakening—the marriage of Lugh and the old hag Ireland, who is transformed by the sun's caresses into a young beauty, a variation on the sun-and-earth union. But Thomas F. O'Rahilly disputes this sun deity claim in *Early Irish History and Mythology*.

Carmel McCaffrey and Leo Eaton, authors of *In Search of Ancient Ireland*, identify Lugh as god of the harvest and of the Underworld, from which he rose to defend the earth against insects that threatened the crops. Though there is surely some humor in the image of the great warrior who defeated the one-eyed giant now waving his masterfully forged sword at insects, the story reminds us of other vegetation gods and grain goddesses who spend the gestation half of the year ruling or roaming the Underworld.

This theme is acknowledged in another common explanation for the origin of the Lughnasa games, that they were instituted by Lugh in honor of his foster-mother Táiltiu, who gave her name to Teltown, the actual site of the festival in Tara. Jones and Pennick remind us that the name of this ancient burial ground is thought to mean "fair" or "lovely" and speculate that a goddess associated with it would share characteristics of the Greek Demeter/Persephone, who "ruled both the Underworld and the fruits which sprang from it."

In *Kindling the Celtic Spirit*, Mara Freeman recounts the story of Táiltiu, the last queen of the Fir Bolg, on her website:

> She died from exhaustion after clearing a great forest so that the land could be cultivated. When the men of Ireland gathered at her death-bed, she told them to hold funeral games in her honor. As long as they were held, she prophesied Ireland would not be without song. Táiltiu's name is from Old Celtic Talantiu, The Great One of the Earth, suggesting she may originally have been a personification of the land itself, like so many Irish goddesses. In fact, Lughnasadh has an older name, Brón Trogain, which refers to the painful labor of childbirth. For at this time of year, the earth gives birth to her first fruits so that her children might live.

The Tailtean Games, or all-Ireland Olympics, survived well into Christian times. Although the last ceremonial ones were held in the twelfth century under Rory O'Conor, the last high king of Ireland, informal gatherings continued into the eighteenth century. And in the late 1920s, after the founding of the Free State, the games and festival were revived.

The idea of funeral games, athletic events to honor a recently deceased hero, is a tradition at least as old as Homer, whose *Iliad* recounts Achilles' temporary suspension of the Trojan War for the funeral of Patroklos and the games held in his honor (a sharp contrast to the modern era, when the Olympic Games were suspended for the two World Wars).

Whether the mourning at Lughnasa was for the dying sun god, or for Lugh's foster-mother Táiltiu, who sacrificed herself to feed her people, or for the old king who must die each year so that the new king might (literally or symbolically) take his place, "funerary rites and processions were a common practice," writes Sue Ellen Thompson in *Holiday Symbols and Customs*. She also reports,

> The festival was an occasion for paying homage to the dead—particularly warriors and heroes in the style of Lugh—and eulogies or poems praising ancient gods and heroes were often recited. Even today, mock-funeral processions are occasionally held in Yorkshire and Lancashire, England, with groups of young men carrying an empty coffin for many miles along an ancient path.

In her study *The Festival of Lughnasa*, Máire MacNeill concludes that the ancient Celtic festival was characterized by a number of rites. The first of the grain was ritually harvested and taken to a hilltop, where it was offered to the deity. All participants ate a meal that included food from the grain harvest as well as blueberries and the meat of a sacred bull that had been sacrificed and then replaced by a young bull. Dancers ritually enacted a play that may have dramatized the struggle of rivals for a goddess. Other plays may have reenacted Lugh's triumph over the head of the enemy and his confinement of the monster blight or famine.

Whatever the features of the ancient Irish festival, it evolved over time, according to Freeman, "into a great tribal assembly, attended by the high king, where legal documents were made, political problems discussed, and huge sporting contests were held. . . ." On this day, as on the cross-quarter days, tenants paid their rents. People entered into contracts of employment or purchase, and some into a particular type of marriage contract that took place only at Lughnasa—called the Tailtean or Teltown marriage after Lugh's foster mother. It was a trial marriage that lasted only a year and a day. If it didn't work out, the couple could return to the following year's festival and, without social disapproval, officially dissolve their union by standing back to back and walking away from each other. Tailtean marriages were legal in Ireland up to the thirteenth century.

A less startling custom associated with Lughnasa, which has persisted to the present, is the climbing to hilltops to gather blueberries. Indeed MacNeill notes that the rites of Lughnasa themselves often took place on hilltops. And what better place? Mircea Eliade reminds us in *Cosmos and History* that many cultures had a "Sacred Mountain" that was considered the center of the world, where heaven and earth meet, the place of epiphanies where humans encounter the divine.

Not surprisingly, many of the berry-picking sites became sites of Christian pilgrimage (just as many of Lugh's attributes came to be assigned to the Saint Patrick of legend). One such site is Croagh Patrick in County Mayo, one of the many mountains St. Patrick is supposed to have climbed (though scholars doubt he was ever there). According to McCaffrey and Eaton,

> The church knew it was an important pre-Christian ritual site and wanted to claim it. . . . Scholars believe that the mountain was once the domain of . . . Lugh. This may be the reason that the annual climb is on the last Sunday in July . . . within the pagan feast time of Lúnasa.

These authors believe that of all the Irish festivals, Lughnasa is "probably the one most associated with partying and holiday time." In her program notes for the Abbey Theatre's production of Brian Friel's *Dancing at Lughnasa*, MacNeill tells us that dancing competitions were held at a number of Lughnasa festivals. (The play, set in early August of 1936, itself dramatizes the struggle between the Dionysian impulse in five spinster sisters and the culture bent on repressing it.) This view of the prevalence of a party atmosphere at Lughnasa is confirmed by Freeman: "Artists and entertainers displayed their talents, traders [convened] to sell food, farm animals, fine crafts and clothing, and there was much storytelling, music, and high-spirited revelry."

With the arrival of Christianity, Anglo-Saxons celebrated the Gule of August, or Feast of August 1, as Hlaef-mass, or Loaf mass, which in medieval England and Scotland became Lammas, the "feast of first fruits." In England it was customary on this day to harvest the first of the ripened grains, mill them, bake them into loaves of bread, and present them at church for blessing. Hutton reports that a book of Anglo-Saxon charms advised dividing the blessed bread into four pieces and crumbling it into the corners of the barn to make it safe for storing the grain about to be harvested.

This mixing of Christian and pagan practices might also be seen in the Scottish Highlands, where people protected their homes from evil spirits by putting crosses made of rowan twigs over their doors or protected their animals by putting a ball of cow's hair into the milk, a dab of tar on the animals' ears, or colored strings on their tails, or spoke incantations over the udders. Hutton sees these practices as an autumn renewal of the rites of protection given to homes and livestock at Beltane, the opening of summer. Thompson reports that Highlanders "sprinkled their cows and the floors of their houses with menstrual blood, believed to be especially potent against evil on May 1 and August 1."

Another Lammas custom in Scotland was enacted by the young herdsmen of the village, who formed groups to build sod towers about eight feet tall and decorated them with flags and multicolored ribbons. From these mock fortresses, they ventured forth with clubs to attack rival towers. A less violent outlet for youthful exuberance, according to MacNeill, featured an Irish hilltop ceremony on the Sunday nearest Lammas in which a girl or her effigy was decorated with ribbons and garlands of flowers. Dancers circled the figure, the girls among them picking the flowers or ribbons off the figure in the center. Perhaps this focal female was a remnant of the grain goddess, for Walker contends, "the secret worship of Ops, Ceres, Demeter, or Juno Augusta continued throughout the Middle Ages in the rites addressed to the Lammas corn-mother who ruled the harvest-month."

Whatever rituals attended it, Hutton assures us, "Lammas remained an extremely important date throughout the Middle Ages, for holding fairs, payment of rents, election of local officials, and opening of common lands." Some of the fairs still survive, and in the 1940s some farmers in parts of southern England revived the custom of presenting the first sheaf of grain at church.

Nearly all mythologies celebrate goddesses who supply humans with life-sustaining grains. The crop differs depending on the locale—wheat, barley, oats, corn, rice—as does the name of the deity. The Greek grain mother was Demeter (her daughter Kore/Persephone representing the young shoot). For the Romans it was Ceres, associated with both life-sustaining cereals and the rituals of death. Patricia Monaghan tells us in *The New Book of Goddesses and Heroines* that Ceres was a funeral goddess

> to whom sacrifice was made to purify homes after a death had occurred therein. Ceres was also goddess of the death of plants that makes them edible—and the death of human beings that returns them to *Tellus Mater*, the earth.

The Sumerians relied on Ashnan for their grain, the Aztecs on Chicomecoatl, and the Norse on Freya. The Cambodians called their giver of rice Po Ino Nogar. The Javanese honor Saning Sari as their rice mother, and according to Michael Jordan's *Encyclopedia of Gods*, the finest of the planting grain is sown in the nursery bed in her image. At transplanting time, these shoots are given a special place in the paddy field and these same plants are harvested separately and used for the next year's planting.

The ancient Peruvians believed their Corn Mother, Zaramama, sometimes came to earth in cornstalks. Monaghan tells us that these stalks were then hung on willow trees that became the focus for festive dances, after which the stalks were burned to assure a plentiful harvest.

Among the agricultural tribes of North America, the origin of maize is attributed to the Corn Mother or Corn Maiden, whose story has as many variations as there are tribes. The *Encyclopedia Britannica* entry on the topic distills the basic two versions. In the "immolation version" the Corn Mother is an old woman who frequently adopts a foster child. She secretly produces kernels of corn by rubbing her body. When the tribe discovers her secret and her method, they are disgusted and determine to kill her. But before her death—to which she consents in some variations—she gives the child specific directions for what should be done with her corpse. Wherever her body is dragged or buried, corn sprouts. (This self-sacrificing spirit is akin to what we see in the story of Lugh's mother, Táiltiu, who died from exhaustion after clearing a field for cultivation.)

In the "flight version," the Corn Mother is a beautiful young woman who marries into a tribe suffering from hunger. When her secret of producing the corn is discovered, her in-laws insult her, causing her to flee back to her heavenly home. When her husband pursues her, she gives him seed corn and directions on how to cultivate it.

For the Keetoowah people of the Cherokee Nation, the corn mother is Selu ("maize") and the Green Corn Dance honoring her traditionally lasted for four days (when the men danced) and four nights (when the women danced). The Green Corn Festival is celebrated by other tribes as well, including the Choctaw, Creek, Seminole, Yuchi, and Iroquois. During the first days, the people purify their homes as well as their bodies, fasting and drinking an herbal concoction. The first ears of corn are offered to the Great Spirit. After eating the corn themselves—roasted or in the form of soup, bread, or tortillas—the people celebrate with singing, dancing, and games. Among the Creek, the women, adorned with colorful ribbons, shells, and rattles, perform a Ribbon Dance lasting up to three hours. Although traditionally the ripening of the corn has determined the timing of the festival, in some places a specific date is observed. For example, the Santa Ana Pueblo north of Albuquerque celebrates the Green Corn Festival on July 26.

Not only do the grain mothers provide the secret of growing the grain, they also protect it while it is vulnerable to blight and drought, thus making its harvesting possible. In *The Goddess Obscured*, Pamela Berger concludes,

> The evidence for the worship of a mother goddess of vegetation is multifaceted, and veneration of her through history is complex. Perpetuated in agrarian contexts, the figure remained part of humankind's religious history for millennia. Agriculturalists, seeking to understand the relationship between the tangible world and another, transcendent reality, devised a figure who could protect family and community from crop calamity and resulting starvation. The basic human fear of uncontrollable, malevolent forces assured that each successive culture would incorporate a form of this protectress into its religious life.

Although grain goddesses abound, there are male grain deities as well. Examples (besides Lugh) include the Aztec Cinteotl, the Mayan Ghanan, the Egyptian Neper, the Roman Liber, and the Phoenician Dagon, who is also credited with inventing the plow.

Ancient vegetation gods—like the Sumerian Dumuzi (or Tammuz), the Greek Adonis, the Anatolian Attis, and the Christian Jesus—all experience an annual death and resurrection, like the seed of life they personify. Their worshipers commemorated them in rituals that often involved the breaking and eating of bread. Sometimes the dough was shaped in the figure of the deity. Barbara

Walker suggests in *Women's Rituals* that the original form of holy communion—which certainly predated Christianity—was the "flesh" of grain gods like Osiris, Adonis, and Tammuz being "ceremonially eaten by their worshipers, who thus became symbolically one with each other as they also internalized their deity."

In *The Golden Bough*, James Frazer theorizes that as human communities abandoned the nomadic life of hunting and herding and turned instead to tilling the land, their energies became more "engrossed by the staple of their life, the corn . . . accordingly the propitiation of the deities of fertility . . . and . . . the corn-spirit . . . tended to become the central feature of their religion." An essential element in this propitiation is the harvest rite of mourning the god who is being sacrificed. Thus the Egyptian reapers lamented when they cut the first corn and called upon Isis, who breathed life back into the dead Osiris. Similarly the women worshipers wept profusely for Adonis while the men applied their sickles to the grain god. And the Syrian women bewailed Tammuz at the festival where he was slain and his bones ground in a mill. Frazer draws a parallel between Tammuz and John Barleycorn, the subject of an English folk ballad published in the sixteenth century (but likely of much older origin) and immortalized in a poetic adaptation by Robert Burns:

> They wasted o'er a scorching flame
> The marrow of his bones;
> But a miller us'd him worst of all—
> For he crush'd him between two stones.

The vegetation god, who dies and is buried (planted), rises in due time (sprouts) and grows to maturity—only to be slain again (reaped), for the cycles of his life are the cycles of the agricultural seasons. As such they are the sustenance of our own cycles of birth, growth, and death.

Contemporary Celebrations Around the World

As we shall see in more detail in the next chapter, celebrating the harvest is a universal phenomenon. Whether the crop is rice, wheat, or yams, its first harvesting is cause for ritual celebration. The Buddhists of Sri Lanka, for example, have a first fruits ceremony at which they offer the Buddha a large bowl of milk and rice.

Slavic peoples take a ritual walk around the circumference of their fields when the grain is beginning to form ears. Tatyana Agapkina, author of "The Mytho-Ritual Complex of Going into the Grain," explores the various ritual actions associated with this practice (wearing a twig or small cross, throwing upward, eating a ritual meal that involves burying some of the food), as well as the alleged effect of drawing a line around one's field on the growth and fruitfulness of the grain.

Some scholars believe Lammas is related to the Jewish Shavuot, or Feast of Weeks, celebrated in late spring. (The harvest comes earlier in warmer climates.) Although in later tradition the feast emphasizes gratitude for the law given on Mount Sinai, in biblical times it was a thanksgiving for the grain harvest. According to Virtual Jerusalem's Jewish Holidays website, Jews from all over Israel traveled to Jerusalem on Shavuot to offer their first harvest of the season.

Not coincidentally, Shavuot services include reading the Book of Ruth, whose main drama is set in a barley field at harvest time. Boaz, its owner, is so impressed with the young widow's kindness to her mother-in-law that he marries Ruth. Their son becomes the grand-father of King David, founder of the Judean dynasty and patriarch of the house from which the Messiah is to come. Traditionally, Shavuot also marks the day of David's birth and death.

For the tribes of West Africa, yams are the primary crop and the first to be harvested—at the beginning of August, the end of the rainy season. At the Yam Festival, a popular holiday in Ghana, Nigeria, and Côte d'Ivoire, the first yams are offered to the gods and the ancestors. According to Professors G. Kranjac-Berisavljevic and B. Z. Gandaa of the University of Ghana, the Dagomba people of northern Ghana forbid yam consumption before the festival; individuals are allowed to eat them only after the communal celebration. This emphasis on community is also reflected in the Dagomba practice of each farmer working a neighbor's plot to gather seed yams. They believe that such interdependence earns the blessing of the gods and produces high yields.

Harvest Customs

For those who live in cities and suburbs, far removed from "amber waves of grain" and the first of their harvesting, perhaps the appreciation of the rites of Lughnasa may be best experienced at county or state fairs. Here the rows upon rows of pies, cakes, muffins, and cookies pay homage to the grain goddesses. The stacks of jars filled with preserves of summer fruits—golden peaches and red, black, and blue berries—honor the vegetation gods.

At fairs, in parks, and by lakes, craftspeople exhibit their wares—pottery, quilts, woodworking, jewelry—a celebration of the host of skills attributed to Lugh, the master craftsman. At summer camps, in back alleys, in neighborhood playgrounds, and in pools, Lugh's athletic prowess is imitated by children learning to swim, cycle, skate, and maneuver their way through any number of ball games.

At a legion of Renaissance Festivals, craftspeople and horse-borne jousters join singers, musicians, and storytellers who honor the memory of the patron of harpists and poets celebrated at Lughnasa.

WAYS TO CELEBRATE

Celebrate the summer harvest.

⑥   If your supermarket buys from local farmers, thank the manager; if it doesn't, ask the manager to try it.

◔ Shop for local produce at a farmers' market or a mom-and-pop stand or from the back of a grower's pickup truck on the side of the road.

◔ Go berry picking (blueberries on a hilltop, if possible!).

◔ Visit an orchard where you can pick your own peaches or a field where you can gather your own melons.

◔ Take time to slowly, sensuously appreciate a peach or a tomato.

◔ Learn how to can or preserve and put up jars of vegetables and fruit to enjoy in winter. If you already know how, teach someone else.

Celebrate the first cut of grains.

◔ Make a wheat weaving and hang it on the wall as a house blessing, a reminder of the abundance you enjoy and the importance of sharing it.

◔ Patronize a locally owned bakery.

◔ Learn to bake bread. (It's okay to use a bread machine.) If you already know how, try a new festive recipe or bake bread in the shape of a grain deity or his/her symbol.

◔ Bake a cake, a pie, or muffins and enter the state fair competition. Even if you don't "place," it'll be fun to see your creation on display! Or just go to the state fair and enjoy the cornucopia of food exhibits and the 4-H kids taking loving care of their animals. Be sure to think of the turning of the Wheel of the Year as you ride the Ferris wheel.

◔ Make your own granola. It's labor-intensive but worth it. It also makes a great gift. Here's my recipe, which I've modestly named:

GREAT GRANOLA

Ingredients:

3 cups oats
½ cup wheat bran
½ cup wheat germ
¼ cup dry milk
⅓ cup sesame seeds
⅛ cup peanuts
⅛ cup soy nuts
¼ cup sunflower seeds
¼ cup pumpkin seeds
⅛ cup walnuts or pecans
⅛ cup almonds
¼ cup canola oil
¼ cup honey
¼ teaspoon vanilla
½ cup raisins

Preheat oven to 325°. In a 4-quart bowl, mix first 5 ingredients. In a small saucepan, heat on low flame (do not boil) oil, honey and vanilla. While this is heating, chop nuts and seeds and stir into grain mixture. Drizzle the heated liquid mixture into bowl of dry ingredients and mix *thoroughly*. It is important that all dry ingredients be dampened. Spread on 2 large cookie sheets. Bake for 9 minutes. Stir. Bake for another 7 minutes, until golden. Cool on racks. When thoroughly cool, sprinkle raisins over granola on cookie sheets. Loosen granola from sheets, spoon into jar(s) for storage (or for giving away).

Celebrate the "harvesting" of an idea.

☙   Confer with members of your household to determine what you have "harvested" in the past year—things that were in the development or growing stage and have now been completed. Has a child learned how to swim or gotten a driver's license? Did you fix the back porch or paint the guestroom? Did you clean out the attic or have a successful yard sale? Did your supervisor accept your proposal?

⚜ Rejoice in the harvest! Reward yourselves. Drive to the beach to show off your new driving/swimming skills. Invite neighbors to an open house on the refurbished back porch. Invite a friend to stay in the spruced-up guestroom. With the yard sale proceeds, take the family out for a pasta dinner. Take a box of pastries to the office to share with your colleagues who helped with the proposal.

Nourish yourself.

⚜ Take a hard look at your diet and, if necessary, adjust your nutritional intake to make it healthier.

⚜ Discover what nourishes your spirit and feed it. What activity makes you feel most energized, most creative, closest to the source of life? Is it dancing? Gardening? Making music? Cycling? Cooking? Reading or writing poetry? Meditating? Making love? Climbing a mountain? Playing with your grandchildren? Whatever it is, *do it*! And do it mindfully; be deliberate, unrushed, and fully aware and appreciative of the joy it brings your spirit.

⚜ Think of a place that nourishes your spirit. Is it a mountaintop? The ocean? The theater? The tennis court? The concert hall? Your bathtub? A cabin in the woods? A workroom in the basement? A cathedral? A fishing hole? A hiking trail? A museum? A baseball field? An aquarium? A treehouse? A sunporch? A room of your own in the attic? Remember (or discover) such a place—and go there! Let it feed and invigorate your spirit.

Nourish others.

⚜ Volunteer to work at your local food bank.

⚜ If you have a vegetable garden of your own, share its produce with folks who don't have one, or use the produce from your garden to prepare a dish for a soup kitchen or for someone elderly or infirm or alone. Make enough for you to share the meal and have leftovers to leave behind. This is my favorite recipe for putting leftover corn-on-the-cob to use—with green beans and tomatoes from the garden:

THREE VEGGIE SALAD

Combine:

cooked corn cut from the cobs (about 4 ears)
tomatoes, chopped (2 small or 1 large)
cooked green beans (about a cup)

Toss the above with whisked dressing:

1 teaspoon red wine vinegar
1½ tablespoons virgin olive oil
⅓ teaspoon salt
¼ teaspoon black pepper
¼ cup chopped fresh herbs: cilantro or oregano/basil

Celebrate Lughnasa as the Celts did.

⑥ Honor Lugh's famed athletic prowess by organizing games, meets, or races that give everyone in your family, neighborhood, or community the chance to join in the fun.

⑥ Volunteer to help at a Special Olympics. Get involved at the state, provincial, national, or international level, or offer your services locally at a Special Olympics program in your community. Some volunteers offer a few hours of their time a year at specific events, while others work several hours a week year-round. If there isn't a program in your community, start one. Go to **www.specialolympics.org/** for details.

☙ Enhance your own prowess. Join (or start) a softball team, join a gym or a local YMCA or senior center and use the pool or workout room, or develop an exercise program at home. Start (or join) a "walking group" in your neighborhood, take an aerobics class, dance for your morning meditation, or learn T'ai Chi or another form of moving meditation based on martial arts.

☙ Honor Lugh's reputation for being multiskilled by learning a new craft like woodworking, metal-working, or quilting. Or just learn to change the oil in your car, make a pie crust, install a dimmer switch, or darn a sock.

CELEBRATE THE FIRST CUT OF GRAIN

A LUGHNASA/LAMMAS RITUAL

Gather outdoors if possible, and sit in a semicircle on chairs, benches, blankets, or grass. Baskets with loaves of bread baked by volunteers are arranged on a table. Narrator and Leader take positions where they can be easily seen.

Narrator   Welcome to our celebration of First Fruits. At the beginning of August, the ancient Celts celebrated the feast of Lughnasa [*LOO-nah-sah*], honoring their harvest god Lugh. It was adopted by medieval Christians as the feast of Loaf-mass, or Lammas. We are now at the midpoint of the warm half of the year that began at Beltane on May 1 and will end with Samhain on November 1. We are about halfway between Summer Solstice and Fall Equinox. This cross-quarter day, the first of three harvest festivals, marks in some climates the first cut of grain and the baking of bread from that new grain. Wherever in the northern hemisphere we live, whether our fields are ripe with wheat or corn, barley or oats, rye or rice, let us be mindful of the many hands and hearts that bring the bread to our tables.

A Man and a Woman—preceded by a young Girl and a young Boy garlanded with seasonal blooms—ceremonially carry in a large wreath made of sheaves of wheat and/or corn, in which are set four large candles. They set it on a table or platform where all can see it. During this procession, a guitarist sings "Pastures of Plenty" by Woody Guthrie.

Honoring the Harvesters

The wreath has been set down. The four who carried it stand around it, each at a candle.

Narrator This wreath, made of many sheaves of grain, represents the circle of our community and the fruits of our harvest. The candles represent those whose work makes our lives possible, those who labor for our nourishment. We invite you to join in blessing them as we light the candles. The response is in your program.

Leader We light the first candle for all the farmers who plow and plant the seeds of the world's grains.

Man lights first candle.

All We bless the labor of their hands and the kindness of their hearts.

Leader We light the second candle for all who harvest the world's grain, whether by hand or machine, whether migrant or settled, for those who thresh and mill it, and for the animals who help them.

Woman lights second candle.

All We bless the labor of their hands and hooves and the kindness of their hearts.

Leader We light the third candle for all who transport the flour, for the bakers who transform it into bread, for the merchants who make both flour and bread available to us.

Boy lights third candle.

All　　We bless the labor of their hands and the kindness of their hearts.

Leader　We light the fourth candle for those who feed us—for our parents who first put bread on our tables and taught us to enjoy its taste, for those in our households who prepare the food, for friends who invite us to share a meal, for all those who cook and serve food in soup kitchens and hospitals, in school cafeterias and restaurants, and at every hearth around the world.

Girl lights fourth candle.

All　　We bless the labor of their hands and the kindness of their hearts.

Remembering Bakers

Narrator　Some of us can remember from our growing up the magic of the neighborhood bakery, where a tinkling bell announced our entry into a sanctuary of sweets. It was a bright, clean place that smelled of dough baking, where sparkling chrome and glass cases were laden with fruit-filled buns and honey dips, apple strudel and crumb cakes, ginger men, éclairs, and tea cakes. The back racks bore crusty loaves of different shapes and shades. And on display was a three-tiered wedding cake with fluted ribbons of sugary white icing.

　　　　For others of us, the best baking memories are of our mother's kitchen. While cookies cooled on racks, we could eat the broken ones still warm, and despite the warning to be careful, we hovered over the oven as the opening door released a hot, sweet wave of cinnamon or chocolate. Cherish these memories, for it is often near the hearth that the heart is best revealed.

Reader 1   (*a woman*)
I want to die
an old bakerwoman
with my hands floured
white,
white apron stretched across a clean (at last) heart,
white vitals spilling from measuring cups and spoons:
sugar, salt, shortening, soda, powder, milk,
eggshell jaws agape on marble,
white-noise whirr of beaters,
wash of morning sun on porcelain oven door
and ivory-lace floor.

I want to die
    spooning cookie batter into ragged globes,
    shaping doughy embryos into rounded loaves,
    rolling pie crust into waxing moons,

my baker mother waiting in the white light
with leaven for my rising.

Narrator   While some see themselves as bakers, others think of themselves as the bread—kneaded by the hands of the universe or of a divine baker.

Reader 2   Bakerwoman God,
I am your living bread,
Strong, brown Bakerwoman God.
I am your low, soft, and being-shaped loaf.
I am your rising
bread, well-kneaded
by some divine and knotty
pair of knuckles,
by your warm earth hands.
I am bread well-kneaded.

Put me in fire, Bakerwoman God,
put me in your own bright fire.

I am warm, warm as you from fire.
I am white and gold, soft and hard,
brown and round.
I am so warm from fire.

Break me, Bakerwoman God.
I am broken under your caring Word.
Drop me in your special juice in pieces.
Drop me in your blood.

Drunken me in the great red flood.
Self-giving chalice swallow me.
My skin shines in the divine wine.
My face is cup-covered and I drown.

I fall up
in a red pool
in a gold world
where your warm
sunskin is there
to catch and hold me.
Bakerwoman God, remake.
          —Alla Renee Bozarth, "Bakerwoman God"

Meditation on the Gift of Grain

Servers hand out paper and pencils.

Leader   Grain is the most basic of foods, the staff of life, the
           staple of our diet. Whatever form it takes, grain ap-
           pears on our tables and bed trays, in our lunch boxes
           and picnic baskets, at our large, lavish banquets and
           our lonely midnight snacks with comforting, nourish-
           ing regularity. Let us meditate on the gifts of grain. I in-
           vite you to count these blessings—literally. To write

down as many forms as you can think of in which grain appears in your diet. After a few minutes, we'll collect and collate your responses and later in the ritual offer them as a litany of grains.

Instrumental meditation music for three to five minutes. Then the Servers collect the paper and pencils, privately collate the responses to eliminate duplicates, and organize them into a list appropriate for the litany. See below for examples.

Remembering Lugh

Narrator   The original feast of Lughnasa was the celebration of Lugh, one of the most powerful and popular of the Celtic gods. He was patron of the arts and crafts and an accomplished blacksmith, carpenter, and metal worker, as well as a talented harpist, gifted poet, sorcerer, physician, and champion chess player. Beyond this, he was a handsome young athlete and a warrior who defended his people against their enemies and protected the wheat crops against disease.

Leader   At the Festival of Lughnasa, the first of the grain was ritually harvested and taken to a hilltop, where it was offered to the deity. Everyone ate a meal that included bread made with the new grain as well as blueberries and the meat of a sacrificial bull. Dancers enacted a play that may have dramatized the struggle of rivals for a goddess (possibly symbolizing the struggle of light and darkness for the day or of summer and winter for the earth). There were dance contests as well. Other plays may have reenacted Lugh's victory over the rival tribe or his defeat of blight or famine. We are about to see a contemporary version of that battle in the play "Lugh Among the Locusts."

A group of children, each holding a wheat sheaf in each hand, run onto the stage and sit on the ground, forming rows, to represent a wheatfield. The rest of the characters can be played by youth or adults. Music accompanies this entrance. When the field has been established, a musician gives the signal and the children move the sheaves back and forth so that they appear to be swaying in the breeze. A Male Grasshopper enters, sees the wheat, rubs his legs together with joy, and makes a stridulating, chirping sound.

Grasshopper   Oh-boy-oh-boy-oh-boy! Get a load of those eats. (*chirps*) It's my lucky day!

Grasshopper chirps again and hops toward the field. Female locust enters.

Locust   Pssst! Hey Grassy!

Grasshopper stops, turns around.

Aren't you gonna invite me to lunch?

Grasshopper   Yo, Locust! (*They embrace, slap each other on the back.*) Where you been, Cuz?

Locust   Oh, here and there. We had a little . . . eh, population explosion in our neck of the woods. I hadda hit the road. (*gesturing to field*) But this here is lookin' good. (*rubbing hands together*) Real good.

Grasshopper   Yeah, I think this'll do for lunch and dinner for the rest of the summer. Whatta you say?

Locust   I say get out your napkin.

Locust takes bib from pocket and ties it around her neck. Female Wheatbug and Male Stinkbug enter together, see field, and react appreciatively.

Wheatbug   Whoooaaaa! Did somebody ring my lunch bell?

Stinkbug	(*rapidly and repeatedly stroking his throat*) I think I'm having a . . . a . . . religious experience!
	Stinkbug turns and spits. All respond as though a foul smell has been released and look at Stinkbug with disgust.
	Well, I'm sorry. I can't help it, you know.
Locust	Why not?
Stinkbug	I'm a stinkbug.
	All groan. Grasshopper turns to Wheatbug.
Grasshopper	And who are you?
Wheatbug	I'm a wheatbug, and this (*indicating field*) is my destiny!
Grasshopper	Oh, no it isn't. We got here first.
Wheatbug	So?
Grasshopper	So you and your smelly pal can just find yourselves another field.
Locust	(*aside*) Or at least another deodorant.
Wheatbug	Why should we? We found this one.
Grasshopper	No. *We* found this one.
Stinkbug	And then we found you finding this one.
Locust	Finders keepers.
Stinkbug	So we get to keep you.
Locust	(*about Stinkbug, to others*) What's he talking about?
Wheatbug	I don't know, but don't get him excited or he'll do that spitting thing again.
Stinkbug	Listen! Why can't we . . . share?

Others gasp in disbelief.

Nobody ever wants to share. It's not nice.

Grasshopper   Who has time for nice? It's the survival of the fittest out here.

Stinkbug   But we could all be fit if we had enough to eat.

Locust   Stinky's got a point there. With an adequate diet, we'd have the energy to exercise.

Grasshopper   (*to Locust*) Hey, cuz, don't go getting all squishy on me.

Wheatbug   Exercise, smexercise. It's time for lunch.

Wheatbug starts toward field. Grasshopper intercepts her.

Grasshopper   Oh no you don't!

Stinkbug rapidly and repeatedly strokes his throat.

What's with him anyway?

Wheatbug   He doesn't like violence. It excites him. It makes him reek.

Grasshopper lets go of Wheatbug and tries to calm Stinkbug down.

Grasshopper   Whoa. Let's not get excited. Do you see any violence? I don't see any violence. Who said anything about violence?

Stinkbug calms down.

Why don't you two just stay for lunch, and we'll see what we can work out.

Stinkbug   Lunch?

Locust   Lots of lunch. Let's go!

They all head for the field and start munching on sheaves of wheat, which the children grip tightly. Happy music segues into action music. Lugh enters.

Lugh   This looks like a job for Lugh of the Long Arm, Harvest God of the Celts! (*draws his sword and shouts to Bugs*) Get away from that field!

Bugs freeze.

Wheatbug   Why?

Lugh   Because my people need that wheat to make bread.

Wheatbug   Who's stopping them?

Lugh   You are, my nasty Wheatbug. You have an enzyme in your saliva that drastically modifies the nature of the gluten, which, when it comes in contact with water, disintegrates.

Stinkbug   Not our problem.

Lugh   And you, my smelly friend, affect the taste of the plant; you actually make it nauseating.

Stinkbug   Oh.

Locust   Imagine that.

Grasshopper   So what are we supposed to do about it?

Lugh   Get out of that field!

Grasshopper   (*to other Bugs*) You heard him, Mates. Let's get out of this field!

Grasshopper, Locust, and Wheatbug swarm about Lugh, stinging and biting him. He swings his sword at them and smacks his neck and body where they bite, all the while making growling, gasping, and threatening battle noises. Stinkbug grows increasingly agitated at this violence, rapidly and repeatedly stroking his throat. When he has worked himself into a frenzy, he spits. The battle comes to a grinding halt as Lugh and the others hold their noses and make noises of disgust.

Stinkbug   I'm sorry. I can't help it. I'm a—

All others   (*interrupting*) Stinkbug!

All wave away the air near them, trying to clear the stench.

Lugh   Now listen up, all of you! I want every one of you out of this field. Now.

Grasshopper   (*sarcastic*) Or what?

Lugh   (*taking a can of pesticide spray from his belt*) Or else!

Locust   He wouldn't do it.

Wheatbug   He wouldn't think of it.

Stinkbug   He wouldn't even dream of it.

Grasshopper   (*to Lugh*) You wouldn't. Would you?

Pause.

Lugh   Of course not. (*puts pesticide away*) But I would dream of other things.

Locust   Like what?

Lugh   (*matter-of-factly*) Diversified farming. Crop rotation.

Wheatbug   (*not impressed*) Yeah, yeah.

Lugh   Planting pest-deterrent species of wheat.

Stinkbug   (*slightly threatened*) Hmm.

Lugh   Pest-management techniques.

Stinkbug   Say what?

Lugh	Like releasing predators of pests . . .
Grasshopper	Let's not get carried a—
Lugh	(*interrupting*) Or sterile male insects.
Stinkbug	And just where would you get *them*?
	Lugh steps between Grasshopper and Stinkbug and puts an arm around each of them.
Lugh	Oh, I'd *fix* them to be that way.
	The two register the meaning of this with the utmost dismay, then break away. Stinkbug starts rapidly and repeatedly stroking his throat and then runs off. Grasshopper looks after him and back at the smiling Lugh.
Grasshopper	I'm outta here.
	Grasshopper makes a quick, hopping exit.
Locust	What about us?
Wheatbug	Yeah?
Lugh	Ladies, I'm afraid motherhood will not be part of your future.
Locust	No eggies?
Lugh	Not in this field.
Wheatbug	Bummer.
Locust	There's something unnatural about this.
Wheatbug	Yeah. Why do you take their side? The humans.
Lugh	(*shrugging*) I'm their god. What do you expect?
Locust	How about a little cross-species justice?
Lugh	Hmm . . . I'm afraid we're not there yet.

Wheatbug   And in the meantime?

Lugh   I can let you have a tiny corner of the field . . . if you promise to keep quiet about it.

            Locust and Wheatbug look at each other. Lugh puts his hands out, palms up.

Lugh   Deal?

Locust and (*slapping Lugh's palms*) Deal.
Wheatbug

            All, including the Wheatfield, exit quickly.

Leader   We hope you've been inspired by "Lugh Among the Locusts" and will join in a song celebrating all creation.

            All sing "All Creatures of the Earth and Sky," words by St. Francis of Assisi.

All sing   All creatures of the earth and sky,
            come, kindred, lift your voices high, Alleluia, Alleluia!
            Bright burning sun with golden beam,
            soft shining moon with silver gleam: Alleluia, Alleluia,
                Alleluia, Alleluia, Alleluia!

            Swift rushing wind so wild and strong,
            white clouds that sail in heav'n along, Alleluia, Alleluia!
            Fair rising morn in praise rejoice,
            high stars of evening find a voice: Alleluia, Alleluia,
                Alleluia, Alleluia, Alleluia!

            Cool flowing water pure and clear,
            make music for all life to hear, Alleluia, Alleluia!
            Dance, flame of fire so strong and bright,
            and bless us with your warmth and light: Alleluia,
                Alleluia, Alleluia, Alleluia, Alleluia!

            Embracing earth, you, day by day,
            bring forth your blessings on our way, Alleluia, Alleluia!

All herbs and fruits that richly grow,
let them the glory also show: Alleluia, Alleluia,
    Alleluia, Alleluia, Alleluia!

Enjoying Seasonal Foods

Narrator   At Lughnasa, people celebrated the season by climbing
hills to pick the blueberries that were plentiful there.
This practice reminds us of the pleasure that only seasonal fruits and vegetables can provide. Even in the
twenty-first century, when miracles of transportation
and electricity make it possible to ship produce around
the world, we can still tell the difference between the
imports in winter and the home-grown or local produce in season. The corn that goes from field to pot in
six hours, the tomatoes from our own garden, the
peaches we pick from nearby orchards, the melons we
buy from roadside stands—this is the joy of August,
this is the taste of the earth at its finest.

Reader 3   Facing the sunset
Peaches and sugar
And the sun inside the evening
Like the stone in a fruit

The ear of corn holds intact
its hard yellow laughter

August
Children eat
Dark bread and tasty moon
                    —Federico Garcia Lorca, "August"
                    translated by Alan S. Trueblood

Guitarist sings "Homegrown Tomatoes" by Guy Clark.

Litany of Grains

The litany includes the responses written by participants in the Meditation on the Gift of Grain (page 235), which the Servers have organized and delivered to the Leader. Examples follow.

Narrator Our delight in the taste of seasonal flavors is matched only by our joy in the first fruits of the grain harvest. We have counted our blessings and will now share our responses. Let us celebrate the many forms of grain and the richness they bring to our lives. Your response to the litany will be: "Blessed be the bread of the earth!"

Leader Let us rejoice in wheat and corn, oats and barley, rye and rice,

All Blessed be the bread of earth!

Leader In whole wheat, cracked wheat, sour dough, and pumpernickel,

All Blessed be the bread of earth!

Leader In French bread, Italian garlic bread, Russian black bread, Irish soda bread, Indian pita bread,

All Blessed be the bread of earth!

Leader In corn pone, corn chips, corn pudding, cornflakes, tacos, tortillas, and popcorn,

All Blessed be the bread of earth!

Leader In raisin bread and bagels, muffins and crumpets, scones and brioche and croissants,

All Blessed be the bread of earth!

Leader In pancakes and waffles, blintzes and crêpes,

All Blessed be the bread of earth!

Leader   In donuts and buns, crullers and beignets, and Danish
           pastry,

All   Blessed be the bread of earth!

Leader   In challah and matzoth, biscuits, won ton, and
           dumplings,

All   Blessed be the bread of earth!

Leader   In oatmeal, bran flakes, wheat flakes, and grits,

All   Blessed be the bread of earth!

Leader   In breadsticks, rolls, and granola bars,

All   Blessed be the bread of earth!

Leader   In rice cakes, rice pudding, fried rice, and sushi,

All   Blessed be the bread of earth!

Leader   In saltines, graham crackers, animal crackers, and
           pretzels,

All   Blessed be the bread of earth!

Leader   In spaghetti, macaroni, lasagna, fettuccine, ravioli, and
           pizza,

All   Blessed be the bread of earth!

Leader   In layer cakes, loaf cakes, shortcake, pound cake, coffee
           cake, cupcakes, and jelly roll,

All   Blessed be the bread of earth!

Leader   In bread pudding, cookies, pies and tarts, brownies,
           biscotti, and baklava,

All   Blessed be the bread of earth!

Honoring the Deities of Grain and Vegetation

Narrator   We are blessed with an abundance and variety of grains. Ancient peoples had fewer choices, but they understood the importance of cultivating and caring for the grains they had. And they relied on their gods for help. Lugh was not alone. Mythologies around the world celebrate deities that provide grains to sustain human life. The Greeks called upon Demeter and her daughter Persephone; the Romans called upon Ceres. The Sumerians relied on Ashnan, the Aztecs on Chicomecoatl, and the Norse on Freya. The Cambodians called their giver of rice Po Ino Nogar. The Javanese honor Saning Sari as their rice mother and dedicate the finest of the planting grain to her. The ancient Peruvian Corn Mother Zaramama was believed sometimes to come to earth in cornstalks, which then became the focus for festive dances. Native North Americans attribute the origin of maize to the Corn Mother, whose story has many variations. Here is one from a New England tribe.

Reader 4   Now the people increased and became numerous. They lived by hunting, and the more people there were, the less game they found. As the animals decreased, starvation came upon the people. And First Mother pitied them. The little children came to First Mother and said, "We are hungry. Feed us."

But she had nothing to give them, and she wept. She told them, "Be patient. I will make some food. Then your little bellies will be full." But she kept weeping.

Her husband asked, "How can I make you smile? How can I make you happy?"

"There is only one thing that will stop my tears."

"What is it?" asked her husband.

"It is this: You must kill me."

"I could never do that."

"You must, or I will go on weeping and grieving forever."

Then the husband traveled far, to the end of the earth, to the north he went, to ask the Great Instructor, his uncle Kloskurbeh, what he should do.

"You must do what she wants. You must kill her," said Kloskurbeh.

Then the young man went back to his home, and it was his turn to weep.

But First Mother said, "Tomorrow at high noon you must do it. After you have killed me, let two of our sons take hold of my hair and drag my body over that empty patch of earth. Let them drag me back and forth, back and forth, over every part of the patch, until all my flesh has been torn from my body. Afterwards take my bones, gather them up, and bury them in the middle of this clearing. Then leave that place."

So it was done. The husband slew his wife. And her sons, praying, dragged her body to and fro as she had commanded, until her flesh covered all the earth. Then they took up her bones and buried them in the middle of it. Weeping loudly, they went away.

When the husband and his children and his children's children came back to that place after seven moons had passed, they found the earth covered with tall, green, tassled plants. The fruit of these plants, corn, was First Mother's flesh, given so that the people might live and flourish. And they partook of First Mother's flesh and found it sweet beyond words. Following her instructions, they did not eat all but put many kernels back into the earth.

In this way her flesh and spirit renewed themselves every seven months, generation after generation.

Leader   There were also male grain deities, including the Aztec Cinteotl, the Mayan Ghanan, the Egyptian Neper, the

Roman Liber, and the Phoenician Dagon, believed to have invented the plow. Ancient vegetation gods—like the Sumerian Tammuz, the Greek Adonis, and the Anatolian Attis—all experienced a yearly dying and rising, like the seed of life they personified. Rituals honoring them often included the breaking and eating of bread. By thus eating the flesh of the grain gods, their worshipers achieved a "holy communion" with one another and with their deity. James Frazer, author of *The Golden Bough*, draws a parallel between the ancient vegetation god and John Barleycorn, the subject of an English folk ballad.

Guitarist sings "The Ballad of John Barleycorn."

The Taste of Fellowship

Narrator With the coming of Christianity, Anglo-Saxons celebrated the Feast of August 1 as *Hlaf-mass or* Loaf mass, which in medieval England and Scotland became Lammas, the Feast of First Fruits. On this day in England it was the custom to harvest and mill the earliest of the ripened grains, then bake them into loaves of bread and carry them to church for blessing.

Certainly bread has played an important role in the Judeo-Christian tradition. When Moses leads the Israelites out of Egypt, they are hungry in the desert until Yahweh sends daily manna, which the Psalmist calls the "grain of heaven." Part of the prayer that Jesus teaches his followers includes the petition, "Give us this day our daily bread," using bread as a metaphor for the satisfaction of all human needs. And in John's gospel, Jesus refers to himself as "the bread of life."

Just as the vegetation god dies and is buried and in time rises, only to be slain again, and born again, so is the grain planted in the earth, in time rising, only to be harvested and planted again. For this is the cycle of all life—the cycle of the earth's seasons, the cycle of our own lives.

Leader   To honor these life cycles and to celebrate our communal appreciation for the first fruits of this year's grain harvest, some of you have baked bread to share with us today. We give thanks to the bakers and invite you to come forward, take up your loaf, and tell us what kind of bread you chose to bake and why.

Bakers come forward and take up their loaves and talk about them in turn.

Leader   And now we invite all to come forward and share the bread of fellowship.

Bakers hold baskets and others come forward and take pieces of bread, while all sing the following words to the melody of "Let Us Break Bread Together," repeating as necessary until all have returned to their places.

All sing   Let us break bread together at our feast.
Let us break bread together at our feast.
Let us nourish our friends
And give thanks for the good they do.
Let us break bread together at our feast.

Let us share in the harvest of the grain.
Let us share one another's joy and pain.
Let us comfort our friends
And rejoice in their blessings too.
Let us share in the harvest of the grain.

Let us open our hearts to humankind.
Let us serve both with body and with mind.
Learn to share, learn to give,
Learn that loving is how to live.
Let us open our hearts to humankind.

> Let us cherish the beauty of the earth.
> Let us yield to each dying and each birth.
> Praise the hills, praise the fields,
> Praise the bounty that nature yields.
> Let us cherish the beauty of the earth.

Narrator   May the bread we have shared feed our bodies and our spirits. And may all who hunger find nourishment in the generosity of others.

While this ends the formal ritual, the Lughnasa/Lammas celebration may continue with less formal activities like the following. In this case, the Narrator may wish to make the appropriate announcements.

☙ Hold athletic events and games to celebrate the legendary prowess of Lugh. They might include such standards as tug-of-war, sack races, three-legged races, wheelbarrow races, relay races, egg-carrying (with spoon) races, egg tosses, watermelon seed-spitting contests, horseshoes, croquet, or volleyball.

☙ Have a bake sale and give the proceeds to an organization to combat world hunger such as Oxfam.

☙ Have a baking contest with awards in different categories and different age groups.

☙ Have a crafts booth where children and adults can try their hands at wheat weaving.

☙ In honor of the dancing at Lughnasa, have a dance exhibition featuring individuals, couples, or groups demonstrating various dance forms, for example traditional ethnic folk dances like Irish step dancing, Scottish contra dancing, the Polish polka, the Greek syrtos or tsamikos, the Russian troika, the Spanish flamenco, the Mexican hat dance, and the American square dance. You might also feature ballroom dances like the waltz, the tango, the rumba, and the fox trot and modern dances like the Charleston, the jitter-bug, the Watusi, disco dancing, line dancing, and salsa.

A final word: This might be a good time to set aside some ears of corn to dry for use as decorations in the Fall Equinox Ritual.

Autumn Equinox

September 21-22

School buses are on the road again and footballs spiral through the air. Bowling leagues are back in the lanes and book groups are buzzing. Lawnmowers have quieted down, walnut trees have splattered the ground with yellow leaves, and mum's the word in the garden. Yellow jackets are coming to lunch. Bears are bulking up and ground squirrels and chipmunks are storing nuts and acorns. Elk are starting down the mountain, whales are heading for tropical waters, monarch butterflies for Mexico, and sparrows for South America. Wild geese follow the sun south, their vibrant squawking drawing our amazed attention to their determined Vs.

The Seasonal Calendar

Once again we come to a balance of the light—the second time of the year when the hours of day equal the hours of night, the *equinox*, when everyone on earth experiences twelve hours of each. On the equinox the sun rises due east and sets due west on the horizon, but each day from now until Winter Solstice in the northern hemisphere, it will continue to rise and set a little farther south. The nights will grow still longer and the days shorter. The gods of darkness begin their victory over the gods of light; the wheel of the year turns.

Surely our ancient ancestors experienced a certain sadness, even fear, at the withdrawal of the sun since they depended on it for light and warmth. Yet in many places this was also a time of harvest, and if the crops were plentiful, they provided a store of food sufficient for the winter as well as grain and seeds for the next year's planting. Then it was also a time for celebration.

The full moon nearest the Fall Equinox is the harvest moon because it provides brighter and longer-lasting light than the ordinary full moon and so enables farmers to harvest crops after sunset. The scientific explanation for this phenomenon is that the moon rises due east during this time—opposite the setting sun. Further, as naturalist Don Hendershot points out in his column in the North Carolina weekly *Smokey Mountain News*, the moon rises about fifty minutes later each evening during the rest of the year. But at the time of the equinox—due to the relative position of the moon in relation to the earth—it rises only about ten minutes later each night and climbs at a lower angle. Thus it seems to hang longer on the horizon. In addition, "since the light from the moon travels through more atmosphere near the horizon, there is more refraction which creates the illusion of a larger moon." This phenomenon is repeated to a lesser degree, providing more than usual illumination at the next full moon, called the hunter's moon.

Both the Fall and the Spring Equinoxes are marked by ancient structures around the world. In Europe, Asia, Africa, and the Americas, we find stone cairns, pyramids, temples, and earthen mounds whose deliberately precise, east-west orientation enabled them to announce to their dedicated builders both Spring and Fall Equinoxes.

These astronomical markers, in some cases clearly dedicated to deities, also served other purposes related to agriculture or hunting or safety. We have already noted that the desert people of the Nabta Playa would have been able to use their Summer Solstice marker to warn them of the monsoon season. The Egyptians of Karnak could use the Great Temple of Amen-Ra to prepare for the flooding of the Nile. Native Americans and others used solstice and equinox markers—as well as the stars—to formulate a planting and harvesting calendar.

Crops are ready for harvest at different times of the year in different places, depending on the crop as well as on distance from the equator, altitude, temperature, and other topographical and climatic features. We are accustomed to think of late summer and fall as harvest time, but in some places it is spring or even winter. And of course, below the equator, summer and fall extend from late December through late June. Although this chapter deals with Fall Equinox, the following survey includes ancient and contemporary harvest festivals around the world—even ones celebrated in other seasons—in the hope of identifying common purposes and practices that suggest a global kinship with regard to this tradition, despite differences in particularities. The Australian Media Family Network provides brief sketches of many of these celebrations on its website "Harvest Festivals from Around the World."

Mythology and History

The ancient Sumerians of Uruk revered Inanna as, among other things, goddess of the storehouse. Their harvest festival featured a celebration of the marriage of Inanna and Dumuzi, or Amaushumgalana (a form of the vegetation deity), who represented the power of growth. As the newlyweds found security in their marriage, so did the community feel safe with its storehouses full of provisions.

The Egyptians celebrated their harvest in the spring with a festival dedicated to the fertility god Min, sometimes called Min-Horus. His statue, which featured an erect phallus, was carried in procession while the people sang hymns and performed ritual dances. Then the pharaoh, believed to descend from a line that identified him with Min-Horus, presumably engaged in a mating ritual with his queen, enacting a sacred marriage that reflected the union of the human and the divine as well as the life-giving power evidenced in the harvest. After this, the pharaoh took his throne and gave orders to shoot four arrows and release birds toward the four directions.

The Canaanites' harvest festivals extended from March to September. They celebrated their barley harvest around the time of Spring Equinox, when the moon was full. On the first night they sacrificed a lamb, and on the second they dressed in white and processed to the temple to offer the first barley sheaf to the gods while chanting prayers. Meanwhile, they had carefully removed from their homes all leavening and leavened foods—things associated with the old harvest. They ate unleavened barley bread, bitter herbs, fresh greens dipped in salted water, and fruits with nuts and spices. In the light of the full moon, they performed sacred dances and sang sacred songs.

Seven weeks later, when the wheat was harvested, a portion of it was ritually desacralized—winnowed, threshed, and parched—to release the spirits and make it safe for human consumption. From this grain each family made two loaves of bread to offer the deities. Two months later, bonfires and dancing marked the beginning of the grape harvest. And two months after that, at the Fall Equinox, the people performed rituals of expiation and purification. Then at the full moon they celebrated the week-long festival marking the end of the grape harvest with processions through the fields, sacrifices of animals, flour, oil, and wine, and revels to mark the conclusion of the agricultural year and the onset of the rainy season.

Ancient Hebrews marked this time of year—as do modern Jews—with three different holy days. Sukkot, a festival of thanksgiving beginning on the fifteenth day of Tishri (September or October), was also known as the Feast of the Ingathering or harvesting of grains and fruits. The word *sukkot* means "huts" and recollects the temporary shelters in which the Israelites lived while in the desert before entering the Promised Land. It might also refer to shelters that they set up in the fields once they had settled to maximize the time they could spend there during the harvest.

The other two, Rosh Hashanah and Yom Kippur, are the most important of all Jewish holidays. They are observed over a ten-day period starting on the first day of Tishri. Rosh Hashanah begins a time of penitence and prayer, a time to examine one's behavior of the past year and ask forgiveness for sins, and a time for families to gather for special meals. Yom Kippur, the Day of Atonement, which falls on the tenth day, is a time of fasting from food, drink, and sexual intercourse, among other things (though the day preceding it features a good deal of eating and little praying). It is also a time for reflection, for ritual prayer that includes communal confession of sins, and for asking forgiveness—of Yahweh and of fellow humans—for promises broken. In the days when the Temple in Jerusalem was the center of Judaism, the high priest ritually transferred the sins of the people to a goat, which was then taken into the wilderness and thrown over a precipice, giving rise to the term *scapegoat*.

According to Anthony Aveni's *Book of the Year*, as early as the seventh century BCE, the Chinese celebrated the Great Cha at the end of each agricultural year. At this thanksgiving event, "offerings were presented to the spirits, animals, and cultural heroes connected with agriculture." It also provided an occasion for an eating-and-drinking orgy "accompanied by music, dance, and masquerading."

For the ancient Greeks, the autumn festival was dedicated to Demeter, goddess of the earth's fruits, especially those requiring cultivation. The Mysteries at Eleusis—where, according to myth, she had ordered a temple built in her honor—were celebrated from at least the fifteenth century BCE to the fourth century CE, nearly two thousand years, until the Christian Emperor Theodosius I suppressed them.

In *The Myth of the Goddess*, Anne Baring and Jules Cashford describe the nine-day event that welcomed initiates from all over the Greek and Roman world. It began with a procession of sacred objects, including a statue of Dionysus, accompanied by singing, dancing, and ecstatic shouting. The initiates were summoned and prepared through rites of purification, which included fasting, cleansing in the sea, and the sacrifice of young pigs. Once inside the *Telesterion* or Hall of Initiation (which held several thousand), they participated in a ritual that was and remains a secret. The ini-

tiates were forbidden to speak of it, and the only accounts are
from cryptic classical writers or unsympathetic Christian writers
condemning its pagan "abominations." From what we can piece
together, the initiation seemed to involve the lighting of a fire,
possibly the ritual drinking of a special (perhaps hallucinogenic)
potion that intensified the experience, the reenacting of
Persephone's descent into the Underworld and her return to her
mother Demeter, and possibly a ritual sacred marriage enacted by
the *hierophant*, or chief priest, and priestess to assure Persephone's
return. The heart of the initiation involved "things done, things
said, things revealed." At the culminating moment, the hierophant
chanted, "The great goddess has borne a sacred child...." Then, in
profound silence, he held up a single ear of grain. The ceremony
was followed by singing, dancing, and feasting on a sacrificial bull.
Finally the priest poured water from two vessels onto the ground
as the people looked to heaven crying "Rain!" and then looked to
earth crying "Conceive!"

What did the initiates experience that made Sophocles ex-
claim, "Thrice-blessed are these mortals who have seen these rites
and thus enter Hades. For them alone there is life; for the others
all is misery"? Perhaps the epiphany of the single ear of grain,
which must die and be buried in the earth in order to rise again as
a new life, reinforced by the story of Persephone's descent and rising, the sacred marriage rite, the wedding of water and earth, and
the proclamation of the new birth, enabled the initiates to better
understand and accept their own mortality and the mystery of the
cycle of life. The fruit is mother of the seed is mother of the fruit
is mother of the seed.

For the Romans, Ceres, who gave her name to our word *cereal*,
was the grain goddess who oversaw the harvest at the beginning of
August. This was her month, and to her the reapers gave thanks as
they cut straw and did a second mowing of their fields.

In medieval and early modern Europe, some of the harvest customs corresponded with those of the Greco-Roman world. In *The*

Stations of the Sun, Ronald Hutton describes some of these customs in the British Isles. All over Scotland and the arable districts of Wales, as well as in much of England and Ireland, the last sheaf of grain to be harvested was given special treatment. For one thing, it was generally named, though the name differed depending on the locale and whether possession of the sheaf was considered a liability or an asset. Names included the Cailleach, the Lame Goat, the Bitch, the Witch, the Maiden, the Neck, the Old Sow, the Frog, the Mare, the Winter, and the Hare. As some of these names suggest, there was, in some places, a palpable fear of the last sheaf, which was believed to contain an unlucky spirit, so that nobody wanted to be the one to cut it. In other places this fear was transmuted to jest, and the harvesting of the last sheaf was treated humorously. For example, in some cases blindfolded reapers competed by throwing sickles at it while watchers cheered or taunted. In Devon and Cornwall, the ceremony was called "crying the neck." After the reapers completed their work, they formed a circle and held aloft the ears of the last stalks of corn. The people would bow and shout "a neck, a neck, a neck, we have one" several times and cheer.

In some places, there was simply a great cheer at the end of the reaping, and the womenfolk tossed the harvest master in the air and kissed him. Sometimes there were customary shouts in rhymed verse. In other places, reapers tied the last sheaf with ribbons and took it to a nearby hilltop, where everyone cheered as the harvest queen held it aloft.

Often there was a competition among harvesting teams, and the first team to finish might send its last sheaf to the rivals as a mockery or insult. On the other hand, in many places the last sheaf was viewed as a trophy borne triumphantly home, where it was displayed until the following harvest, ground and baked into bread, or fed to horses. In the triumphal procession, the Maiden was sometimes carried by a young female worker. In another case, two sheaves were honored: the Old Woman, representing the harvest of the past year, and the Maiden, representing that of the coming year.

Eventually the decorating with ribbons escalated to dressing the sheaf in varying degrees of finery or weaving it into a rough human figure, sometimes crowned with flowers. The figure, variously named kern baby, corn dolly, harvest queen, maiden, or Cailleach, was sometimes identified with its bearer, who herself became the harvest queen.

On larger farms, the strongest image of the completed harvest was the cart that carried the last load home. It was "decorated with green boughs, flowers, and ribbons, drawn by beribboned horses, and had children, or womenfolk, or a chosen man, or . . . the harvest lord, sitting on top." All involved in the procession shouted or sang some variation of this chant:

> We have ploughed, we have sowed,
> We have reaped, we have mowed,
> We have brought home every load,
> Hip, hip, hip, Harvest home!

Once home, the reapers and gleaners enjoyed a harvest feast provided by the farm's owner. This included a meal (in the farmhouse kitchen or decorated barn, depending on the size of the company) that amply demonstrated the farmer's largess, as well as entertainment consisting of "toasts, drinking games, singing . . . dancing . . . [and] at times charades and short dramatic sketches."

During the nineteenth century, as social tensions between classes increased, the harvest suppers declined and farmers began to pay workers in cash. Advances in technology finished off the tradition. With the introduction of the mechanical reaper and baler, the number of harvesters needed in the mid-nineteenth century was a quarter of those required in the eighteenth. And by the mid-twentieth century combines had reduced the figure to two percent.

The Church stepped into the breach in the person of Rev. R. S. Hawker who, in 1843, invited his congregation in Cornwall to receive the sacrament "in the bread of the new corn." By the end of the century, it was an almost universal custom for villagers to process to the church, which was decorated with harvest symbols, for a morning communion service and to enjoy dancing and games at a community feast afterward. But in the twentieth century, this custom disappeared in most places where village communities declined, though in some places it was revived in the 1950s. Hutton notes the irony:

> The present ritual celebration of harvest consists principally of a Christian religious service which is itself much less than two centuries old. Nonetheless, the feeling persists in different forms that the season belongs to older deities as well. . . . Elizabethan observers of English harvest customs, after all, instinctively recalled the Roman worship of the corn-goddess Ceres.

Hutton reminds us that nineteenth-century folklore scholar Wilhelm Mannhardt demonstrates the similarity of then-current agricultural customs and those of the Greco-Roman world. James Frazer reinforces his arguments, suggesting that the treatment of the last sheaf provides evidence of a fertility cult and belief in an animating corn spirit. But Swedish scholar Carl von Sydow, writing in 1934, discounts this theory by demonstrating that the evidence all points to practical rather than religious explanations for the customs. Subsequent scholars suggest that the religious interpretation is speculative, not susceptible of disproof.

As might be expected, the Roman Church had early on assigned a major saint to this equinoctial harvest time: Michael the Archangel whom the Book of Revelations credits with defeating the rebellious "dragon" (Lucifer) who was then cast out of heaven. *The Catholic Encyclopedia* notes that as early as the sixth century, Michael was mentioned in three of the five masses for September 30. By the seventh century, he was assigned his own feast day, September 29. In the Middle Ages, Michaelmas was important enough to be designated a holy day of obligation; Christians were obliged to attend Mass as they were on Sundays. Some parishes had processions. Many families baked St. Michael's bannocks and enjoyed a meal of dressed goose. Though it is no longer a holy day of obligation, Catholics today still celebrate St. Michael on September

29. Early Church fathers claimed he was the "cherubim with the flaming sword" assigned by Yahweh "to guard the way to the tree of life" after the expulsion of Adam and Eve from paradise.

Perhaps it was this role of gatekeeper that Latvians had in mind when they insisted that by the celebration of Mikeli, all gardens should be harvested and all crops be stored, since "after Mikeli the gates are open for winter." Mara Mellena of the Latvian Institute describes a harvest ritual related to the Jumis, a field spirit viewed as the embodiment of fertility:

> Upon the completion of reaping, a Jumis-clump was left uncut, the ears were tied in a knot, bent to the ground, and weighed down with a stone or surrounded with soil. The grain was rubbed out of the ears in the clump and scattered in the prepared soil. The spirit and strength of the harvest was directed back into the earth, so that it could appear again in the new sowing. Later the last sheaf is plaited into a wreath or braid, taken home with great honor, and given to the mistress, who saves it in a place of honor until the next sowing. In the spring the grain rubbed from the wreath is sown, or the entire wreath is placed under a rock in the field.

Neighbors worked together for the harvest and celebrated its completion with a feast that included dancing, responsorial singing, and fertility rituals. One of these was an attempt by the boys to capture from the girls the *stebere*, a mock phallus made from a carrot and a pair of onions.

In Poland the harvest wreath, or *wieniec*, was given honored treatment. According to Stanley Garczynski of the Polish Genealogical Society of America, it was made of wheat and rye "in the shape of a large domed crown and decorated with ribbons, flowers, hazelnuts, and the fruit of the mountain ash tree." The exemplary young female harvester honored to wear it sat atop "a wagon pulled by four horses decorated in greenery and surrounded by other young maidens wearing flowers in their hair." The other workers followed as the wreath was taken to church for blessing. (Generally the conclusion of the harvest fell around August 15, the Feast of Mary's Assumption into Heaven.) After the blessing, the procession, accompanied by singing, headed for the manor house. Here the workers stopped at the gate but kept singing. When the owner came out, the young woman presented him with the wreath or even placed it on his head. The owner rewarded the harvesters, signaled the musicians to play, and danced with the young woman. All joined in the dancing and the feast began. The wreath "was cherished and given much care . . . hung in a prominent place . . . as a symbol of prosperity."

A similar custom of making and presenting the harvest wreath was found in Slovakia and the Czech Republic. It was called *obzinky* and followed the religious thanksgiving service, *Posviceni*. Here too the last sheaf was believed to have special powers of healing and fertility. It might be woven into wreaths for a bridal couple, placed in a pregnant woman's bed for safe delivery, or even put in hen houses to increase output. Part of the last sheaf was planted with the new seed the following spring.

One Czech/Slovakian tradition left a single shock of wheat standing in the field. Called the *boroda*, or beard, it was tied with ribbon or straw and left as an offering for the field mice in the hope they would not raid the barn's supply in winter. Another custom was to deliver the last sheaf—called a *dido*, or grandfather, if decorated with flowers or a *baba* if dressed as an old woman—to the landlord, who displayed it prominently until Christmas or possibly the next year's harvest.

Although enthusiasm for these customs had waned in an increasingly industrialized Europe by the twentieth century, some were still practiced in traditional agrarian communities.

Contemporary Celebrations Around the World

The Erntedanktag is an official holiday in Germany. Here, too, the *erntekrone*, or harvest crown of ears of grain, flowers, and fruit, is taken to church in solemn procession at the harvest festival, generally celebrated the first Sunday in October, which is usually the first Sunday following Michaelmas. (The nearly two-hundred-year-old Oktoberfest has its official roots not in the traditional harvest festival but in the wedding feast of Crown Prince Ludwig I of Bavaria and Princess Therese of Saxony-Hildburghausen on October 12, 1810.)

The grape harvest has traditionally received the primary focus in some places, especially in the Mediterranean area. Even today the Festa del Uva, or Festival of Grapes, in Tuscany marks the culmination of the grape-picking month of September with parades featuring floats constructed by various wards and outdoor feasts of roasted meat and specialty breads and sweets.

In *Festivals of Western Europe*, Dorothy Spicer describes a Spanish thanksgiving for the grape harvest, the Fiesta de la Vendimia, or Vintage Feast, which takes place each September in Jerez. "The morning is devoted to church services and parades" in which men in traditional attire sit atop magnificent Andalusian horses and accompany flower-decked carriages of women, also in traditional costumes.

> In the afternoon there are bullfights, horse racing, and other sports events, but in the evening people sit and sip the famous golden sherry of Jerez and listen to the haunting improvisations of flamenco singers.

Farther north, in pastoral societies, the occasion for rejoicing is the return of the herds from summer pasture. In Belalp, Switzerland, the second Sunday in September is Schäfer Sonntag, or Shepherd Sunday, which begins with a religious service to pray for the safe return of flocks. The villagers eagerly wait below as the shepherds start the animals down the mountain. When they are safely penned, a hearty lamb dinner concludes the event.

In Norway the summer mountain farms, or *saeters*, are run by young women who put out the cows and goats to lush pastures, milk and tend them, and make butter and cheese. When they return to the valley homesteads at Mikkelsmesse (Michaelmass), "with fat, flower-decked animals and full butter tubs," it is "occasion for great rejoicing—for dancing, singing, and feasting."

Of course Europeans are not the only ones who celebrate the harvest. According to the oral tradition of the African Ga people, they were plagued by famine during the migration that first brought them to what is now Accra, the capital of Ghana. After years of hardship, those who survived were motivated to undertake massive food production initiatives, which eventually yielded a huge harvest. Overjoyed at the end of their hunger, they celebrated by mocking the enemy; they called their festival Homowo, or "hooting at hunger."

In some African tribes, no one may enjoy the fruits of the harvest until the chief, as representative and leader of his people, ritually partakes of them. The Ngoni of Eastern Zambia, for example, have a religious rite of thanksgiving for the harvest in February (the equivalent of August in the northern hemisphere). At the Incwala, the paramount chief tastes the first fruits, which are offered to him by twelve local chiefs. Dancers from each tribe compete and the paramount chief names the winner. A cow is killed as symbol of the first harvest food, and once the chief drinks his blood, the people may eat.

Perhaps nowhere in Africa is this identification of the welfare of the king with the welfare of the tribe seen more clearly than in Swaziland. Celebrated just after the full moon nearest December 21 (their Summer Solstice), the Incwala, though it is often translated as First Fruits Festival, is best rendered, according to Richard Patricks of the Swaziland National Trust Commission, as Kingship Ceremony. It actually serves three purposes: to gain the blessing of the ancestors, to strengthen and even sanctify the kingship, and to celebrate the harvest season.

Preparation begins a month in advance when members of the Bemanti clan set out to collect water—some from the rivers, but most from the sea—in the form of foam. After a month, they return to the royal capital, where the king chews sacred foods prepared with the foam and spits them to the east and west to show he has broken off with the old year and opened the new. This marks the beginning of Little Incwala, two days of ritual dancing and singing. Two weeks later, Big Incwala begins with young boys walking over twenty-five miles to gather branches of the sacred lusekwane bush. The next day, the elders weave these between poles, creating a private sanctuary for the king, who withdraws therein and is administered traditional medicines. On the third day, a charging black bull is overpowered and slaughtered and provides ritual ingredients for doctoring the king. Warriors dance around the king's enclosure and entreat him to emerge. He does so the following day, in full warrior attire. He performs a sacred dance, bites and spits out certain plants of the first harvest, and throws the sacred gourd. On the fifth day he returns to seclusion and no one in the tribe is permitted to touch water, wear ornaments, sit on chairs or mats, shake hands, scratch, sing, dance, or engage in sexual activity. (As with the Hebrews, the end of the old year is marked by abstinence and purification.) On the final day, the elders prepare a great fire and burn articles symbolizing the old year, including the king's bedding and other household items, while others dance and sing and beg the ancestral spirits for rain. When the king emerges, his sanctuary is dismantled, and the New Year begins with feasting.

Asians traditionally celebrate the rice harvest. The timing varies depending on the geography. The people of Sabah in Malaysia celebrate the Pesta Ka'amatan in May. They consider rice a sacred food given to them by their creator god, who sacrificed his only daughter Huminodun so that her body parts might become food: Her flesh became rice, her head the coconut, her fingers ginger, her teeth maize, her knees yam, etc. Before dying, she requested that the people hold a great feast so that they would not forget her sacrifice. During the feast, her grief-stricken father played his bamboo flute and called out her name. Suddenly, from the jar containing the remains of the threshed rice, she arose, causing much rejoicing.

In gratitude, the people honor Bambaazon, the spirit of Huminodun embodied in the rice. Knowing that the rice spirit is at risk from pests and natural disasters, they perform the ritual of Magavau to protect, restore, and appease it. Traditionally, according to the Sabah Tourism Board, the ritual is conducted in the rice fields under the first full moon after the harvest. Preceded by a warrior brandishing his sword to ward off disruptive evil spirits, the high priestess and her assistants slowly process through the fields, chanting prayers to enable them to enter the spirit world in search of Bambaazon. Each time a priestess meets and recovers a stray part of Bambaazon, she emits a piercing cry of joy and encouragement to the others to keep searching. When all member-spirits have been summoned, they find a meal ritually laid out for them on banana leaves: chicken, eggs, betel leaves, nuts, tobacco, and the finest rice wine. A second offering is placed on a bamboo platform for the Bambaazon to take back to the spirit world for the creatures that would otherwise eat the rice in the field. There follows a great feasting that includes traditional dancing and the enthronement of a harvest queen, a maiden judged to resemble the sacrificed Huminodun in beauty of heart, mind, and body.

Contemporary Chinese, Taiwanese, Japanese, Vietnamese, and Koreans call their harvest festival Mid-Autumn Festival or Moon Festival and celebrate it around the time of the Fall Equinox. Originally a day of thanksgiving for the rice harvest, in modern times the emphasis has been on families gathering in parks or gardens or on hilltops to view the harvest moon and to enjoy a special meal that includes moon cakes, whose shape and sweetness symbolize not only the beauty of the heavenly body but also the unity of the family itself.

One of the three major festivals in the Chinese calendar and dating back to the Song dynasty of over a thousand years ago, Chung Ch'ui, a public holiday, is acclaimed the birthday of the moon and observed over a three-day period at the time of the harvest moon. Families gather to eat a thanksgiving meal of roasted pig, harvested fruits, and moon cakes, usually stuffed with bean paste and egg yolk or fruit and preserves and believed to bring good luck and a plentiful harvest for the next year. Sometimes they are stamped, like the moon itself, with the image of a rabbit. Children enjoy puppet shows and make colorful paper lanterns shaped like flowers or animals, inside of which a candle provides soft "moonglow" as they join in processions. Traditionally this is also a time for lovers to rendezvous and enjoy their cakes with wine while viewing the full moon and perhaps reciting from the host of poems honoring the occasion.

The Taiwanese mark Tiong-cchiu Choeh by climbing to the top of a hill and enjoying a picnic that includes moon cakes. They give thanks to the earth god Tu-ti-Gong for the year's harvest and pray for the next year's harvest as well.

The Japanese celebrate Hounen-Odori; the literal translation is "year of wealth and richness" combined with "dance." Rural villages often hold festivities under the full moon in the harvested fields or other open areas. Musicians from all over Japan supply entertainment. Parades of floats bear images of the gods, while at the Imperial Palace, the emperor offers the first fruits of the paddy fields to them. Even urban dwellers enjoy *tsukimi* or moon viewing, a ritual believed to purify the world. Facing the moonrise, people sit at tables laden with offerings to the moon spirit: the seven grasses of autumn, cooked vegetables, and rice dumplings.

On the island of Aguni, near mainland Okinawa, prayers are offered during the Yagan Orimi not just for a good harvest of crops but also for the safe delivery of infants, making clear the connection between the life-giving qualities of the earth and those of its people.

In Korea half the population is on the move on Ch'usok, traveling to family reunions, usually at the home of the eldest son, and visiting ancestral gravesites. Preparations begin with the women shopping for ingredients for the feast, the specialty of which is *song pyun*, crescent mooncakes made with dough of finely ground, newly harvested rice and filled with a sweetened mixture of beans, peas, persimmons, toasted sesame seeds, and/or chestnuts. As they make the cakes, several generations of women share their life stories and sing traditional songs. On Ch'usok morning, the family performs a memorial ceremony at the table, which includes ritual kneeling and bowing to the floor and offering wine and food to the ancestors. After this, the ceremonial food is removed and family members enjoy their meal and reminisce about their departed loved ones. Often they then take some of the food to the cemetery, where they clean and prepare gravesites for the winter. The rest of the day's activities include singing folk music, performing a traditional circle dance, and enjoying athletic events like tug-of-war, wrestling, archery, and "turtle tag." Koreans see the holiday as an occasion to give thanks for the harvest and affirm family and community bonds.

Children are the focus of the Vietnamese mid-autumn Tet-Trung Thu, also called the Children's Festival. Tradition has it that parents neglected their children of necessity during the hard work of harvesting. To make amends, they used the festival to show their affection. Children make masks and paper lanterns in the shape of boats, cranes, dragons, hares, and unicorns. Then in the light of the harvest moon, they carry their lighted lanterns in processions, perform traditional dances accompanied by drums and cymbals, and compete for prizes and scholarships. As in other Asian countries, people celebrate the harvest by eating moon cakes or presenting them as gifts and honor their deceased relatives by burning incense.

As the Roman Catholic Church did in the West, Buddhism reinterpreted preexisting seasonal festivals with an overlay of its own liturgical feasts and practices. The thanks offered to local deities at Tibetan harvest festivals, though reflecting an earlier tradition, are externally Buddhist, and harvest celebrations in many Buddhist countries include a ritual enactment from the life of a *buddha* or *bodhisattva*, an enlightened being who, out of compassion, forgoes nirvana in order to save others. Tibet and Thailand have become famous for these professional performances.

In eastern and northern India, the harvesting of the winter crops of rice and wheat is celebrated at Holi. This was once a fertility festival and incorporates a pole similar to the European maypole that may be a phallic symbol. This full-moon festival marks the end of the year and celebrates the arrival of the New Year and spring at a time equivalent to February or March in the Gregorian calendar. On the first night, people gather around a great bonfire, giving thanks to Agni, the fire god, and offering fruits of the harvest for his consumption. The fire heralds the hot days of summer to come and celebrates the mythological Prahlad, who, because of his goodness and faith, was miraculously saved from a fiery death and therefore symbolizes the triumph of good over evil. At the bonfires loud horns and drums accompany street dancing. The next day people rub ashes from the fire on their foreheads for good luck. In a spirit of joyful, reckless abandon, they make colored water using a variety of powders and "play Holi" by filling buckets, balloons, squirt guns, and sundry containers and noisily dousing neighbors, friends, and strangers—young and old. Everyone wears old clothes and joins in the celebration. As with Saturnalia, the usual rules regarding caste, sex, and status are in abeyance and vocal and gestural obscenities are permitted. Revelry rules.

The rice harvest is celebrated at Onam in late August or early September in Kerala in southwestern India. After preparing for the feast by cleaning their homes and decorating the entrances with flowers, families give thanks at the temple and offer prayers to King Mahabali and Lord Vishnu. Upon their return, the head of the household gives everyone new clothes and a lavish feast follows. The celebration lasts ten days and includes singing and dancing as well as boat races, fireworks, performances of Kathakali dance, and parades featuring decorated elephants.

Bonfires and feasts also mark Pongal, a four-day harvest festival celebrated in South India in January. This festival of the Tamils, which some historians believe to be almost two thousand years old, lasts for four days. On the first day, people clean out their houses and light a bonfire to burn old and useless items and herald a fresh beginning in the New Year. They create *kolam* on the floors of their homes—designs drawn with a white paste made from newly harvested rice and outlined in red mud. On this day, they offer *pongal*, a sweet rice dish for which the holiday is named, to the rain gods Bhogi or Indran in thanksgiving for the harvest. On the second day, they offer pongal to Lord Surya, the sun god, and kolam are drawn in his honor. Newly harvested sugarcane, turmeric bulbs, and coconuts are arranged on plantain leaves and placed on the kolam. On the third day, they honor the cattle for providing milk and pulling the plows by bathing them, polishing and decorating their horns, garlanding their necks, and feeding them the pongal that had been offered to the gods. This is followed by cattle races and a bullfight. On the last day, they honor the birds by offering them colored balls of cooked rice.

Reminiscent of the British Harvest Home described by Hutton, the traditional harvest celebration of Barbados begins as the last caravan of carts wends its way into the mill yard and a laborer strikes a gong, the signal to shout "Crop over!" Originating in the 1780s when Barbados was the world's largest sugar cane grower, the festival declined with the industry there and disappeared in the 1940s. But in the 1970s it was revived and now Crop Over is the one of the most colorful events in the West Indies, a five-week extravaganza culminating on the first Monday in August. It begins when the last canes are ceremonially delivered and the most productive male and female cutters are crowned king and queen of the festival. The carnival-like festivities include competitions for costumes, band music, singing, and calypso dancing.

Each autumn in Alaska when the salmon-fishing season draws to an end and the berries are harvested, the people celebrate with a series of festivals and religious ceremonies, including ritual songs and dances executed in masks and ceremonial dress to the accompaniment of drums, rattles, and whistles. They appeal to the spirits who have influence over their lives as well as to the souls of animals on whom they depend.

The Cherokee tribe of North America celebrates the Ripe Corn Festival in September, giving thanks to Selu, spirit of the corn and First Mother, and honoring Mother Earth for providing food. They call the September moon *Duliidsdi*, the nut moon, and the gathering of fruits and nuts (chestnuts are a staple) from the trees and shrubs culminates in the Brush Feast Festival. During their October *Nowatequa*, or harvest festival, they give thanks to all creatures of the earth and fields on whom they rely for sustenance and to the Apportioner, the sun goddess Unelanuhi, who divides the year into seasons.

Aveni recounts the history of what is now celebrated as Thanksgiving Day in the United States. When the first English immigrants to the New World survived a hard winter in Plymouth, Massachusetts, and harvested a bountiful crop in the fall of 1621, they invited the local natives to celebrate with a feast and games. Two years later, after a drought compelled the Pilgrims to fast and pray and late summer rains saved the crop, Governor William Bradford issued a proclamation calling for a second feast on November 29, 1623, to thank Almighty God for "an abundant harvest of Indian corn, wheat, beans, squashes, and garden vegetables . . . [as well as] game . . . fish and clams." Gratitude was also to be rendered to the great Father who "has protected us from the ravages of the savages, has spared us from pestilence and disease, [and] has granted us freedom to worship." (The decree made no mention of giving thanks to the "savage" Native Americans who contributed much to the survival of the poachers.)

For the next century and a half, end-of-harvest thanksgiving was sporadically observed in October, November, or even December, depending on the colony. In 1789 George Washington declared Thursday, November 16, a national Thanksgiving holiday, and six years later, taking a decidedly political turn from Bradford's edict, proclaimed February 19 an annual celebration on which to give thanks to God "for the manifold and signal mercies which distinguish our lot as a nation; particularly for the possession of constitutions of government which . . . establish liberty within order."

Some states, however, preferred to keep their own harvest celebrations. At the urging of Sarah Josepha Buell Hale, an editor and activist who organized a letter-writing campaign, Abraham Lincoln proclaimed that Thanksgiving was to be observed in all the states, recommending that all implore the Almighty "to heal the wounds of the nation, to the full enjoyment of peace, harmony, and Union." In the nineteenth century, the holiday was observed by attending church in the morning, followed by a family feast featuring a roasted turkey. It remained for the 1941 Congress, in response to Franklin Delano Roosevelt's proposal, to set the annual celebration on the fourth Thursday in November.

Today more Americans travel on Thanksgiving weekend than at any other time of the year. Some families still attend church together. While the original Plymouth Thanksgiving featured playing games, contemporary Americans are more likely to be spectators— either in stadiums or in front of televisions—of football games, which are often preceded by extravagant parades boasting lavish floats. While thanks is typically offered for the food on the table and the family gathered around it, there is not always a conscious acknowledgment of the event as a harvest feast. Despite the contention of some scholars that the American Thanksgiving is a direct descendant of the British Harvest Home, the connection is not necessarily appreciated by average Americans. Perhaps this is because the feast comes as much as two months after the harvest. Or perhaps because, with the exception of a dwindling number of farm families, modern Americans are generally out of touch with the seasonal cycles of agriculture, now largely controlled by agribusinesses.

The array of harvest festivals is stunning in its diversity. Yet despite the differences in crops and the seasons of harvesting them, despite the differences in climate, culture, and religion, despite, even, the differences in historical time, we see common themes and elements running through the festivals.

Preparation often involves some kind of purification of participants and/or dwellings. Individuals fast, pray, reflect on past offenses, confess sins, do penance, and are cleansed in the sea. They build bonfires, throw away old clothes, and strip their homes of useless items or things reminiscent of the old harvest. In a few cases, they construct temporary shelters for the event.

The religious rituals themselves often involve the marriage of deities or their human representatives (or at least the selection of a harvest king and queen). Other common features are processions to a temple or church with revered objects such as a statue of a deity, the last sheaf of wheat, or an image made from it; the sacrifice of an animal; and the offering of newly harvested food to deities, animals, and/or spirits of ancestors. There are also chanting, singing of sacred songs, ecstatic shouting, ritual dances, and the enactment of stories of gods or religious heroes. The last sheaf generally gets special treatment: a threshing that releases its spirit to the earth or a transformation into a doll, a crown, or a wreath that is honored and preserved until planting time when it is buried with the new seed.

Always there is a harvest feast. It may be a supper supplied to the reapers by the landowner, a meal for which family members have traveled long distances to be reunited, or a large community affair. But it always features traditional foods of the locale and is considered a time to give thanks—to the deities, to the harvesters and their animal helpers, and to all deserving gratitude for the gifts of the season and of the year.

The feast is often followed by more secular diversions: singing, dancing, and musical competitions; fireworks; races and games; parades, floats, and masquerades; and new clothes—all to mark the beginning of the new (agricultural) year. For our ancestors living close to the earth, surely it was the happiest time of the year!

WAYS TO CELEBRATE

Decorate your home to celebrate the harvest.

☙   Make a swag of dried ears of corn to hang on the door of your home.

⑥ Make a grapevine wreath for the door.

⑥ Fill a shallow basket with small pumpkins, gourds, Indian corn, acorns, etc., and use it as a table centerpiece.

⑥ Make a corn doll and display it in your home until Winter Solstice. Then take it down and store it until spring. When you prepare your garden or window box, crumble the corn doll into the soil where you bury your seeds or plant your cuttings, offering Mother Earth's honored fruits back to her. For suggestions for making a corn doll, see Judith Corwin's *Harvest Festivals Around the World*. There are also many websites that offer instructions and ideas.

Prepare for the new year.

⑥ Clean out the garage, attic, or basement and have a yard sale. Use the money to provide a "harvest" for the hungry by donating it to Oxfam.

⑥ Exorcise the "clutter demons" from the house.

⑥ Clean out the car and wash and wax it for the colder months to come.

⑥ If you are a teacher, make a New Year's resolution. For example, give yourself a challenging deadline to know the names of all your students at the beginning of this new term. Resolve to read one important book a month related to your field. Research ways to make your teaching more student-centered. Resolve to be more thorough in your preparation for each class, or more organized in your presentations.

⑥ If you are a student, determine to set up a realistic, adequate study schedule and stick to it, start right away on projects or papers whose deadlines are mid-semester, do assigned homework on time, or bring an open mind to required courses and subjects you don't especially like.

    If you have completed your formal education, start the New Year by learning something new. Sign up for an enrichment class at a local college's Continuing Education Program or at the YMCA or the local senior center, or online.

Welcome the change of seasons into your home and garden.

    Change the tablecloth and place mats, the bed and bath linens, or the sofa throw to reflect the cooler, quieter time of the year.

    Get out the heavier blankets.

    If frost is possible in your locale now, bring in the houseplants that summered outdoors and harvest herbs for drying.

    Plant mums in the garden or window box.

    If you've already done this and they're blooming, bring fresh mums into the house.

Practice hospitality.

    This is a good time (a full two months before the traditional family Thanksgiving dinner in the United States) to host a harvest meal for some of the people outside your family who have been good to you. It could be simple (barley vegetable soup, salad, bread, grapes, and beverage) or more elaborate, depending on your resources.

    Another way of being hospitable is to volunteer to cook or serve at a soup kitchen.

    Using the Internet or your local library, research recipes for the special foods people in different parts of the world eat at their harvest festivals; prepare one dish to include in your Thanksgiving meal. Or have a potluck Thanksgiving and ask each guest to bring a harvest festival dish from a different part of the world.

Celebrate the harvest moon.

☾ Check your calendar or newspaper to see when the harvest moon will appear and make a date to admire it with someone you love.

☾ Make paper lanterns of different colors, install a candle in each, and set them outside to mark the transition from twelve hours of light to twelve hours of dark on the equinox.

☾ Here's my recipe for cookies that have the shape and color of the full moon:

————————

MOON CAKES

Ingredients:

½ cup (1 stick) butter
½ cup confectioners' sugar
1 cup sifted flour
1 cup chopped nuts of choice (pecans, walnuts, almonds)
½ teaspoon vanilla
additional confectioners' sugar for coating

Preheat oven to 350°. In mixer, cream butter and sugar. Beat in flour, nuts, and vanilla. Pinch off small pieces of dough, roll between palms, and place on cookie sheets. (Children might have fun helping with this part.) Bake for about 15 to 20 minutes. Remove from sheets and roll in bowl of confectioners' sugar. Cool on rack. Makes 2-3 dozen, depending on size. (Note: If coating melts and browns, roll again when cookies have cooled down a bit, but not altogether or the coating won't stick.)

Send thank-you notes.

☾ Write one to your significant other explaining why you are grateful to be sharing your life with him/her.

⑥ Write to your parents and grandparents (whether living or dead) thanking them for the gift of life and the lessons and values they passed on to you. Let them know how you have used them. Mail the ones written to the living.

⑥ Write to aunts, uncles, cousins, brothers, and sisters, thanking them for all they contributed to your life while you were growing up—and since.

⑥ Write to your children, grandchildren, nieces, and nephews, thanking them for enriching your life.

⑥ Write to your best friends from elementary school, high school, and college, even if you haven't been in touch for years. Remind them of the good times you shared and the hard times they helped you through, and thank them.

⑥ Write to the teachers who taught you how to read, write, think for yourself, and discover your creativity. Tell them about your current projects and thank them for their role in making them possible.

⑥ Write to the coaches and trainers who helped you learn to respect your body and tell them what a difference it's made.

⑥ Write to the friends and colleagues and neighbors who are there for you and thank them for their loyalty and generosity.

⑥ Write to the civic leaders you think have done a good job this year: your local mayor or governor, your council persons, your senators and representative, national leaders of your own and other countries. Thank them for taking their job seriously and making the world a little better.

⑥ Write to the people you serve who keep you in business. Thank them for trusting you.

⑥ Write to the people who serve you with care and honesty—your doctor, minister, therapist, mail carrier, financial adviser, social worker, hairdresser, newspaper carrier, waitpersons at your favorite restaurants, the people who service your car and house. Thank them for their expertise and kindness. (If you don't know the address, leave the note where the recipient will be pleasantly surprised to find it, like in the mail box or on top of the trash can or recyclables pile.)

◐ Make a special effort to say thanks to the folks who provide for your day-to-day needs: the bank teller, salesperson, grocery checkout clerk, medical technician, cafeteria worker, and insurance representative (even though you were on hold for ten minutes).

◐ Write to a filmmaker, musician, writer, or scientific researcher whose work has changed your life for the better. Thank her/him for this contribution.

Celebrate the season with your body and spirit.

◐ Enjoy a fall festival.

◐ Take a hayride.

◐ Play football or soccer with the kids.

◐ Dance your feelings of light and dark, and end with balance.

◐ On the Fall Equinox, when everyone on earth experiences the same number of hours of light and darkness, honor this common experience by calling or e-mailing someone you know in another country: a pen pal from childhood, an exchange student you went to school with, a friend you made on a visit to another country, or a colleague or family member who now lives in another part of the world. Share your experiences of this time of year.

CELEBRATE THE HARVEST

AN AUTUMN EQUINOX RITUAL

Gather indoors or out, depending on the weather. A large cart wheel decorated with seasonal flowers and harvest symbols has been set flat on a table on a small lazy Susan. Four large candles in autumnal colors are set in it to symbolize the four seasons.

Narrator   Once again this year the sun comes to the midpoint on its journey between its highest and lowest paths in the sky. The days have grown shorter and the nights cooler as the sun moves irrevocably toward the Winter Solstice. The riot of colors and smells in the summer gardens has quieted down. Now classrooms and football fields are noisy with life. Bears and chipmunks are preparing for hibernation. Wild geese and gray whales are heading south. The crops are harvested for another year. It is the Autumn Equinox.

All sing the following words to the melody of "Holy, Holy, Holy."

All sing   Holy, holy, holy, is the ground we stand on.
Blessed earth, our mother dear to all her children here.
Bountiful and giving is our land in fall.
Now at the harvest, we give thanks for all.

Narrator   On this day—as at the Vernal Equinox—everyone on earth experiences the same number of hours of light and darkness. It is time once again to think about our brothers and sisters in other countries and continents and hemispheres, our human kin in other time zones and climate zones. It is time once again to remind ourselves that our differences of culture, race, government, and religion do not matter. Our differences in clothing, diet, and lifestyle do not matter. On this day we have an important common experience. On this day nature reminds us that we are the same. We depend on the same sun for warmth and light. We rely on the same sky for rainwater, the same earth for food. We breathe the same air. Our differences are superficial compared to this most basic, most vital commonality: We share this dazzling and dangerous natural world. May this sharing unite us. We light candles now in honor of the light we share with all humankind on this day.

Four participants who have volunteered or been recruited in advance come forward. Each lights a candle while speaking. If acoustics pose a problem, the Leader can speak as the Lighters light the candles.

Lighter 1   In the name of everyone here, I light this candle for all those who live in Asia and Europe.

Lighter 2   In the name of everyone here, I light this candle for all those who live in Africa, Australia, and Antarctica.

Lighter 3   In the name of everyone here, I light this candle for all those who live in South and North America.

Lighter 4   In the name of everyone here, I light this candle as a pledge of our promise to work for peace among all peoples.

Turning the Wheel of the Year

Two Turners come forward and stand on either side of the wheel. After each statement from the Leader, they turn the wheel one quarter clockwise.

Narrator   The circle of the autumn wreath here symbolizes the Wheel of the Year, the complete cycle of the four seasons, represented by four candles. It is decorated with the flowers of fall and symbols of the harvest.

Leader   We invite you to join in turning the wheel, responding as indicated in your programs.

Leader   This equinoctial light we share—

All   And join with people everywhere.

Leader   We turn the wheel; we urge the sun—

All   To stay the course that's now begun.

Leader   We turn the wheel of death and birth.

All   We change the seasons of the earth!

Leader   We turn the wheel to beckon fall.

All   And honor the light that's shared by all!

Narrator   Let us celebrate our oneness in song and send this song to every corner of the universe.

Choir sings "Gather the Spirit" by Jim Scott.

Choir   Gather the spirit, harvest the power.
Our separate fires will kindle one flame.
Witness the mystery of this hour.
Our trials in this light appear all the same.

Gather in peace, gather in thanks.
Gather in sympathy now and then.
Gather in hope, compassion, and strength.
Gather to celebrate once again.

Gather the spirit growing in all,
drawn by the moon and fed by the sun.
Winter to spring, and summer to fall,
the chorus of life resounding as one.

Gather in peace, gather in thanks.
Gather in sympathy now and then.
Gather in hope, compassion, and strength.

Gather to celebrate once again.

Striking the Balance

Leader   The equinoxes are a time of astronomical equality. All over the earth, in Europe, Asia, Africa, and the Americas, we find ancient structures—stone cairns, pyramids, temples, and earthen mounds—whose precise east-west orientation marks the midpoint of the sun's journey, the balance point of light and dark, when neither has the advantage, when all is balanced for the moment, like a gymnast perfectly extended on parallel bars or a dancer defying gravity in a leap of longing. Only in silence do we appreciate song. Or as T. S. Eliot reminds us in *Four Quartets*, "only at the still point of the turning world" can we have the dance, "and there is only the dance."

A Dancer or group of Dancers performs a ballet or modern dance reflecting the tone of the ritual.

Narrator   As the dark waxes and the daylight wanes and the temperature drops, so sometimes do our spirits. Numbered are the days when we can take after-dinner walks, visit on neighbors' porches or stoops, and gather at parks or courts for evening games. The swimming pools are closed. Vacation is spent. The garden begins to wilt, some trees begin to yellow. We have left behind the brilliance and heat and extroversion of summer and are set irrevocably on the path to the dark and cold and introspection of winter. It is a palpable, poignant reminder that zeniths are short-lived, that every prime is followed by decline, that there must be balance in the universe and in our lives. On this day of equal light and dark, let us acknowledge this need by responding to the following litany: "May we find the balance."

Leader	In our busy daily lives with demands of work and family,
All	May we find the balance.
Leader	In our pursuit of health: physical, mental, spiritual,
All	May we find the balance.
Leader	In our striving for professional success and our treatment of co-workers,
All	May we find the balance.
Leader	Between our desires and our duties,
All	May we find the balance.
Leader	Between our rights and our responsibilities,
All	May we find the balance.
Leader	In our loving and our letting go,
All	May we find the balance.

For suggestions on a spontaneous litany rather than a scripted one, see page xvii.

Reader 1 To every thing there is a season,
and a time to every purpose under heaven:
A time to be born, and a time to die;
a time to plant, and a time to uproot the plant.
A time to kill, and a time to heal;
a time to tear down, and a time to build.
A time to weep, and a time to laugh;
a time to mourn, and a time to dance.
A time to scatter stones, and a time to gather them;
a time to embrace, and a time to be far from embraces.
A time to seek, and a time to lose;
a time to keep, and a time to cast away.
A time to rend, and a time to sew;
a time to be silent, and a time to speak.

A time to love, and a time to hate;
a time of war, and a time of peace.

—Ecclesiastes 3:1-8

Guitarist sings "Turn! Turn! Turn!" by Pete Seeger.

Celebrating the Harvest

Narrator   As the sun withdrew, our ancient ancestors surely ex-
            perienced a degree of sadness, even fear, for they de-
            pended on it for light and warmth much more directly
            than we do. Yet in many places, the Fall Equinox was
            also a time of harvest, and if the crops were abundant,
            providing a food supply for the winter as well as grain
            and seeds for the next spring's planting, then it was also
            a time for thanksgiving. But whether the harvesting is
            done in late summer and fall, as is our practice, or in
            spring or even winter as in some other places, it is al-
            ways cause for celebration.

Leader   At harvest time the ancient Sumerians expressed their
            feeling of security by celebrating the marriage of
            Inanna, goddess of the storehouse, and Dumuzi, god of
            vegetation.

Narrator   The Egyptians dedicated their spring harvest celebration
            to Min-Horus, whose descendant, the pharaoh, ritually
            united with his queen in a sacred marriage, mirroring
            the power of life visible in the fruits of the fields.

Leader   The Canaanite festivals began at Spring Equinox with
            the barley harvest and continued two months later
            with the wheat harvest. Two months later still the
            grape harvest began, and Fall Equinox marked the end
            of the agricultural year.

Narrator   Ancient Hebrews—like modern Jews—celebrated
            three different holy days at this time of year. Sukkot

was originally a festival of thanksgiving for the harvest. Rosh Hashanah begins a time of penitence and prayer and family gatherings for special meals. Yom Kippur, the Day of Atonement, observed ten days later, is a time of fasting, reflection, and ritual prayer that includes communal confession of sins.

Leader   The Chinese celebrated the Great Cha at the end of each agricultural year.

Narrator For the ancient Greeks, the autumn festival was dedicated to Demeter, goddess of the earth's fruits. Her Mysteries at Eleusis were celebrated for two thousand years. Initiates underwent a ritual purification, relived Persephone's descent into the Underworld, and experienced a revelation when viewing a single ear of grain held on high in silence.

Leader   For the Romans, Ceres was the grain goddess who oversaw the harvest at the beginning of August.

Narrator When the carts loaded with sheaves were brought in at Harvest Home all over the British Isles, special treatment was accorded the last sheaf harvested. It was generally named, sometimes feared for containing the only remaining spirit of the grain, and almost always treated with respect—cheered, bowed to, decorated, dressed as a human figure, carried aloft in procession by a harvest queen to church or to a hilltop or to the home of the landowner, where it was displayed in a place of honor until plowing time, when it was mixed with the spring seed. This corn doll, often named Maiden or Old Woman was a symbol of continuity. The Maiden grew into the Old Woman, which then fed the seedling that became the Maiden, which ripened into the Old Woman. They were one, even as Demeter and Persephone were one.

Leader   In Latvia the last sheaf was plaited into a wreath or braid, which was buried at spring sowing. In Poland the wreath of wheat and rye was made in the shape of a large domed crown, decorated, and worn by the harvest queen, who sat atop a beribboned wagon drawn by horses in procession. A similar custom was practiced in the Czech Republic and Slovakia, where the last sheaf was believed to have special powers of healing and fertility. Germany still features a procession of the harvest crown as part of its official holiday on the first Sunday in October.

Narrator The grape harvest often receives primary focus in the Mediterranean area. The Festa del Uva (Festival of Grapes) in Tuscany and the Fiesta de la Vendimia (Vintage Feast) in Spain are both observed in September. Later in our ritual, we'll join in spirit with people there to celebrate the fruit of the vine.

Leader   The Quechua Indians of the Andes Mountains, more commonly known as the Incas, gave thanks to their sun god Inti for their wheat, corn, barley, and sugar cane. They sang this song to celebrate the harvest.

          Choir sings "Sung at Harvest."

Choir   Come my sisters, come my brothers,
          At the sounding of the horn;
          On the hillsides, on the mountains,
          Harvest we the yellow corn.
          Golden shines our father sun;
          Silver shines our mother moon;
          Sickles flashing, fill our baskets,
          Reaping in the yellow noon.

          Praise to thee, O mighty Inti,
          For the barley and the cane!
          In the wheat fields, in the cornfields,

> Harvest we the yellow grain.
> Softly blows the autumn wind;
> Gently wave the silken leaves;
> Reapers singing, press we onward,
> Tying up the yellow sheaves.

Narrator The people of Ghana in Africa called their harvest festival Homowo, "hooting at hunger." In eastern Zambia, the February harvest celebration is marked by dance competitions, and no one may partake of the fruits of the harvest until the chief ritually tastes them.

Leader The Incwala (First Fruits Festival) serves three purposes in Swaziland: to gain the ancestors' blessing, to strengthen the kingship, and to rejoice in the harvest.

Narrator Asian peoples generally celebrate the rice harvest. The people of Sabah in Malaysia believe rice was given to them by their creator god, who sacrificed his only daughter Huminodun so that her flesh could become rice. They celebrate Pesta Ka'amatan in her honor.

Leader People in China, Taiwan, Japan, Vietnam, and Korea call their mid-autumn festival Moon Festival. Initially a day of thanksgiving for the rice harvest, the focus is now on the gathering of families outdoors—on hilltops when possible—to admire the harvest moon and enjoy a meal that features a sweet delicacy shaped like the moon.

Narrator In many Buddhist countries, especially Tibet and Thailand, harvest celebrations include a ritual enactment of an episode from the life of a saintly hero.

Leader In eastern and northern India, the harvesting of the winter crops of rice and wheat is celebrated at Holi, a full moon festival in February or March. It marks the end of the old year and the beginning of the new and features bonfires and revelry.

Narrator   The people of Kerala in southwestern India celebrate Onam, a ten-day harvest festival in late August or early September. They clean and decorate their homes, wear new clothes, and give thanks at the temple. Then they enjoy a family feast, singing and dancing, parades, boat races, fireworks, and dance performances.

Leader   In South India, the festival of Pongal, possibly two thousand years old, lasts four days. People strip their homes of useless things, burn them in a bonfire, and mark the beginning of the New Year with *kolam*, designs made on the floors with a rice paste. In thanksgiving, they offer *pongal*, a sweet rice mixture, to the gods of rain and sun, as well as to the cattle who helped with the harvest.

Narrator   In Barbados, when the final cart arrives in the mill yard, everyone shouts, "Crop Over!" and the last sugar canes are ceremonially delivered. The best cutters are crowned king and queen, and the festival begins.

Leader   Alaskans celebrate the harvest of berries and salmon with ritual songs and dances, praying to the spirits who influence their lives and to the souls of animals on whom they depend.

Narrator   The Cherokee of North America hold their Ripe Corn Festival in September, honoring Mother Earth and thanking Selu, spirit of the corn. The Brush Feast Festival celebrates the gathering of fruits and nuts. And at the harvest festival in October, the Nowatequa, they offer thanks to all creatures who provide for their livelihood and to the sun goddess, who divides the year into seasons.

Leader   The official Thanksgiving Day in the United States is celebrated on the fourth Thursday in November. Despite its original association with the sharing of a harvest meal by Pilgrims and Native Americans, it is late in the year for a harvest festival. Still it is an occasion for giving thanks for the nourishment of food and family.

All sing "Give Thanks for the Corn."

All Sing   Give thanks for the corn and the wheat that are reaped,
for labor well done and barns that are heaped,
for the sun and the dew and the sweet honeycomb,
for the rose and the song and the harvest brought
home.

Give thanks for the mills and the farms of our land,
for craft and the strength in the work of our hands,
for the beauty our artists and poets have wrought,
for the hope and affection our friendships have
brought.

Give thanks for the homes that with kindness are
blessed,
for seasons of plenty and well-deserved rest,
for our country extending from sea unto sea,
for ways that have made it a land for the free.

Taking Stock

Narrator   Now is the time to look within. For many cultures and religions, the end of the agricultural year is the end of the calendar year, the time to take stock, to examine what has been accomplished over the past year, a time for getting rid of old baggage, for fasting and praying and purifying, a time for new resolve to do better, to be kinder, to love more generously. Let us listen to this poem by Elizabeth Bishop and then take a few minutes to think about where we have been in the past year and where we want to go in the coming one. Perhaps if we

carefully plant the tears of the past year, they will water
the hopes of the coming year.

Reader 2 September rain falls on the house.
In the failing light, the old grandmother
sits in the kitchen with the child
beside the Little Marvel Stove,
reading the jokes from the almanac,
laughing and talking to hide her tears.

She thinks that her equinoctial tears
and the rain that beats on the roof of the house
were both foretold by the almanac,
but only known to a grandmother.
The iron kettle sings on the stove.
She cuts some bread and says to the child,

It's time for tea now; but the child
is watching the teakettle's small hard tears
dance like mad on the hot black stove,
the way the rain must dance on the house.
Tidying up, the old grandmother
hangs up the clever almanac

on its string. Birdlike, the almanac
hovers half open above the child,
hovers above the old grandmother
and her teacup full of dark brown tears.
She shivers and says she thinks the house
feels chilly, and puts more wood in the stove.

It was to be, says the Marvel Stove.
I know what I know, says the almanac.
With crayons the child draws a rigid house
and a winding pathway. Then the child
puts in a man with buttons like tears
and shows it proudly to the grandmother.

But secretly, while the grandmother
busies herself about the stove,
the little moons fall down like tears
from between the pages of the almanac
into the flower bed the child
has carefully placed in the front of the house.

Time to plant tears, says the almanac.
The grandmother sings to the marvelous stove
and the child draws another inscrutable house.

—"Sestina"

Silence

Litany of Thanksgiving

Narrator   The harvest season is a time to give thanks—not just for our food but for all the other things and people we need in order to live a meaningful life. Let us offer our Litany of Gratitude. We invite you to respond with "We give thanks!"

Leader   For the miracles of sun and moon and stars,

All   We give thanks!

Leader   For oceans and seas and bays and rivers and lakes and streams,

All   We give thanks!

Leader   For the beauty of the earth in all its seasons, its mountains and valleys, its forests and deserts, and all its vegetation,

All   We give thanks!

Leader   For all the critters of the earth, wild and tame, great and small,

All   We give thanks!

Leader   For the bounty of the harvest and all those who made
          it possible,

All   We give thanks!

Leader   For life, liberty, education, the right to vote, and the
          freedom to pursue happiness,

All   We give thanks!

Leader   For the blessing of our families: spouses, significant
          others, parents, children, brothers, sisters, grandpar-
          ents, aunts, uncles, nieces, nephews, and cousins,

All   We give thanks!

Leader   For the blessing of good friends, old and new, who sup-
          port and encourage us,

All   We give thanks!

Leader   For the blessing of kind colleagues and co-workers and
          neighbors,

All   We give thanks!

Leader   For our teachers and coaches and trainers, our doctors
          and ministers and therapists, our social workers, fire-
          fighters, police officers, and all who care for our bod-
          ies, minds, and spirits,

All   We give thanks!

Leader   For all civic leaders who work to make the world a bet-
          ter place,

All   We give thanks!

Leader   For all who serve us with care and kindness,

All   We give thanks!

Leader   For philosophers and scientists, musicians, artists, and poets who enrich our lives,

All   We give thanks!

Leader   For idealists, activists, and all people of courage who inspire us to help others,

All   We give thanks!

For suggestions on a spontaneous litany rather than a scripted one, see page xvii.

All sing the following to the melody of "We Gather Together." The words are from "We Sing Now Together" by Edwin T. Buehrer.

All sing   We sing now together our song of thanksgiving,
            rejoicing in goods which the ages have wrought,
            for Life that enfolds us, and helps and heals and holds
                us,
            and leads beyond the goals that our forebears once
                sought.

            We sing of the freedoms which martyrs and heroes
            have won by their labor, their sorrow, their pain;
            the oppressed befriending, our ampler hopes defending,
            their death becomes a triumph, they died not in vain.

            We sing of the prophets, the teachers, the dreamers,
            designers, creators, and workers, and seers;
            our own lives expanding, our gratitude commanding,
            their deeds have made immortal their days and their
                years.

            We sing of community now in the making
            in every far continent, region, and land;
            with those of all races, all times and names and places,
            we pledge ourselves in covenant firmly to stand.

Celebrating the Taste of Life

During the above song, Servers come forward with trays containing small cups of grape juice and plates of moon cookies.

Narrator   Common to harvest festivals all over the world is the sharing of food and drink. While these may differ depending on the place and the crops, the impulse to celebrate by sharing this most basic of all human activities is the same. By eating and drinking, we nourish our bodies; by eating and drinking together, we nourish our spirits.

Leader   We invite you to come forward for moon cookies and grape juice. After you have returned to your place and all have been served, we'll toast one another and share them together.

Instrumental music plays until all have been served. The Narrator holds up a moon cookie.

Narrator   Behold the glowing harvest moon:
to all who live below, a boon.

All   We join our Asian kin to take
much joy in sharing this moon cake.

All eat. The Leader holds up a cup of grape juice.

Leader   The harvest of the vine is here,
which brings us sweetness and good cheer.

All   As many grapes are here made one,
we drink to all who share the sun.

All drink, then sing the following words to the melody of "Now Thank We All Our God."

All sing   Now give we all our thanks with minds and hands and voices,
And celebrate the earth, where every heart rejoices.

The harvest we have reaped, we owe to sun and rain;
Our planting of the seed has not been done in vain.

Across the great divide of wealth and class and chances
There lies another world where hunger's pang
    advances.
To those in need of food for body and for soul,
May we give of our store, that they and we be whole.

When all are fed and clothed, and none are poor and
    needy,
When all have homes and schools and none are mean
    and greedy,
Then may we celebrate the bounty of the earth
And bring the harvest home that all may share its
    worth.

Samhain, All Souls
and Day of the Dead

November 1-2

As the light and warmth wane, vegetation withers. Maple leaves shimmer golden in the strong, sideways light of afternoon, then float to the ground and shrivel. The grass has settled down and will need but one more mowing. Once-stalwart mums succumb to the chill. The smell of smoke from hearth fires singes the air. With clocks falling back to standard time, outdoor play is curtailed and it's dark by dinner.

For gardeners it's time to prune, snip off dead flowers and seed pods, pull up annuals, spread a light fertilizer, and mulch. It's time to winterize our cars, our homes, our bodies, our psyches. We change the oil in the auto and the filter in the furnace, put away the deck furniture, and exchange screens for storm windows, blankets for comforters, T-shirts for turtlenecks, exuberant outdoor activities for quiet indoor pastimes. At this dying time of the year, we remember our beloved dead but celebrate the cycle of life as we harvest the last of the crops and prepare treats for the spirits of our ancestors, who come as costumed children begging at our doors.

The Seasonal Calendar

The Celts marked the end of the warm season of the year and the beginning of the cold season on November 1 with the feast of

Samhain or Samain or Samuin (all pronounced "SOW-in," rhymes with "now"). At Beltane the herds were driven to high summer pastures where the grass was green and plentiful; at Samhain they were returned to home pens, where the strong ones were kept for breeding and the weaker ones, who would be a drain on the winter feed yet had little chance of surviving, were slaughtered. These slaughtered animals, together with the fruits of the harvest, provided a sacrifice to the gods and food for the festival that, like those of the three other Celtic quarter days, began the evening before the actual date of the feast. Since the agricultural year closed with the end of the harvesting period, Samhain is believed to have marked not just the beginning of winter (the Welsh term is *Calan Gaeaf*, the first day of winter) but also the beginning of the Celtic New Year, when trading and warfare were suspended, land leases were renewed, and tribal assemblies convened. In addition, some scholars maintain Samhain was a day for honoring the dead.

Mythology and History

Festivals commemorating the dead did not begin with the Celts. They are also found in older civilizations. In *The Book of the Year*, Anthony Aveni, reports that some five thousand years ago the Babylonians at Ur honored Ninazu, god of the Underworld, at a time in their calendar equivalent to our end of August. At Nippur they celebrated the sacred Mound Festival, dedicated to the dead at October, a time between life cycles when the harvest was complete and the fallow fields awaited seeding in the rainy season. These festivals marked the "return of the spirit for a brief visit to the family. Setting fires and lighting torches near the household guided the ghosts to the funeral meal that awaited them."

Ancient Egyptians commemorated Isis' search for her dead husband/brother Osiris, lord of the Underworld, and her bittersweet recovery of him at a November festival, during which, Aveni tells us, people burned oil lamps on the eaves of their homes in a nightlong vigil to honor Osiris. This practice eventually became a commemoration of all the dead and included setting out food for the departed.

However, not all festivals of the dead occurred in the fall. In ancient Greece, the last of the three days of the Anthesteria festival, celebrated in February and March in honor of Dionysus, god of wine, was dedicated to the dead, who were believed to return from the Underworld and roam abroad. Fearful residents took precautions by chewing whitethorn leaves and tarring their doors for protection. The Romans also celebrated a festival of the dead in February, the Parentalia. As the name implies, it was originally a private remembrance of deceased family members, but eventually it became generalized and included a public ritual, the Feralia, at which offerings were placed on graves.

Like the Celts, the ancient Finns marked the end of the agricultural year and the return of herds from the summer pastures on November 1. During this feast of Kekri, poised between the old year and the new, spirits of the ancestors were believed to visit their former homes, where food and drink and a heated sauna awaited them.

In their book, *In Search of Ancient Ireland*, Carmel McCaffrey and Leo Eaton identify Samhain as the "central feast in the Celtic calendar," a time when the barriers between this world and the Otherworld temporarily disappeared so that the living and the dead could meet. These encounters might be pleasant if the ancestors had been treated with respect, if offerings of food were left out for them, and if they approved of how their offspring had been behaving. But encounters might be unpleasant if the living had done something to distress the gods or the dead. In the latter case, the living might even wear a disguise to avoid being recognized by the avenging dead. A disguise might also conveniently enable the wearer to "get up to all sorts of mischief without being detected." Like other turning-point festivals, Samhain offered a license to behave inappropriately, sometimes exceeding the bounds of rank or class. In a close-knit world, this temporary suspension of the rules of behavior—when folks relieve tension without consequences—is believed to have the effect of strengthening those rules.

But humans might not be the only ones getting up to mischief, according to McCaffrey and Eaton:

> Samhain was also a time of sacrificial ritual because the gods and goddesses had to be given special treatment to please them. There is a sense that mischief might occur if the deities were not pleased. In this the Celtic religion seems to be no different from other religions. The supernatural has great power to do good or bad. Yet the idea of festival and celebration seems paramount, and there is a very strong sense of interaction between the two worlds of the living and the dead.

Among the gods to be honored at Samhain were the Dagda, the "good god," also known as Ollathair, the Great Father, who is often depicted with a giant cauldron of food that is never depleted and a large club, with which he both kills tribal enemies and revives the dead. The other deity central to this feast was the Morrigan, the tribal mother and goddess of war, who sometimes, in the midst of battle, shape-shifted to a raven, the symbol of death. Samhain provided the occasion for the ritual mating of these two powerful deities.

While one translation of Samhain is "summer's end," Barbara Walker contends in *The Woman's Encyclopedia of Myths and Secrets* that this Celtic feast of the dead was "named for the Aryan Lord of Death, Samana, 'the Leveller,' or the Grim Reaper, leader of ancestral ghosts" and points out that the name appears in the Bible as Samuel, from the Semitic Sammael, the underworld god. She reminds us further that "in Lithuania, the last European country to accept Christianity, the pagans celebrated their New Year feast at Halloween, sacrificing domestic animals to their god Zimiennik," or Samanik, another name for Samana.

Some scholars believe Samhain was, like Beltane, a fire festival, with hearth fires extinguished and then relit at the New Year from the communal bonfire. The bonfires might also have served to strengthen and encourage the sun as it waned as well as to scare off unwanted spirits or even to provide illumination for the spirits, wanted and unwanted, to return to the Otherworld. Miniature versions of the bonfire were created in lanterns carved out of hollowed gourds or turnips.

As a transition time, when the veil between the worlds was thin and the living and the dead had access to each other, Samhain was also believed to be a favorable period for divining the future, especially concerning marriage and health.

In *The Stations of the Sun*, Ronald Hutton acknowledges that Samhain was a major festival marking the start of winter in medieval Ireland but insists that the records "furnish no evidence that November 1 was a major pan-Celtic festival" and no evidence of religious ceremonies, even where it was observed. He further attributes to James Frazer the allegedly unsupported idea that Samhain was a feast of the dead. However, Hutton does admit that in mid-October, pagan Scandinavia celebrated the start of winter—the Winter Nights—with feasts and sacrifices.

Although some Wiccans and followers of James Frazer, among others, claim that Samhain was taken over by the Church with the Christianization of the Celts and transformed into All Saints' (or All Hallows') Day, Hutton questions this assertion. A history of that liturgical feast suggests an origin independent of Samhain. By the middle of the fourth century, Christians in the Mediterranean world were celebrating a feast on May 13 to honor all those who had been martyred under the pagan emperors. Although the Eastern orthodox churches eventually transferred this celebration to a moveable feast tied to the timing of Easter, the Roman church kept May 13, a date formally approved by Pope Boniface IV when, in 609, he dedicated what had been the Pantheon (temple of all the gods) as a church in honor of the virgin Mary and all the martyrs. Pope Gregory III changed the date in the next century when he consecrated a chapel in the Basilica of St. Peter to all the saints on November 1. By 800 the feast was being observed on November 1 in Germany, England, Gaul, and Austria. In 837 Pope Gregory IV extended the celebration to the entire church, which would have, of course, included Ireland. So while the Church may have indeed imposed its own feast for honoring the saintly deceased on the Irish Samhain, it does not seem to have relied on the latter as inspiration for the former.

Honoring the common-folk dead was universalized later. According to the *Catholic Encyclopedia*, the names of the faithful departed in the early Christian church were entered into the *diptychs* of the dead, tablets whose liturgical use suggests the inscribed names might have been recited at the celebration of Mass. In the sixth century it became customary in Benedictine monasteries to commemorate the deceased members at Whitsuntide (late spring). The Spanish did it either at the end of February or in late spring. By the tenth century, the Germans were doing it on October 1. From the monasteries the practice spread to the dioceses. In the twelfth century the feast was introduced into Milan for October 15, gradually settled on November 2, and was called All Souls' Day.

The theological basis for the feast is the doctrine that souls who, at the time of death, "are not perfectly cleansed from venial sins, or have not fully atoned for past transgressions" are temporarily denied heaven, and that "the faithful on earth can help them—by prayers, almsdeeds, and especially by the sacrifice of the Mass"—to shorten the time they must spend in the purifying flames of Purgatory. Those who die in a state of mortal sin are believed condemned to hell. Those who die in a state of grace are believed admitted directly to heaven, where they can be called upon to intercede with God for those on earth. But the souls in Purgatory are themselves in need of help and can benefit from the prayers of those on earth as well as from the intercession of the saints in heaven. Thus the back-to-back commemoration of All Saints and All Souls is not coincidental; nor perhaps is their assignment to the dying time of the agricultural year, when the thoughts of the living turn to their beloved dead as well as to consideration of their own deaths.

Hutton describes the customs associated with All Saints' and All Souls' on the British Isles, among them the giving of soul cakes to groups of poor people, especially children, who went begging door-to-door. This offering to the poor was sometimes done in the name of the dead and was believed to have a salutary effect on the souls in Purgatory. Among people whose cultural inheritance included a pagan festival and a Christian feast of the dead, putting a dish of food or a bit of bread on the windowsill could be interpreted as welcoming ancestral spirits, bribing evil spirits to stay away, making an offering to the poor, feeding the poor for the benefit of the dead, or all of these. Although soul cakes were originally oatcakes, the term came to be applied to any treat, whether food or coins. Some of the soulers' songs—for example, a late nineteenth-century one from Wales that ends with the implied threat, "Give us good alms and we'll be gone"—make it a likely forerunner of our trick-or-treaters' presentation of ultimatums.

One Hallows' Eve custom was wearing masks or the guises of evil spirits, a practice that prepared the way for playing pranks. For illumination, the pranksters depended on lanterns made of hollowed-out turnips, carved with the grotesque faces of goblins and used to scare people. In eastern England these were called jack-o'-lanterns, another name for marsh flames, or balls of methane gas that ignited spontaneously from dead vegetable matter decomposing in the fields. A more fanciful suggestion is that these mysterious, flickering lights were spirits of the condemned (or of a damned individual named Jack O'Lantern) carrying their share of personal hellfire while wandering the earth. More kindly is the interpretation that the function of the jack-o'-lantern—when placed in windows rather than in the hands of mischief-makers—was to serve as a beacon to welcome the roaming spirits.

Another Halloween custom was using nuts or apples to predict the future. In *Holiday Symbols and Customs*, Sue Ellen

Thompson describes a divining method used by young people in Scotland who put pairs of nuts named after certain couples in the fire: "If the pair burned to ashes together . . . the couple could expect a happy life together. If they cracked or sprang apart . . . quarrels and separation were inevitable." Apples, an acknowledged fertility symbol, were also used to predict one's romantic future. A girl would pare an apple in a single peel, throw it over her shoulder, and then read in the fallen peel the initial of her future husband. Young people bobbed for apples in a tub of water, a game that may have arrived in Britain with the Romans, who dedicated orchards to their goddess Pomona (*pomum* means "fruit"), who was honored at this harvest time. Coming up with an apple in your teeth meant your love would be reciprocated. Of course, as Walker reminds us, "The original divinations were [believed to be] oracular utterances by the ancestral dead, who came up from their tombs on Halloween." And the apples in tubs of water represented "soul symbols in the Cauldron of Regeneration."

The Reformation, which condemned the notion of Purgatory as well as the veneration of saints as semidivine intercessors, snuffed out the religious holiday for Protestants in Europe and it was forbidden among the Puritan American colonists, but Halloween traditions survived among some Southern colonists. The wave of mid-nineteenth-century Irish immigrants popularized the holiday in the United States, where pumpkins replaced turnips as lanterns and children went trick-or-treating in their neighborhoods wearing homemade costumes. Today, according to Aveni, Halloween is "a $2 billion annual business (second only to Christmas) . . . celebrated on the new turf of the shopping mall," where merchants dole out treats to children and teens who often wear elaborate, commercial costumes.

The costume, especially the mask, has a long history of association with ritual. Oscar Brockett, author of *History of Theatre*, tells us,

> A fundamental premise of many rituals is that a desired
> result—such as success in battle, adequate rainfall, or the favor

of a god—can be achieved by acting it out. Masks and costumes are often used to represent supernatural powers in the belief that a spirit is attracted by and enters into its likeness.

Operating on a related belief, primitive hunters often draped themselves in the skins of the powerful animals they had slain, hoping to absorb some of their power. Perhaps some of us hope to retain the positive spirit of deceased relatives by wearing clothing or jewelry inherited from them.

The idea of "dressing up" often means assuming the appearance of the more powerful. Children habitually dress up in their parents' clothes. On Halloween, they frequently do their trick-or-treating and even go to school dressed up as adult action heroes or fantasy figures, characters who seem to be even more powerful than their parents and with whom they identify. Now that Halloween is also celebrated in bars and nightclubs across America, adults also assume disguises, often dressing "up" the social ladder as royalty, rich and famous rock stars and athletes, or political or historical figures. In addition to dressing "up," dressing "across" gender lines was practiced in nineteenth-century Wales (Glamorgan) and twentieth-century Scotland (Orkney Islands) and has its counterpart in contemporary American celebrations of Halloween. Perhaps the popularity of this custom is due to the opportunity it provides to escape, for one night, culturally assigned sex roles, even as dressing "up" enables people to escape their socioeconomic class.

On the other hand, dressing "down" the social ladder can give one the freedom to behave as badly as one's "inferiors" are thought to. For example, Hutton reports that early in the last century on the Isle of Skye, young men put on old clothes and dirtied their faces and were given great license when visiting houses on Halloween, "sitting where they pleased in a kitchen, singing, conversing, and ignoring the inhabitants of the house . . . who were expected to set scones, cakes, and fruit before them." Even worse pranks seem only appropriate on Mischief Night to those disguised as rebellious, criminal, or lethal figures like Jack the Ripper, Frankenstein, and Darth Vader. This license to behave badly also

extended to those dressed as variations of the dead: ghosts, goblins, skeletons, mummies, vampires, the grim reaper, the devil
himself, or any "evil spirit" who roamed about looking to terrify
the living. Indeed, one way to deal with our fear of dying is to
ridicule death by seeming to appropriate its dangerous powers.

Despite the changes in tastes and fads over the centuries, one costume that has remained a staple is that of the witch, a figure be-
longing to neither the dead nor the supernatural but associated
with both, for she was accused of using demonic powers to deal
death and suffering to unsuspecting innocents. The Church's ha-
tred of witches, which resulted in the persecutions of the sixteenth
and seventeenth centuries in Europe, was an intensified version of
the institutional misogyny reflected in the *Malleus Maleficarum*,
the manual used by the Dominican priests who served as officers
of the Inquisition:

> When a woman thinks alone, she thinks evil, for the woman
> was made from the crooked rib which is bent in the contrary
> direction from the man. Woman conspired constantly
> against spiritual good. Her very name, femina, means "ab-
> sence of faith." She is insatiable lust by nature. Because of
> this she consorts even with Devils. It is for this reason that
> women are especially prone to the crime of witchcraft, from
> which men have been preserved by the maleness of Christ.

The term *witch* is from *wicca*, believed by some to be a nature
and fertility religion of pre-Christian Europe whose adherents, especially in rural villages, resisted conversion. (*Pagan* was originally
a term applied to people who lived in the country, or *paganus*, and
held fast to their nature religion—the last holdouts against
Christianity.) Some of these "evil" witches were, in reality, simply
unattached females—old and weak and therefore a drain on the
community's resources; widowed and occupying coveted lands; or
simply single, independent, and therefore dangerous. Others accused of witchcraft, as suggested by Adrienne Rich in *Of Woman*

Born, were herbalists, healers, and midwives whose "sin" may have been easing women's labor pains and thus circumventing the just punishment recorded in Genesis for daughters of Eve. Still others may have been the wise elders of their village, whose authority and practice of the Old Religion were seen as a threat to the new. With time and persecution, the original wise crones were demonized and exterminated; in their place arose the unsavory Weird Sisters of Shakespeare's *Macbeth*, the grotesque seductresses of fairy tales, and the trivialized ugly (or cute) cartoons of Halloween greeting cards.

A similar fate befell the witch's cauldron. In *The Grail Legend*, Emma Jung and Marie-Louise Von Franz tell us that nearly all mythologies feature a "miraculous vessel" that sometimes "dispenses youth and life," sometimes possesses the "power of healing," and occasionally inspires "strength and wisdom," effecting transformations. According to Joseph Campbell's *The Masks of God: Occidental Mythology*, the cauldron of the Celtic father-god, the Dagda, was just such a vessel. Its contents not only provided unlimited nourishment but "restored the dead and produced poetic inspiration." Campbell believes that the Dagda's cauldron originally belonged to a goddess and that its assignment to him "betrays the appropriation by a patriarchal deity of matriarchal themes." This idea finds support in Barbara Walker's *Crone*, which points out that the cauldron was always understood in pre-Christian religions to symbolize the cosmic womb, the source of regeneration: "All life, mind, matter, and energy arose in various forms from the ever-boiling vessel, only to return thereto, when each form came to its destined end, in a perpetual cyclic recurrence."

With the discrediting of its guardian priestess, the crone, this sacred vessel of ancient religions was reduced in the popular imagination to its opposite—a pot for brewing disgusting, poisonous concoctions that would induce spells or cause sickness or death. Like the witch, the cauldron was both demonized and caricatured, reduced to a trivial prop for Halloween parties.

Although in the minds of most modern people who celebrate it, Halloween is now a secular holiday that has lost its religious association with saints and souls of the beloved dead, there are still many people around the globe who celebrate festivals of the dead, many of them at this time of year.

Contemporary Celebrations Around the World

Wiccans around the world regard the feast of Samhain as the most important of their four quarter days. A common ritual is the Dumb Supper, which Anne Lafferty describes in "A Seeker's Guide to Modern Witchcraft and Paganism."

> The table is laden with potluck dishes. There is a place setting for each person present, as well as one in front of an empty chair. This place is for the Beloved Dead, who are being honored by this meal. The first plate filled is given to them. The living eat in silence, thinking about their ancestors and others they cared about who have passed on. When the meal is over, the leftover food, including the food that was on the plate for the spirits of the dead, is taken outside and placed on the ground.

> Participants might then tell stories and share memories about their beloved dead or sing a song honoring them. Sometimes the food prepared for the supper includes favorite dishes of the departed in whose honor the ritual is observed.

Ullambana, the festival of All Souls popularly known as Festival of the Hungry Ghosts, is observed by Buddhists and Taoists in China, Korea, Japan, Singapore, and elsewhere. It emphasizes the virtues of filial piety and respect for the dead. Dr. P. Gnanarama, spiritual director of the Purvarama Buddhist Temple in Sri Lanka, suggests it originated in ancient China as a harvest festival and later took on a religious meaning, with its inspiration attributed to a *sutra*, or didactic story, supposedly told by the Buddha. The story's hero discovers through meditation that his dead mother, because of previous karma, has been reborn in Purgatory, where she is hanging upside down (the meaning of *Ullambana* in Sanskrit), emaciated, and suffering intensely from starvation. The son embarks on a rescue mission but is advised by the Buddha that the way to alleviate his mother's suffering as well as that of seven generations of his deceased relatives still in distress, is to make offerings of food, incense, oil lamps, candles, and bedding on the fifteenth day of the seventh month. The Taoist tradition has it that the gates of Purgatory are opened on the first day of that month so that its hungry inhabitants might escape and search for food on earth. Thus it is customary throughout the month to make offerings of animals and other food to satisfy the wandering souls.

Buddhists of the Theravada tradition believe in the transfer of merit to the departed, who indeed expect their living relatives to contribute such merit to relieve the pain of the dead. The living earn merit by religious practice and moral behavior. The transference of merit benefits both the dead, who receive it, and the living, who are inspired to live better lives to earn it. This doctrine bears clear similarity to the Catholic teaching that the prayers and good works of the living can shorten the suffering of souls in Purgatory. The Theravada traditions observe Ullambana at the end of the three-month rainy season in October, though other traditions celebrate it in August.

In many places the return of ancestral spirits is welcomed with ceremonial dances and lanterns floating on water. In Japan, where the festival is called Bon and generally observed August 13 through August 16, offerings accompanied by chanted invocations are made on two altars: one for the spirits of ancestors and the other for restless spirits who died in ways that precluded burial, whose presence among the living is believed dangerous. Often families reunited during this time visit ancestral cemeteries, clean memorial stones, and place incense and flowers on graves. On the last night, bonfires are lit on hills to speed the spirits back after their visit.

Since the late Middle Ages, the dead have been remembered in Christian countries in Europe and elsewhere around the globe in formal church services on All Souls' Day. Although fear of "roaming spirits" was officially declared superstition, pagan beliefs and practices persisted. In Germany, for example, when peasant farmers harvested the hay and brought it to the barn, they broke the first straw and offered it as food for the dead. Even today in Latvia, after the Fall Equinox festival of Mikeli, a quiet shadow period begins. "At this time," according to Mara Mellena of the Latvian Institute, "the shadows—spirits of the dead—visit the farmsteads to look over the life of the household," and to bring blessings for future life and work.

One of the most elaborate festivals at this time of year is El dia de los Muertos, the Day of the Dead, observed on November 1 and 2 in Mexico and other Latin American countries. Typically infants and children are remembered on the first day and adults on the second. Here the dead are not feared but welcomed. Combining Roman Catholic rituals of All Saints' and All Souls' Days with millennia-old Mexican Indian traditions, the holiday includes solemn religious rites such as masses and prayers for the dead in church.

There is also feasting in the home, where scattered petals and burning incense invite the spirits to enter and partake of their favorite foods and special bread, *hojaldra*, which have been set out on tables or home altars decorated with flowers and photos of departed family members. What is not consumed by the dead provides a festal meal for the living. The leftovers from that meal may be taken to the cemetery and laid on the graves of ancestors or distributed in the community. The event includes processions, pageantry, elaborate food, bright decorations, and even fireworks. While this is a time of mourning for the beloved dead, the pervading atmosphere is one of fiesta. Cakes and candies in the shape of skulls, skeletons, coffins, and gravestones "sweeten" the concept of death, perhaps reminding those who eat them of the sweetness of living in heaven as well as in the memories of one's descendants. Some families keep candlelight vigils through the night at the gravesites of their dead and attend open-air memorial masses.

While "sophisticated" North Americans are tempted to view some of these practices as primitively morbid at worst or quaint at best, Peter Morales cautions us in "Bringing the Dead to Life,"

> If we dismiss the Day of the Dead as pure superstition, we can easily miss the profound spiritual and psychological insight that makes this tradition powerful. A Mexican boy spending the night at his uncle's grave has a connection across time with his forebears that our children do not. While we dwellers in a technological age are connected to the World Wide Web, cellular phones, and cable TV, [while we] have message machines, voice mail, pagers and call waiting, we have cut ourselves off from the web of time. Traditional cultures, with their mediums and ghosts and reincarnations, have understood intuitively something we've repressed: the dead don't die; they live on.

For Hindus, the dead live on when their souls are reincarnated in other bodies. One of the major festivals of Hinduism, and possibly the only one that is truly pan-Indian, is Diwali, the Festival of Lights (from the Sanskrit *dipavali*, or "row of lights"), which is observed with temple services that include singing and recitations from sacred texts. Celebrated on dates in the lunar calendar that correspond to late October and early November in our Gregorian calendar, it marks the official end of autumn and the beginning of winter. In upper India, Diwali also marks the beginning of the commercial New Year. People clean their homes, light oil lamps, and set them in rows along the parapets of houses and temples or float them in rivers. They invoke Lakshmi, goddess of fortune and prosperity, to bless their homes and businesses as they open new account books. They wear new clothes, visit friends and family members to exchange gifts, and set off fireworks.

But in Bengal Diwali honors the goddess Kali, the five-millennia-old Creator-Preserver-Destroyer of the Universe, the womb-and-tomb primal mother found in so many ancient religions. Her breathing is the pulse of the universe, for she is at once the menstrual sea of blood that gives birth to the world and the fierce, emaciated hag whose primordial hunger must feast on animals and humans to replenish the energy that drives the cosmos. Thus she is often depicted wearing a necklace of skulls, her hair wild, her tongue red with blood, dancing ecstatically on cremation grounds, gathering up souls to be seeds for new life. In this destroyer mode, Kali may well be our worst nightmare—the nightmare we must come to grips with, for in facing her, we face our own terror of annihilation.

As Monica Sjöö and Barbara Mor remind us in *The Great Cosmic Mother*, primitive peoples seemed to understand that life and death are the same. It was a paradox they strove to be conscious of—just as we strive to escape it:

> Moderns who neither kill nor grow their own food nor bury their own dead would seem to have solved the problem by avoiding it; but in fact the resolution is simply delegated, nowadays, to nightmare, slaughterhouses, torture rooms, death squads, and "snuff" films, in which criminal priests perform obscene sacrifices to the gods of displaced responsibility.

For early peoples, the paradox was somehow made bearable through ritual expression of their fury, which often took the form of bloody sacrifices to the death deity. For us, the paradox remains unbearable and yet, despite our best efforts, inescapable. So we try to trivialize it. The hags of our Halloween cards and costumes are domesticated reminders of the Wiccan wise women who served as midwives and morticians, who themselves represented the hallowed and harrowing goddess of womb and tomb, of life and death. The ghosts and goblins and grim reapers who people our parties and parades are fun versions of the very serious destination that we know deep down we cannot escape.

Such trivialization may put the paradox at arm's length, but it does not resolve it. Yet perhaps it is not too late for us to return to ritual for that resolution. We cannot, to be sure, revert to the bloody sacrifices practiced by some of our ancient ancestors, but perhaps we can embrace other kinds of rituals that will, whether we believe in a personal afterlife or not, enable us to find comfort in the understanding that life and death are one.

For many peoples both ancient and contemporary, belief in an ongoing relationship with their beloved dead and the rituals associated with that belief have provided a means of finding such comfort.

Honoring Ancestors

Ancestor worship, according to John A. Saliba's *Encarta Encyclopedia* entry, is the reverence paid to deceased relatives based on the belief that as spirits they have the power to influence the fate and well-being of the living. Although in some cases ancestors are thought to assume the status of deities, more frequently their "worship" is not the adoration rendered to gods, whose power extends over the whole population. Their concern is generally limited to what affects the family of which they were once living members and whose protection is their chief interest. They are believed to have the ability to intercede with the supreme gods on behalf of the family, whose members might, through dreams or trance, receive communications from them. Often the living have ambivalent feelings about ancestors, for while they are perceived as a potential source of blessings if properly honored with ritual, prayer, and sacrifice, they might also inflict misfortune if these are not offered. Saliba concludes that ancestor worship is

> a strong indication of the value placed on the household and of the strong ties that exist between the past and the present. The beliefs and practices connected with the cult help to integrate the family, to sanction the traditional political structure, and to encourage respect for living elders. Some scholars have also interpreted it as a source of individual well-being and of social harmony and stability.

A search for "ancestor worship" in the *Encyclopaedia Britannica* reveals dozens of entries identifying practitioners of this cult around the world. It is an important element in the religion of many peoples in central Africa, including the Luba, Zande, Lunda, Lugbara, Mongo, and Madi. In some cases, as with the Madi, homage is paid to the chief's lineage ancestors, who are believed to punish erring subjects. In East Africa, ancestor worship is central to the religious practice of some Tanzanians, including the Nyamwezi and the Yao. It originally figured significantly in the Yao puberty rites for males, though under Arab influence, many Yao have been converted to Islam. In Madagascar, although half the population has become Christian and a good number have embraced Islam, the rest still practice ancestor worship and believe that the dead reward or punish the living.

A similar situation obtains in Burkina Faso where, despite inroads made by Christianity and Islam, half the population remain animists (believing that natural objects such as rivers and rocks possess a soul or spirit) and worship ancestors. The practice is still strong among other peoples of West Africa as well, including the Fon (Dohemy) of Benin and the Bamum and Bamileke of Cameroon. Farther south, although Christianity has gained many converts, ancestor worship provides the foundation of the traditional religions of the Herero of Namibia and Botswana and the Zulu of South Africa. Whether performing rituals to ensure fertility, win a war, or end a drought, the traditional Zulu king invoked his royal ancestors on behalf of all the people. The matrilineal Baule of Côte d'Ivoire believe that the ancestral spirits of each lineage are embodied in ceremonial stools and are famous for these genuine works of art as well as their carved ceremonial masks and small wooden statues representing spirits—all originally used in the rites of ancestor worship.

Half a world away, the indigenous people of New Guinea also created small devotional figures of wood or stone, called *telum* figures, believed to represent not just human forebears but also gods whom the natives worshiped as their mythical ancestors. Elsewhere in Melanesia, as well as in the Republic of Vanuatu, traditional ancestor worship is still practiced, sometimes alongside Christianity.

This mixture is also the case in parts of Indonesia. For example, people on the island of Samosir in Sumatra are primarily Christian but still practice ancestor worship. And on the island of Timor, though Christianity and Islam have been welcomed by some, animism and ancestor worship still dominate.

While the majority of educated people among the Oraon of Bihar in northeastern India have converted to Christianity, the traditional religion includes ancestor worship, as does that of the Gond people of central India.

As might be expected in China—where reverence for even living parents and grandparents is legendary—ancestor worship has been the most universal form of religion throughout the country's history, with heads of households responsible for making regular offerings to the deceased. The ethical principles of Confucianism emphasize devotion to family, including the spirits of ancestors. Taoism advocates transcending all distinctions, even that between life and death. Yet even before the rise of these two great philosophical schools, Chinese thought was formed by ideas basic to ancient agrarian religion, which included the oneness of humans and the natural world, the cyclical nature of time, and the worship of ancestors.

Even today, the elements of animism and ancestor worship are found in the religious practices of the She people and the Yi people of South China, as well as among the Kansu in the north central part of the country, where Chinese temples, monasteries of lamas, and mosques draw respective worshipers. In most places in China, folk religion, Taoism, Buddhism, Christianity, and Islam enjoy a peaceful coexistence, though ancestor worship pervades all. This is also true in South Korea, where there is no national religion and where Buddhists and Christians live side by side, yet most families still practice the ancestor worship inspired by Confucianism, which provided the country's ethical basis for the five centuries of the Choson dynasty, which ended in 1910.

Some might see a similarity in the Chinese worship of ancestors and the Catholic veneration of saints (spiritual ancestors). Yet
the former became a sticking point in the famed "Chinese rites
controversy" of the seventeenth and eighteenth centuries. Jesuit
missionaries advocated a tolerant approach to the veneration of
Confucius and of ancestors and wanted to adapt these rites for
Christian purposes, but purists in the West resisted these efforts. In
1645 the Church condemned the rites, forbidding Catholics to
practice them. This condemnation was reiterated by Pope Clement
XI in 1704 and again in 1715 and by Pope Benedict XIV in 1742. It
took nearly three hundred years for the Church, by edict of Pope
Pius XII, to permit Catholic schools in China to display images of
Confucius and to allow missionaries to assist in civil ceremonies
honoring the dead.

In most indigenous religions characterized by ancestor worship, human elders die and become powerful spiritual beings, but
the reverse is claimed when living human rulers are assigned divine ancestors. In the Japanese Shinto religion, whose deities tend
to embody natural forces, the sun goddess Amaterasu Ōmikami
was claimed as the emperor's ancestor until the mid-twentieth
century. According to legend, she gave her grandson the sacred
mirror (which lured her out of her cave at Winter Solstice) as well
as a sword and a jewel and sent him to earth. This grandson's
great-grandson, Jimmu, became Japan's first emperor. For other
examples of sun deities claimed as ancestors, see the chapter on
"Summer Solstice and Midsummer."

Some scholars see evidence of ancestor worship in the megalithic
communal tombs of Britain and Ireland, some of which have elaborately decorated stones. Constructed as early as 4000 BCE, these
monuments are thought to have served, among other functions, as
ritual centers for the worship of ancestors.

Ancestor worship was central to the religion of early Slavic
peoples, according to Evel Gasparini, professor of Slavic philology
at the University of Padova. Their seasonal festivals were almost

entirely dedicated to the dead. At one such annual feast, the spirits of the dead were believed to visit all the village homes disguised as beggars. Communal banquets (called Love Feasts and still enjoyed in modern Russia, Serbia, and Bulgaria) were dedicated to a deceased founder of the clan. These mainly legendary founders were sometimes venerated as divine ancestors, especially among the Finns and Ugrians, but burial practices provide evidence of veneration of actual human ancestors as well. Until the nineteenth century, in various places in the Danubian-Balkan area, reinterment was practiced. Graves were reopened a few years after the first burial and bones were washed, wrapped in linen, and reburied. In other times and places, they may have been burned. The multiple cinerary urns found in the mortuary mounds of the Krivichi suggest the practice of periodic, collective cremation of exhumed bones:

> It is possible that the bones of the disinterred were kept for a long period inside the dwellings, as is still sometimes done in the Tyrol of Austria, and that the sacred corner—now occupied by the icon—was the place where they were kept.

As with other ancestor-worshipers, the Slavs both revered and feared the spirits of their dead, especially the "unclean dead," those whose premature passing deprived them of fulfillment in this life and who might therefore return to claim what now belonged to the living. For example, maidens who died before marriage might try to kidnap a bridegroom or a newborn. The Semik festival in late spring was devoted to expelling such dangerous spirits. The *domovoy*, on the other hand, is a more friendly household ghost whose roots are in ancestor worship. As protector of the family and its well-being, its disapproval of resident slackers might be manifest in mysterious creaks and knocks. The Slavs are responsible for introducing the concept of the vampire, a dead person who doesn't decompose and must be terminated by setting fire to the corpse or thrusting a stake through the heart.

Some indigenous peoples of the Americas also practiced ancestor worship. For example, it is central to the religion and society of both ancient and modern Maya. Nearly all their temple pyramids house hidden tombs. This suggests that a ruler buried there—thought to have become one with his own divine ancestor—might have himself become the object of veneration by his descendants. The Incas also venerated the spirits of their ancestors, treating their rulers' corpses as sacred shrines.

For the Hopi and other Pueblo peoples, ancestor worship is demonstrated in their belief in *kachinas* (*ka* means "spirit" and *china* means "respect"). These ancestral and nature spirits are impersonated by ceremonial male dancers wearing elaborate masks and costumes. The dancers, sometimes thought to be possessed by kachinas, invoke these spirits to provide for the needs of the people. The kachina dancers also provide initiation rites at puberty and scold individuals in the community who behave badly.

While ancestor worship was never a universal phenomenon, anyone who has mourned the loss of beloved family members can understand the desire to continue the relationship with them beyond the grave. We miss the wisdom, support, and energy they contributed to our lives. We long still for their presence and protection. We feel the need to honor their lives and, perhaps even by remembering them, to give them a kind of immortality. Possibly this explains the formalizing of occasions to honor the dead and/or deities of the dead in so many cultures.

WAYS TO CELEBRATE

Honor your beloved dead.

◉   Set up an altar on a table, bookcase, or shelf in your home to honor your beloved dead. Display framed photos of your ancestors and other deceased relatives, friends, and heroes. (You may want to include pets as well.) Perhaps add a special heirloom—a piece of jewelry or cherished artifact—or a small vase of seasonal flowers. Leave the altar up from October 31 through November 2. Each time you pass it, let the photos bring back good memories. If you are saddened by loss, acknowledge the grief and then give thanks for the positive experiences and relationships.

☾ Light a candle and read aloud from letters or saved e-mails you have from persons now dead who have been important in your life. Let them speak to you again through their own words. Let the memory of them comfort you.

☾ Make a list of the people now dead who had a positive, significant influence on your life. You could include not just relatives and friends but historical figures, writers, musicians, scientists, teachers, and others. Get out any photos you may have of these people. Light a candle. Then write a paragraph about each beloved dead one, describing what it has meant to you to have had this person in your life. Write it in the form of a letter if you wish. Read each one aloud, pausing afterward to let yourself respond emotionally and mentally to what you have just said. You might want to follow this moment by saying or chanting a phrase like "So long as I remember, you live." Then go on to the next. (The older you get, the longer your list, and possibly the more daunting this practice. If you are overwhelmed by the prospect, choose the three most significant to honor this year, and three others for next year, and so on.) If it is comfortable and appropriate to do so, share either/both of these last two rituals with your family or a small group of friends.

☾ Using photo albums, or videos if they are available, tell your children, grandchildren, younger siblings, or nieces or nephews stories about the relatives now dead that they didn't have the opportunity to know well. Pass on your best memories and the values best exemplified by each.

☾ Ask your parents or grandparents to tell you what they most admired about their parents or grandparents. A good way to introduce this subject is to ask for their help working on the family tree or updating photo albums.

⑥   Ask your spouse, partner, or best friend to share with you his or her memories of deceased loved ones, to tell stories about people you didn't have a chance to know.

⑥   Visit the cemetery where your beloved dead are buried. Make sure the gravesites are well ordered. Then take some time to think about your relationships with the deceased. Be grateful for what was good; let go of what wasn't. Leave a flower if you like.

⑥   Give a memorial gift in honor of your beloved dead—to a cause she or he believed in or worked for. Or make your contribution in hours of work.

⑥   Donate to a food pantry or soup kitchen the ingredients for a meal that was the favorite of one of your beloved dead.

Honor your living ancestors.

⑥   Show your gratitude to elders for the wisdom and care they have provided you by taking them out to lunch or dinner, having them to your home for a meal, or preparing a meal to take to and enjoy with them. Use the occasion to tell them how much you appreciate their gifts.

⑥   Arrange an outing for an elder relative: a drive in the country, a walk in the park, or a visit to a museum, movie, or sporting event—whatever would be most appreciated.

⑥   Send an elder relative a greeting card or an arrangement of fall flowers or deliver a bouquet of mums or a basket of fruit in person.

⑥   Rake leaves for an elderly neighbor who can no longer do it, or help one who has difficulty.

Comfort those in mourning.

⑥   Invite a friend or relative who is in mourning for someone who died this year to join you for a meal. Try to provide whatever is needed at this stage: a listening ear, a tissue for tears, encouragement to tell stories or share pain, permission to get on with life, or to laugh again.

☉   Visit someone who is dying. Listen. Talk. Read poetry aloud. Listen to music together.

Think about your own death.

☉   If you enjoy classical music, play a CD of the Requiem of Fauré or Verdi. Or listen to the Gregorian chant version. Or Andrew Lloyd Webber's "Pié Jesu." Or attend a concert featuring any of these.

☉   Write your own eulogy. How do you want to be remembered? For your relationships? For your accomplishments? Read it aloud to yourself. Determine what you would have to do to make it true, and take a first step in that direction. Distill the eulogy into an epitaph. Write it on a card, put it on your nightstand, and leave it there for a month. Each night as you go to bed, ask yourself how your behavior that day reflects the description of you in the epitaph.

☉   Draw up a will. Who will be your heirs? Family members? Friends? Organizations (religious, political, social, cultural, environmental) that you believe in enough to invest time and energy in while you are alive? Those you value but regret not having time to invest in? Draw up a spiritual will. Who will be heirs to your values? Who will benefit from your accomplishments? What can you do now to assure that you will pass on this spiritual legacy?

☉   Make preparations—as far as possible—for your own death. Do you have a living will? Have you designated someone to have medical power of attorney to make decisions in the event you are unable to? Have you registered as an organ donor? Have you formulated your wishes for the disposal of your body? Burial? Cremation? Or will you donate it to your State Anatomy Board to be used for medical education and research? If your children are old enough, talk about these things with them. If your parents are still alive, ask them to talk about these things with you.

Winterize your home.

⑥   Put the garden to bed. Prune, snip off dead flowers and seed-pods, pull up annuals, spread a light fertilizer, and mulch.

⑥   Rake and mulch leaves for the compost heap.

⑥   Put away the outdoor furniture, shut off the outside water, and drain the hoses.

⑥   Change the furnace filter and exchange screens for storm windows.

⑥   Get the comforters out of storage.

⑥   Retrieve boots, turtlenecks, corduroys, and woolens.

⑥   Mend what needs mending.

Prepare for the inwardness of the cold half of the year.

⑥   Start keeping a dream journal.

⑥   Make time for daily meditation.

⑥   Try chanting or drumming.

⑥   Develop the habit of "spiritual reading." Select a sacred text or a collection of such texts or a book of thoughtful essays on theology, ethics, or spirituality, and read from it for fifteen minutes each day.

⑥   Keep a book of poetry by your bedside, and read one poem each night before you go to sleep.

⑥   Listen for a little while each day to music that nourishes your spirit—or play it.

Celebrate the Halloween season.

⑥   Carve pumpkins or turnips with symbols of the season. Burn candles inside to illuminate the design.

⑥   Create your own costumes or help children create theirs with ragbag clothes, scraps of fabric, or yard-sale paraphernalia. Make masks with children. Try this simple, inexpensive method suggested by Gertrud Mueller Nelson in *To Dance with God*:

MASKS

Begin with a sheet of 8½ x 11 paper or cardstock or a paper plate. Fold it in half lengthwise. Measure up 2 inches from the bottom to allow for a chin. Cut into the fold a half of a mouth, frowning or smiling. Measure up 1 inch from the mouth, cut into the fold an inverted 7 for a nose. Poke the scissors through both layers of paper at once to make the eyes. Slash the top of the paper to make hair. Open the paper—now you have the basis for the mask. Round the chin, if you like. Add teeth, lashes, mustache, ears, horns, whatever. Paint, color, or decorate the mask. Refold the mask and make a 2-inch slash into the cheeks from the open ends and a 1-inch-slash in the center of the chin. Open the mask and pull the slash of each cheek over itself to make a little formed cheek. Staple in place. Do the same with the slash in the chin to form a point on the chin. Staple. Now the mask has dimensionality.

Give "soul cakes."

⑥   Create a "cauldron of plenty" by filling a bucket or large bowl with goodies. Dress in costume to distribute these to children who come trick-or-treating.

⑥   Contribute to the Halloween campaign of the United Nations Children's Fund, UNICEF.

⑥   Make pumpkin cookies for your household and another batch to give away. Here's my favorite recipe from Ellen Buchman

Ewald's *Recipes for a Small Planet*:

PUMPKIN COOKIES

Ingredients:

1 ¼ cups whole wheat flour
5 tablespoons soy flour (or more whole wheat flour, if you
    don't have soy)
1 teaspoon baking soda
½ teaspoon salt
½ teaspoon cinnamon
½ teaspoon nutmeg
¼ teaspoon cloves
½ cup butter
⅔ cup honey
1 egg
1 cup cooked and pureed pumpkin (or canned
pumpkin)
1 cup chopped walnuts
½ cup chopped raisins
½ cup chopped dates

Stir together the dry ingredients and spices. In another bowl, cream the butter and honey; beat in the egg until the mixture is smooth. Stir in the pumpkin puree, and don't worry if the texture is strange. Add the dry ingredients to the pumpkin mixture; blend, then stir in the nuts and dried fruit. Drop by tablespoons onto an oiled cookie sheet. Bake at 325° for 15 minutes, until they are golden.

For "gift packaging," wipe clean the inside of several small, empty nut cans. Wrap a piece of orange construction paper around the outside of each and tape to secure. Draw, paint, or color Halloween symbols on it, or use stickers. Put a bow or large sticker on the plastic lid. Line the cans with wax paper. Fill with cookies (about a dozen each) and give to special friends, family elders, or neighbors. (Note: homemade cookies may not be appropriate for trick-or-treating children who have been cautioned to accept only commercially packaged goodies, but could work for children whose parents accompany them and know you.)

☙   Gather the summer clothes you or your children have out-grown and take them to Goodwill.

☙   Prepare bag lunches and give them to homeless people.

☙   Share your riches (resources of time, money, energy) by con-tributing to organizations that directly aid the poor of our own or other countries or by volunteering at a shelter, soup kitchen, or food pantry.

☙   Write to your congressional representatives, urging the revision of our tax system so that wealth will be more equitably distributed.

REMEMBER OUR BELOVED DEAD

A SAMHAIN/ALL SOULS RITUAL

Prior to the ritual, participants have been invited to bring with them photos or other iconic memorabilia of their beloved dead, as well as food—canned or boxed—representing the favorite food of their dead. Two Scribes have volunteered or been recruited in advance. As partic-ipants enter the gathering space, they give to the Scribes the names of one or two of their beloved dead that they wish to be read aloud. The Scribes print the names clearly, indicating pronunciation phonetically where necessary. On separate lists, they record the names of infants born this year or toddlers. After submitting the names, participants place the photos and memorabilia of the beloved dead on a table where they can be viewed by all but keep the food offerings for later in the rit-ual. Music might accompany this preparation.

Narrator   Today we gather to honor the dying and the dead. Nature speaks to us of this passing. As the earth tilts farther away from the sun, the light in our hemisphere is steadily waning—a diminishment made even more dramatic in some places with the end of daylight saving time. The leaves, once shimmering green then gold in sunlight, now fall to the cooling earth, where they will soon become as brittle as the bones of elders. Grass and gardens have hunkered down for the winter, turning their energy downward and inward. Yet before this final loss there is a blaze of color, one last burst of accomplishment, one final hymn of praise to the fullness of the life that is about to dwindle.

Reader 1   O sacred season of Autumn, be my teacher,
           for I wish to learn the virtue of contentment.
           As I gaze upon your full-colored beauty,
           I sense all about you
           an at-homeness with your amber riches.

           You are the season of retirement,
           of full barns and harvested fields.
           The cycle of growth has ceased,
           and the busy work of giving life
           is now completed.
           I sense in you no regrets:
           you've lived a full life.

           I live in a society that is ever-restless,
           always eager for more mountains to climb,
           seeking happiness through more and more possessions.
           As a child of my culture,
           I am seldom truly at peace with what I have.
           Teach me to take stock of what I have given and
                 received;
           may I know that it's enough,
           that my striving can cease
           in the abundance of God's grace.
           May I know the contentment

that allows the totality of my energies
to come to full flower.
May I know that like you I am rich beyond measure.

As you, O Autumn, take pleasure in your great bounty,
let me also take delight
in the abundance of the simple things in life
which are the true sources of joy.
With the golden glow of peaceful contentment
may I truly appreciate this autumn day.
    —Edward Hays, "Autumn Psalm of Contentment"

*All sing the following to the melody of "Cradle Song." The
words are from "In Sweet Fields of Autumn" by Elizabeth
Madison.*

All sing   In sweet fields of autumn the gold grain is falling,
the white clouds drift lonely, the wild swan is calling.
Alas for the daisies, the tall fern and grasses,
when windsweep and rainfall fill lowlands and passes.

The snows of December shall fill windy hollow;
the bleak rain trails after, and March wind shall follow.
The deer through the valleys leave print of their going;
and diamonds of sleet mark the ridges of snowing.

The stillness of death shall stoop over the water,
the plover sweep low where the pale streamlets falter;
but deep in the earth clod the black seed is living;
when spring sounds her bugles for rousing and giving.

Around the World

Narrator   For many ancient peoples, the final harvest, the end of
the agricultural and pastoral year, also marked the end
of the calendar year. At this time they acknowledged
the end of the cycle of the earth's seasons and gave
thanks for its gifts. Often this was also a time to ac-

knowledge the human lives that had come to an end and to give thanks for their gifts.

Leader   Some Celtic peoples celebrated Samhain [*"SOW-in,"* *rhymes with "now"*] on October 31 and November 1. The last of the crops were harvested, and the flocks and herds returned from summer pastures to home pens. It was the end of the warm half of the year that began at Beltane on May 1 and the beginning of the cold half. In Ireland, it marked the official start of winter. Some scholars say it was also a feast of the dead, whose spirits returned to their hearths on the night of Samhain eve to visit their families.

Narrator   The ancient Finns celebrated their new year and honored their dead at the November 1 feast of Kekri.

Leader   Much older even is the Babylonian Sacred Mound Festival, another harvest feast honoring the dead.

Narrator   Ancient Egyptians honored their dead at the November festival of Isis and Osiris.

Leader   The Christian church had, from early on, honored its dead—especially those martyred by Roman emperors. By the middle of the ninth century, the feast of All Hallows or All Saints was observed by Christians all over Europe on November 1. Three centuries later, the Feast of All Souls—those souls believed to be in Purgatory—was officially established as November 2.

Narrator   On these two days, people in Latin American countries celebrate the Day of the Dead, a fusion of Catholic and Mexican Indian traditions.

Leader   Buddhists and Taoists around the world celebrate Ullambana. Originally a harvest feast, it is popularly known as Festival of the Hungry Ghosts.

Narrator Hindus observe Diwali, the Festival of Lights, at this time of year to welcome the winter. It is celebrated as the New Year in northern India. But in Bengal it honors the death-bringing goddess Kali.

Leader Wiccans today still celebrate Samhain, lighting a hearth fire to welcome the cold season and the remembered spirits of their beloved dead.

Choir sings "Samhain Hymn" by Leigh Ann Hussey.

Choir Welcome, Winter, waning season.
Now with night the New Year comes;
all who honor elder kinfolk,
dance the dead to Earthly drums;
souls respected safeguard living,
house we'll hold and hallow hearth;
blessings be on those who bide here,
blessings be on those who bide here,
and indeed on all the Earth!

Honoring Our Beloved Dead

A ring of five candles or a candelabra has been set on a table or altar. Autumn foliage surrounds its base. Lighters, who have volunteered or been recruited in advance, come forward. Lighters light their candles as they speak their lines. Or the Leader can speak the line as each Lighter lights a candle.

Narrator Fire has always been important in festivals honoring the dead. Whether bonfires, hearth fires, or sauna fires, whether candles or oil lamps, torches or lanterns, their light was a symbol of honor accorded the dead or deities of the dead. It provided illumination for the ancestors to find their way to their former homes and guided their spirits away when the visit was over.

Leader We light these candles of remembrance now, so that

our own beloved dead may find their way to our hearts, that we may be open to the wisdom and messages of hope and love that they would offer us if only we would listen and heed.

Lighter 1   We light this candle to beckon our parents, grandparents, and great-grandparents—all the ancestors to whose love and care and sacrifices we owe our very existence.

Lighter 2   We light this candle for other family members who have gone before us—spouses, partners, children, siblings, aunts and uncles, cousins, nephews and nieces— and give thanks for the richness and love they provided in our lives.

Lighter 3   We light this candle for members of our community who have died this year, in thanksgiving for the contributions they made to the life of this community.

Lighter 4   We light this candle for ancestors of another kind, for those who have given life to our minds—for teachers, mentors, writers, and sages; for scientists and artists who imparted knowledge and wisdom that outlives their earthly existence.

Lighter 5   We light this candle for our spiritual ancestors—for all those who have taught us the values by which we live, who have given us confidence in our own spiritual worth and the worth of every creature.

Choir sings "I Cannot Think of Them as Dead," words by Frederick Lucian Hosmer while the two Scribes carry forward the lists of names and present them to the Narrator.

Choir   I cannot think of them as dead
who walk with me no more;
along the path of life I tread
they are but gone before,
they are but gone before.

And still their silent ministry
within my heart has place
as when on earth they walked with me
and met me face to face, and met me face to face.

Their lives are made forever mine;
what they to me have been
has left henceforth its seal and sign
engraven deep within, engraven deep within.

Narrator   In times past, one of the most famous customs of All
Souls' Day was the ringing of church bells to comfort the
departed spirits. Perhaps they also provided a comfort to
the living, signaling that attention must be paid both to
the lives of those who have gone before, passing down
their gifts of hope and love, and to our own lives so that
when it is our turn, we too might leave a legacy of love.

We now call the names of our beloved dead and invite you to respond after each set of five names by singing
the refrain. After the litany of names, the ringing of the
bells will invite us to a few moments of meditation.

Soloist sings "What Is Remembered Lives" by Starhawk &
Reclaiming. Then, if necessary, a Choir Member teaches
participants this phrase of music to be used as the response.
Narrator and Leader alternate in reciting sets of five
names. After each set, all sing. If the gathering is small
and the number of participants few, this litany can be
conducted less formally. Rather than using scribes and
submitting names in advance, individual participants
can call out names and all can sing after each name or
each participant's set of names. A short period of medita-
tion follows, during which bells are rung.

Narrator   We have invoked the spirits of our ancestors and other
beloved dead. Let us hear with our hearts what they
have to tell us.

All sing the following words, adapted from Henry Francis Lyte's "Abide with Me," to the same melody.

All sing   Come to my heart, fast falls the eventide;
The darkness deepens; still with me abide.
When times are bleakest, and all comforts flee,
Light of my young years, come, abide with me.

Swift to its close ebbs out life's little day;
Earth's joys grow dim, its glories fade away;
Yet, thanks to you, I know that deeds will last,
Bearing their fruit, though long the doer's passed.

I fear no foe, with thee at hand to bless;
Ills have no weight, and tears no bitterness.
You taught me well the values dear to me;
Help me to live them; come abide with me.

Offering Soul Cakes

Baskets have been set out in advance for collecting the offering.

Narrator   One of the customs associated with All Saints' and All Souls' Days in the British Isles was the giving of soul cakes to groups of poor people, especially children, who came to the door begging. This offering to the poor was sometimes done in the name of the dead who had lived in the house. This act of kindness by the living was believed to have a salutary effect on the souls of the dead in Purgatory, easing their pain or shortening their stay there. Although soul cakes were originally oatcakes, the term came to be applied to any treat, whether food or coins.

Leader   Let us now make our soul-cake offering to the poor. You have come to this gathering with gifts of food—the ingredients for making a dish or meal that was the favorite of one of your beloved dead. I invite you to come forward with your offering and, in the name of your beloved dead, put them in these baskets, which will be taken to [*name of local soup kitchen or food pantry*] to feed the poor and hungry of our community.

Choir sings "Breaths" by Ysaye Barnwell during the offering. The first verse is the chorus.

Choir   Listen more often to things than to beings.
             'Tis the ancestor's breath
             when the fire's voice is heard.
             'Tis the ancestor's breath
             in the voice of the waters.

             Those who have died have never, never left.
             The dead are not under the earth.
             They are in the rustling trees,
             they are in the groaning woods.
             They are in the crying grass,
             they are in the moaning rocks.
             The dead are not under the earth. So . . .

             Chorus

             Those who have died, have never, never left.
             The dead have a pact with the living.
             They are in the woman's breast,
             they are in the wailing child.
             They are with us in the home,
             they are with us in the crowd.
             The dead have a pact with the living. . . .

             Chorus

Narrator   Every loss we experience in life is a reminder of that ul-
             timate loss to come, the loss of our very life. No matter
             how rich or poor we are, no matter how talented or
             inept, no matter how happy or miserable, we all must
             die. This can be, for many of us, a terrifying realization.

Perhaps it is this ultimate source of grief that lurks behind every other grieving.

Reader 2   Margarèt, are you grieving
Over Goldengrove unleaving?
Leaves, like the things of man, you
With your fresh thought care for, can you?
Ah! as the heart grows older
It will come to such sights colder
By and by, nor spare a sigh
Though worlds of wanwood leafmeal lie;
And yet you *will* weep and know why.
Now no matter, child, the name:
Sorrow's springs are the same.
Nor mouth had, no nor mind, expressed
What heart heard of, ghost guessed:
It is the blight man was born for,
It is Margarèt you mourn for.
      —Gerard Manley Hopkins, "Spring and Fall"

Silent meditation

Leader   For some, the terror of dying is relieved by the joy of living a meaningful and generous life. Rachel Carson, the mother of the environmental movement in the United States, may have been one of these. She had achieved fame and fortune with her books on the sea when she discovered in her mid-fifties that she had cancer. Yet she spent her last years writing *Silent Spring*, a book that would expose the lethal practices of the chemical industry and for which she would be both praised and pilloried. One morning in 1963, approaching the last autumn of her life, Carson sat with her best friend near the edge of the sea in Maine. There they watched a migration of Monarch butterflies. Later, Rachel wrote to her friend:

Reader 3   For me it was one of the loveliest of the summer's hours, and all the details will remain in my memory: that blue . . . sky, the sounds of wind in the spruces, and surf on the rocks, the gulls busy with their foraging, alighting with deliberate grace. . . . But most of all I shall remember the Monarchs, that unhurried drift of one small winged form after another, each drawn by some invisible force. We talked a little about their life history. Did they return? We thought not; for most, at least, this was the closing journey of their lives.

     But it occurred to me this afternoon, remembering, that it had been a happy spectacle, that we had felt no sadness when we spoke of the fact that there would be no return. And rightly—for when any living thing has come to the end of its cycle, we accept that end as natural. For the Monarch butterfly, that cycle is measured in a known span of months. For ourselves, the measure is something else, the span of which we cannot know. But the thought is the same: when that intangible cycle has run its course, it is a natural and not unhappy thing that a life comes to its end.

     That is what those brightly fluttering bits of life taught me this morning. I found a deep happiness in it—so, I hope, may you.

Honoring Deities of Death and Rebirth

Narrator   For some the sting of death is eased by hope of resurrection. Ancient Egyptians, for example, called Osiris the "Resurrection and the Life" and believed that, like him, after death they would be born again into eternal life. Christians also see—in the account of the resurrection of Jesus and in the words attributed to him in the gospels—a promise of their own eternal life and call upon him to grant eternal rest to their beloved dead.

Soloist sings "Pié Jesu" from Gabriel Fauré's Requiem.

Leader   Many religions honor a deity of death, some of whom are also deities of rebirth.

Narrator The Celts honored two deities at Samhain. Ollathair, the great father god whose giant cauldron of plenty is never depleted, carries a club with which he both takes life from enemies and restores life to his own people. Morrigan is both the tribal mother goddess and the agent of death for enemies on the battlefield. On the feast of Samhain, there is a ritual mating of these two deities.

Leader   The Morrigan was also honored as a triple goddess— maiden, mother, and crone. The virgin (the seed, the child) becomes the birth-giving creator-mother (the fruitful plant), who in turn becomes the death-dealing crone (the withering life). This trinity, represented by the waxing moon, full moon, and waning moon, also reflected the stages of human life. By honoring all three, the ancients acknowledged the importance of each in the cycle of life.

Narrator For the Greeks the crone member of the triple goddess was Hecate, a death goddess to whom were attributed magical powers of regeneration.

Leader   Perhaps the most formidable of crones is the Hindu Kali, Creator-Preserver-Destroyer of the universe. She gives birth to the world, yet in her horrible-hag incarnation she dances at cremation grounds, gathering up the souls of the dead. In honoring Kali, we honor not just our final death, which is natural and inevitable, but every phase of darkness and dying that is part of our living.

Reader 4 The kingdom of Kali is within us deep.
          The built-in destroyer, the savage goddess,

Wakes in the dark and takes away our sleep.
She moves through the blood to poison gentleness.

She keeps us from being what we long to be;
Tenderness withers under her iron laws.
We may hold her like a lunatic, but it is she
Held down, who bloodies with her claws.

How then to set her free or come to terms
With the volcano itself, the fierce power
Erupting injuries, shrieking alarms?
Kali among her skulls must have her hour.

It is time for the invocation, to atone
For what we fear most and have not dared to face:
Kali, the destroyer, cannot be overthrown;
We must stay, open-eyed, in the terrible place.

Every creation is born out of the dark.
Every birth is bloody. Something gets torn.
Kali is there to do her sovereign work
Or else the living child will be stillborn.

She cannot be cast out (she is here for good)
Nor battled to the end. Who wins that war?
She cannot be forgotten, jailed, or killed.
Heaven must still be balanced against her.

Out of destruction she comes to wrest
The juice from the cactus, its harsh spine,
And until she, the destroyer, has been blest,
There will be no child, no flower, and no wine. . . .

Kali, be with us.
Violence, destruction, receive our homage.
Help us to bring darkness into the light,
To lift out the pain, the anger,
Where it can be seen for what it is—
The balance-wheel for our vulnerable, aching love.

Put the wild hunger where it belongs,
Within the act of creation,
Crude power that forges a balance
Between hate and love.

Help us to be the always hopeful
Gardeners of the spirit
Who know that without darkness
Nothing comes to birth
As without light
Nothing flowers.

Bear the roots in mind,
You, the dark one, Kali,
Awesome power.

—May Sarton, "Invocation to Kali"

Celebrating Continuity

Narrator   Just as there is a relationship between birth and death within our own lives, there is an important connection between the life of one generation and the lives of the ones before and the ones after. The cycle of individual life swirls out of the lives before and swirls into the lives after, forming one endless human DNA spiral.

The nineteenth-century anthropologist Leo Frobenius studied the burial rites of the planting folk of the tropical jungles of South and East Africa. There he discovered a practice that illuminates and celebrates this connection.

Reader 5   When an old kinsman of the sib dies, a cry of joy immediately fills the air. A banquet is arranged, during which the men and women discuss the qualities of the deceased, tell stories of his life, and speak with sorrow of the ills of old age to which he was subject in his last years. Somewhere in the neighborhood—preferably in a shady grove—a hollow has been dug in the earth, covered with a stone. It now is opened and there within lie the bones of earlier times. These are pushed aside to make room for the new arrival. The corpse is carefully bedded in a particular posture, facing a certain way, and left to itself then for a certain season, with the grave again closed.

But when enough time has passed for the flesh to have decayed, the old men of the sib open the chamber again, climb down, take up the skull, carry it to the surface and into the farmstead, where it is cleaned, painted red, and after being hospitably served with grain and beer, placed in a special place along with the crania of other relatives. From now on no spring will pass when the dead will not participate in the offerings of the planting time; no fall when he will not partake of the offerings of thanks brought in at harvest. . . .

Moreover, the silent old fellow participates in everything that happens in the farmstead. If a leopard fells a woman, a farmboy is bitten by a snake, a plague strikes, or the blessing of rain is withheld, the relic is always brought into connection with the matter in some way. Should there be a fire, it is the first thing saved; when the puberty rites of the youngsters are to commence, it is the first to enjoy the festival beer and porridge. If a young woman marries into the sib, the oldest member conducts her to the urn or shelf where the earthly remains of the past are preserved and bids her take from the head of an ancestor a few kernels of holy grain to eat. And this, indeed, is a highly significant custom; for when this young, new vessel of the spirit of the sib becomes pregnant, the old people of the community watch to see what similarities will exist between the newly growing and the faded life.

—Monumenta Africana

Narrator   We are not a people comfortable with harboring the skulls of grandparents on our bookshelves. Perhaps we even think ourselves somehow more intelligent than these simple folk who imagined their dead could have an effect on the life of the community—on the planting and harvesting, on the outcome of pregnancy and child-rearing. How foolish! . . . Or is it?

If a man learns how to plant and harvest from his father, who learned it from his father, is not the dead grandfather responsible, in part, for the crops?

It is a common myth that maternal behavior is instinctive. Psychologists tell us it is learned—learned from our own mothers and from other mothers in the community, who learned it from their mothers. If a woman takes these lessons to heart, is not her grandmother responsible, in part, for the health of her baby? Are not the ancestors—blood kin and other—who have taught us the practical lessons and spiritual values by which we live to be thanked and honored?

Many of us throw rice at newlyweds, perhaps not even aware that this is a blessing, a wish for fertility in the marriage. How much more powerful it might be for the couple to take the kernels of grain from the skulls of grandparents who perhaps gave them their earliest lessons in love. All right, we are too squeamish (and law-abiding) to use skulls. We might have to substitute a favorite mug or bowl of the ancestor. But the ritual could still provide the powerful experience of continuity.

Life goes on. This we know. What we perhaps need reminding of is that it is the same life—one life—of which we all have a little part.

Leader   We now call the names of our beloved newborn children and toddlers, whose new life is a blessing in our families and communities. We invite you to keep in mind the ancestors whose spirits enliven these children and to respond, after each set of five names, by singing the refrain: "Those who have died live on," using the same melody we sang for the last litany.

Leader and Narrator alternate in reciting sets of five names. After each set, all sing. If the gathering is small, individual participants can call out names at this point with everyone chanting after each name or each set of names.

All chant   Those who have died live on.

Choir sings "Sing of Living, Sing of Dying," words by Thomas Mikelson, while Servers circulate with baskets of apples and distribute them to participants.

Choir   Sing of living, sing of dying, let them both be joined
      in one,
parts of an eternal process like the ever-circling sun.
From the freshness of each infant giving hope in
      what is new,
to the wisdom of the aged deepened by a longer view.

Open to a deeper loving, open to the gift of care,
searching for a higher justice, helping others in despair.
Through the tender bonds of living in a more inclusive
      way,
we are opened more to suff'ring from the losses of each
      day.

Celebrating the Taste of Life

Narrator   Now is the time of year for the harvesting of apples—
a good time to remember the importance of this fruit
in many myths and rituals. At harvest time the Romans
honored Pomona, goddess of fruit, and likely brought
her with them to Celtic countries, where they introduced the game of bobbing for apples in a tub of water
at Samhain. The apples may have symbolized souls in
the Cauldron of Regeneration.

Leader The Greek mother goddess Hera is depicted offering an apple from the Tree of Life to her followers. For the Celts, the Otherworld paradise was named Avalon, or "Apple-land." Scandinavians buried apples with their dead to help with passage to the next life.

Narrator An apple cut in half horizontally reveals a five-pointed star at its core. The Egyptians used this five-pointed star in a circle as the hieroglyph for the underworld womb.

Leader holds up half an apple.

Leader Behold the apple:
flesh and seed.
The flesh for food,
the seed to earth,

All that we may live
by what we need,
the rest to die
and thus give birth.

Narrator As we have come with food for the poor to honor our beloved dead, may we leave with food for our souls to honor all the living.

All sing to the melody of "How Can I Keep from Singing?"

All sing All life flows on in endless song
above earth's lamentation.
I hear the real though far-off hymn
that hails a new creation.
Through all the tumult and the strife,
I hear the music ringing.
It sounds an echo in my soul.
How can I keep from singing!

What though the tempest 'round me roars,
I know the truth, it liveth.

What though the darkness 'round me close,
songs in the night it giveth.
Death comes to all—no one escapes
the anguish of its stinging.
Yet knowing all good deeds live on,
how can I keep from singing!

The old ones die, the newborns cry;
the circle's never-ending.
Each generation learns to love
from others' careful tending.
What gives the meaning to each life?
What keeps the planets ringing?
Our hands across the ages reached
and hearts together singing!

While this is the end of the formal ritual, the All Souls' celebration
may continue as participants carry their photos and memorabilia
to another space, where they may enjoy fellowship and food—
possibly a potluck meal consisting of favorite dishes of the beloved
dead, which they would have prepared and delivered before the
ritual.

Common Ground

We live in an era of religious tension. While a community may be united by its common beliefs and practices, these very things sometimes divide one community from another. Living in the "global village" has made us more aware of other peoples' religions, but not necessarily more appreciative or even more tolerant. The media have brought into our living rooms the rancor and ruin of civil wars fought in the name of religion from Europe and Asia to Africa to the Middle East. In our own country, response to Asian, African, and Middle-Eastern immigrants is increasingly marked by suspicion, even fear, of their religion. And the growing political divide between the Right and the Left is mirrored in the ever-expanding chasm between fundamentalists and liberals who both call themselves Christian. Terrorists wage "holy wars" with bombs, and television evangelists with bombast. In such a culture of mistrust, how do we create community? How do we find common ground?

Common ground.

Perhaps that is the place to start. No matter what we think of one another's religious beliefs or practices, we do all stand on the same ground. We share the same earth. The same sun rises and sets on all of us. Doesn't this transcend our doctrinal differences?

Millennia ago, early peoples personified the sun and earth—made deities of them, worshiped them. Our modern scientific understanding of natural phenomena makes it unreasonable for us to do that. But surely we can share their reverence. Surely we can follow their example of respect for the earth, the air, the water— and be healthier and happier for it.

If there is a theme that runs through the history of rituals related to the earth's seasons, it is renewal. The wheel turns and the old season gives way to the new, the old year to the new, the old life to the new. Each planting of seeds promises new possibilities. Each harvest brings sustenance for yet another year. Each fallow time regenerates the life of the soil. The sun deities retreat and return. The grain goddesses are lost and restored. The vegetation gods die and rise again. The cycle of life goes on and on, birth after death after birth. Perhaps what all the rituals celebrate is this continuity of life, the miraculous natural world that makes it possible, and our abiding connection to it.

For the ancients, interdependence was clear. Humans played as important a role in the renewal of the earth as the earth played in their renewal. On the eve of a new season's beginning, the people (or the king in their name) fasted in order to purify not just their own bodies but the land itself. The fires that encouraged the fecundity of the land also made its people fertile. And the ritual mating of their leaders, replicating that of their deities of earth and sun, produced both children and crops.

For us moderns, distanced from the earth by technology, interdependence is not as clear. And we are paying the price: in polluted air and water, in soil erosion, in deforestation, and in global warming.

How different the condition of the planet might be if we allowed ourselves to be renewed at each turning of the wheel of the year, if we took the time periodically to celebrate the beauty and bounty of nature.

Celebrating the renewal of the earth gives us an opportunity to become new ourselves—to let go of old hurts and failures, to forgive ourselves and others, to get on with life as nature does, to open ourselves to hope and possibilities, to welcome the fertility of spirit that gives life its richness.

And because we all share the same earth, we can celebrate its renewal together, no matter what our theological differences may be. Recognizing our mutual bond with the earth can strengthen our bonds with one another and put into perspective the things that separate us. If together we respect our Mother Earth, will we not learn to respect one another and begin the work of peace?

The ground we stand on is holy—and it is our common ground.

Selected Bibliography

African Network. "African Festivals: Incwala." <u>african.net/incwala.htm</u>

Akhenaten. "Hymn to the Sun," in James Henry Breasted, *A History of Egypt*, 2nd ed. New York: Charles Scribner's Sons, 1912.

Ardinger, Barbara. *A Woman's Book of Rituals and Celebrations.* San Rafael, CA: New World Library, 1992.

Asia for Kids. "Resources." <u>afk.com/resources</u>

AskAsia: Korea. "Chusok: The Korean Thanksgiving." <u>askasia.org/Korea/r14.html</u>

Australian Media.com Family Network. "Harvest Festivals from Around the World." <u>harvestfestivals.net</u>

Aveni, Anthony. *The Book of the Year: A Brief History of Our Seasonal Holidays.* New York: Oxford University Press, 2003.

Baring, Anne, and Jules Cashford. *The Myth of the Goddess: Evolution of an Image.* London: Arkana Penguin Books, 1991.

bbc.co.uk. "Religion and Ethics: Hinduism." <u>bbc.co.uk/print/religion/religions/hinduism/holydays</u>

Berger, Pamela C. *The Goddess Obscured: Transformation of the Grain Protectress from Goddess to Saint.* Boston: Beacon Press, 1985.

Brand, John. *Observations on the Popular Antiquities of Great Britain: Chiefly Illustrating the Origin of Our Vulgar and Provincial Customs, Ceremonies, and Superstitions.* Auburn, CA: Singing Tree Press, 1969.

Butler, Alban. *Butler's Lives of the Saints,* edited, revised, and supplemented by Herbert Thurston, S. J., and Donald Attwater. 4 vols. New York: P. J. Kenedy and Sons, 1956.

Campanelli, Pauline. *Wheel of the Year: Living the Magical Life.* St. Paul, MN: Llewellyn Publications, 1989.

Campbell, Joseph. *The Masks of God: Occidental Mythology.* New York: Penguin Books, 1964.

_____. *The Masks of God: Oriental Mythology.* New York: Penguin Books, 1962.

Canada: Indian and Northern Affairs. "National Aboriginal Day." ainc-inac.gc.ca/nad/index_e.html

Carmichael, Alexander, ed. *Carmina Gadelica: Hymns and Incantations from the Gaelic.* 2 vols. Edinburgh: Floris Books, 2004 [1900].

Celtic Spirit. celticspirit.org

Circle Sanctuary. circlesanctuary.org/pholidays

Cnyantai.com. "Chinese Festivals." cnyantai.com/english/ytfq_en/festivals_1.htm

Condren, Mary. *The Serpent and the Goddess: Women, Religion, and Power in Celtic Ireland.* San Francisco: Harper & Row, 1989.

Corwin, Judith. *Harvest Festivals Around the World.* New York: Julian Messner, 1995.

Del Chamberlain, Von. "Seasonal Markers." Project Astro Utah. clarkfoundation.org/astro-utah/vondel

Dillon, Miles. *The Cycles of the Kings.* Dublin: Four Courts Press, 1994.

Eliade, Mircea. *Cosmos and History: The Myth of the Eternal Return*, translated by Willard R. Trask. New York: Harper & Row, 1959.

Ellis, Peter Berresford. *A Dictionary of Irish Mythology.* London: Constable, 1987.

Finnguide. "Finland Calendar." finnguide.fi/calendar/

Fitzgerald, Waverly. "School of the Seasons." schooloftheseasons.com

Fleming, Fergus, et al. *Heroes of the Dawn: Celtic Myth.* London: Duncan Baird Publishers, 1996.

Fowler, W. Warde. *The Roman Festivals of the Period of the Republic.* Port Washington, NY: Kennikat Press, 1969 [1899].

Frazer, James G. *The Golden Bough: A Study in Magic and Religion.* New York: Touchstone, 1995 [1907].

Friang, Michael. "Rites of Heritage: Spring Festivals in Kyoto, Japan." The World and I. worldandi.com/specialreport/kyoto/kyoto.html

Garczynski, Stanley. "Polish Traditions." Polish Genealogical Society of America. pgsa.org/traditions.htm

Gasparini, Evel. "Slavic Religion." Encyclopedia Britannica. search.eb.com/eb/article?tocId=65464

Gnanarama, Ven. Dr. P. "Ullambana: A Day of Remembrance and Merit-Transfer." 4ui.com/eart/160eart2.htm

Goudsword, David, and Robert Stone. *America's Stonehenge: The Mystery Hill Story.* Kerry, Ireland: Brandon Publishing, 2003.

Hamp, Eric. "Imbolc, Oimelc," *Studia Celtica*, 14 (1979), 106-113.

Harrington, Mary. "In the Wild: The Winter Solstice and Yuletide." Hudson River Audubon Society of Westchester. hras.org/wild/wild101.html

Hazlitt, W. Carew. *Faiths and Folklore of the British Isles*. New York: Benjamin Bloom, Inc., 1965.

Heidorn, Keith. "Celebrating May Day." School of Celtic Studies. islandnet.com/~see/weather/almanac/arc2000/alm00may.htm

Heinberg, Richard. *Celebrate the Solstice: Honoring the Earth's Seasonal Rhythms Through Festival and Ceremony*. Wheaton, IL: Quest Books, 1993.

Hindu, The. "Season of Plenty." hindu.com/thehindu/mp/2002/01/14/stories/2002011400030100.htm

Hutton, Ronald. *The Stations of the Sun: A History of the Ritual Year in Britain*. Oxford: Oxford University Press, 1996.

Internet Library of Serb Culture. "Anthropology and Ethnology: Codes of Slavic Cultures."rastko.org.yu/projekti/kodovi/kodovi_eng.html#agrarian

Janak Community Center of New Delhi. "Mahashivratri." 123mahashivratri.com/shivratri/rituals/

Jones, Prudence, and Nigel Pennick. *A History of Pagan Europe*. London: Routledge, 1995.

Jordan, Michael. *Encyclopedia of Gods: Over 2,500 Deities of the World*. New York: Facts on File, 1993.

Jung, Emma, and Marie-Louise Von Franz. *The Grail Legend*. New York: G. P. Putnam's Sons, 1970.

Kavasch, E. Barrie, and Karen Baar. *American Indian Healing Arts: Herbs, Rituals, and Remedies for Every Season of Life*. New York: Bantam Books, 1999.

Knowth.com. knowth.com

Krupp, E. C. *Echoes of Ancient Skies: The Astronomy of Lost Civilizations*. Garden City, NJ: Doubleday, 1977.

Lafferty, Anne. "A Seeker's Guide to Modern Witchcraft and Paganism." New Directions in Folklore. temple.edu/isllc/newfolk/wicca.html

Leach, Maria, ed. *Funk and Wagnall's Standard Dictionary of Folklore, Mythology and Legend*. Reprint ed. New York: HarperCollins, 1984.

Leeming, David, and Jake Page. *Goddess: Myths of the Female Divine*. Oxford: Oxford University Press, 1994.

Livingstone, Sheila. *Scottish Customs*. St. Paul, MN: Llewellyn Publications, 1989.

Lockyer, J. Norman. *The Dawn of Astronomy*. Cambridge, MA: MIT Press, 1964 [1894].

MacNeill, Máire. *The Festival of Lughnasa*. Oxford, England: Oxford University Press, 1962.

Matson, Gienna. *Celtic Mythology A to Z*. New York: Facts on File, 2004.

Mavor, James W., Jr., and Byron E. Dix. *Manitou: The Sacred Landscape of New England's Native Civilization*. Lacey, WA: Destiny Publications, 1989.

McAlister, J. T. "Solstice Celebrations from A to Z." Echoed Voices: Online Magazine. echoedvoices.org/DecSolstice.html

McCaffrey, Carmel, and Leo Eaton. *In Search of Ancient Ireland: The Origins of the Irish from the Neolithic Times to the Coming of the English*. Chicago: New Amsterdam Books, 2002.

McKenzie, John L. *Dictionary of the Bible*. Milwaukee: Bruce Publishing, 1965.

Mellena, Mara. "Latvian Seasonal Holidays." Latvian Institute. li.lv/old/seasonal_holidays.htm

Monaghan, Patricia. *The New Book of Goddesses and Heroines*. St. Paul, MN: Llewellyn Publications, 1997.

_____. *O Mother Sun! A New View of the Cosmic Feminine*. Freedom, CA: Crossing Press, 1994.

Morales, Peter. "Bringing the Dead to Life." World (June/August 2003).

Nelson, Gertrud Mueller. *To Dance with God: Family Ritual and Community Celebration*. Mahwah, NJ: Paulist Press, 1986.

New Advent. "The Catholic Encyclopedia." newadvent.org/cathen

News India Times. "Diwali: Pan-Indian Festival." newsindia-times.com/2002/11/01/tow42-top.html

Ó Catháin, Seamus. "The Festival of Brigit the Holy Woman." School of Celtic Studies. celt.dias.ie.publications/celtica/c23/c23-231.pdf

Ó Cathasaigh, Donal. "The Cult of Brigid: A Study of Pagan-Christian Syncretism in Ireland," in *Mother Worship: Themes and Variations*, ed. James Preston. Chapel Hill, NC: University of North Carolina Press, 1982.

O'Rahilly, Thomas F. *Early Irish History and Mythology*. Dublin: Dublin Institute for Advanced Studies, 1984.

Order of Nazorean Essenes. "A Canaanite-Phoenician Sacred Year: A Reconstructed Sacred Calendar of Lunar and Solar Festivals." essenes.net/qadeshcalen.html

Orkneyjar: The Heritage of the Orkney Islands. orkneyjar.com/history/maeshowe/

Pollock, Robert. "Stones of Wonder: Prehistoric Observatories in Scotland." stonesofwonder.com/index.html

Putik, Alexandr, Eva Kosáková, and Dana Cabanová. *Jewish Customs and Traditions: Festivals, the Synagogue and the Course of Life*. Prague: The Jewish Museum, 1998.

Quartey-Papafio, A. B. "The Ga Homowo Festival." Journal of the African Society. african-religions.religion.designerz.com/african-traditional.php

Religioustolerance.org. "Easter." religioustolerance.org/easter.htm

————. "Fall Equinox Celebrations." religioustolerance.org/fall_equinox.htm

————. "Spring Equinox Celebrations." religioustolerance.org/spring_equinox.htm

————. "Summer Solstice Celebrations." religioustolerance.org/summer_solstice.htm

————. "Winter Solstice Celebrations." religioustolerance.org/winter_solstice.htm

Rich, Adrienne. *Of Woman Born: Motherhood as Experience and Institution*. New York: W. W. Norton, 1976.

Saso, M. R. *Taoism and the Rite of Cosmic Renewal*. Pullman: Washington State University Press, 1972.

Scandinavica.com. "Traditions." scandinavica.com/culture

Sharkey, John. *Celtic Mysteries: The Ancient Religion*. London: Thames and Hudson, 1975.

Sjoestedt, Marie-Louise. *Gods and Heroes of the Celts*, translated by Miles Dillon. Berkeley, CA: Turtle Island Foundation, 1982.

Sjöö, Monica, and Barbara Mor. *The Great Cosmic Mother: Rediscovering the Religion of the Earth*. San Francisco: HarperSanFrancisco, 1987.

Slovak Spectator. "The Myth of Morena Lives On: The Villagers of Král'ová nad Váhom, Near Sal'a, Welcome Spring," by Tóthová, Lívia. slovakspectator.sk/clanok-19192.html

Spell in Time, A. "Background to Bulgarian Myth and Folklore." spellintime.fsnet.co.uk/Folklore.htm

Spicer, Dorothy Gladys. *Festivals of Western Europe*. Detroit: Omnigraphics, 1994.

Starhawk. *The Spiral Dance: A Rebirth of the Ancient Religion of the Great Goddess*. San Francisco: Harper and Row, 1979.

Stone, Merlin. *Ancient Mirrors of Womanhood: A Treasury of Goddess and Heroine Lore from Around the World*. Boston: Beacon Press, 1979.

Summers, Montague, tr. *Malleus Maleficarum*. London: J. Rodker, 1928.

Tanaka, Masamichi. "Purification of the Universe: Oomoto's Setsubun Festival." Oomoto International. oomoto.or.jp/English/enArkivo/setubun.html

Thompson, Sue Ellen, ed. *Holiday Symbols and Customs*. 3rd ed. Detroit: Omnigraphics, 2003.

Virtual Library—Sri Lanka. "Vesak Festival." lankalibrary.com/rit/vesak.htm

Walker, Barbara G. *The Woman's Encyclopedia of Myths and Secrets*. San Francisco: HarperSanFrancisco, 1983.

_____. *Women's Rituals: A Sourcebook*. San Francisco: HarperSanFrancisco, 1990.

Warner, Marina. *Alone of All Her Sex: The Myth and the Cult of the Virgin Mary*. New York: Vintage Books, 1976.

Waskow, Arthur. *Seasons of Our Joy: A Modern Guide to the Jewish Holidays*. Boston: Beacon Press, 1982.

Waters, Frank. *Book of the Hopi*. New York: Penguin, 1977.

Wilde, William R. *Irish Popular Superstitions*. Dublin: Irish Academic Press, 1979 [1852].

Witches' Voice, The. "Popular Pagan Holidays: The Turn of the Wheel of the Year." witchvox.com/xholidays.html

Music Resources

BB: *Breaking Bread.* Portland: Oregon Catholic Press, 2004.

BH: *Baptist Hymnal.* Nashville: Genevox, 1991.

SFE: *Songs for Earthlings: A Green Spirituality Songbook*, ed. Julie Forest Middleton. Sebastopol, CA: Emerald Earth Publishing, 1998.

SLT: *Singing the Living Tradition.* Boston: Unitarian Universalist Association, 1993.

THE: *The Hymnal 1982, According to the Use of the Episcopal Church.* New York: Church Publishing Incorporated, 1985.

TPH: *The Presbyterian Hymnal: Hymns, Psalms, and Spiritual Songs.* Louisville, KY: Westminster John Knox Press, 1992.

CYB: *The Cyber Hymnal*, cyberhymnal.org

HYM: *United Methodist Hymnal*, hymnsite.com

LUT: *The Lutheran Hymnal Online*, lutheran-hymnal.com/online/tlh_online.html

MID: *MIDI Music*, members.tripod.com/texasmidi/midi.htm

Abide with Me
Tune: Eventide
Score: BB, BH, SLT, THE, TPH
Sound: CYB, HYM

All Creatures of the Earth and Sky
Alternate title: All Creatures of Our God and King
Tune: *Lasst Uns Erfreuen*
Score: BB, BH, SLT, THE, TPH
Sound: CYB, HYM

The Ballad of John Barleycorn
Score and lyrics: folkinfo.org/abctest/getpdf.php?SongID=161
Sound: mudcat.org/midi/midibrowse.cfm?start_letter=I
CD: Jethro Tull. *A Little Light Music.* Chrysalis.

Be Thou My Vision
Tune: Slane
Score: BH, SLT, THE, TPH
Sound: CYB, HYM

Breaths
Score: Sweet Honey in the Rock. *Continuum: The First Songbook of Sweet Honey in the Rock.* Southwest Harbor, ME: Contemporary A Cappella Publishing, 2000.
CD: Sweet Honey in the Rock. *Sweet Honey in the Rock: Selections 1976-1988.* Flying Fish/Rounder Records.

Chant for the Seasons
Score: SLT

Christ the Lord Is Risen Today
Alternate title: Jesus Christ Is Risen Today
Tune: Easter Hymn
Score: BB, BH, SLT, THE, TPH
Sound: CYB, HYM

Come, Thou Font of Every Blessing
Tune: Nettleton
Score: BH, SLT, THE, TPH
Sound: CYB

Cradle Song
Alternate titles: We Rear Not a Temple, Away in a Manger
Score: SLT, THE, TPH
Sound: CYB

Cup of Wonder
Lyrics: cupofwonder.com/songs.html#CupOfWonder
Score: Ian Anderson. *Flute Solos*. Miami: Warner Brothers
Publications, 1999.
CD: Jethro Tull. *Songs from the Wood*. Capitol Records.

De Colores
Score and Sound: montereybay.com/smitty/decolores.html

Dona Nobis Pacem
Score: BB, SLT, THE
Sound: HYM, MID

For All That Is Our Life
Score: SLT

For the Beauty of the Earth
Tune: Dix
Score: BB, BH, SLT, THE, TPH
Sound: CYB, HYM

Gather the Spirit
Score: SLT

Give Thanks for the Corn
Alternate title: How Firm a Foundation
Tune: Foundation
Score: BB, BH, SLT, THE, TPH
Sound: CYB, HYM

Go Now in Peace
Score: SLT, musicnotes.com

Holy, Holy, Holy
Tune: Nicaea
Score: BB, BH, SLT, THE, TPH
Sound: CYB, HYM

Homegrown Tomatoes
Lyrics: <u>john-denver.org/default.asp?id=200</u>
Score: John Denver. *John Denver: The Complete Lyrics*. New York: Cherry Lane Music, 2002.
Sound: <u>singout.org/422toc.html</u>
CD: John Denver. *The John Denver Collection*. Delta.

How Can I Keep from Singing?
Alternate title: My Life Flows on in Endless Song
Score: BB, SLT
Sound: CYB, MID

I Cannot Think of Them as Dead
Tune: Distant Beloved
Score: SLT

I've Got Peace Like a River
Score: BH, SLT, TPH
Sound: CYB

Let Us Break Bread Together
Score: BB, BH, SLT, THE, TPH
Sound: CYB

Lo, the Day of Days Is Here
Alternate titles: Hail the Day That Sees Him Rise, Let the Whole Creation Cry
Tune: Llanfair
Score: BB, BH, SLT, THE, TPH
Sound: CYB, SLT

Now Is the Month of May-ing
Score: sibeliusmusic.com/cgi-bin/show_ score.pl?scoreid=47488
Sound: arach.net.au/~algernon/maying/
CD: Cambridge Singers. *Old English Madrigals & Folk Songs*.
Primarily A Capella.

Now Thank We All Our God
Tune: *Nun Danket*
Score: BB, BH, SLT, THE, TPH
Sound: CYB, HYM

Now the Green Blade Riseth
Tune: *Noël Nouvelet*
Score: BB, SLT, THE
Sound: CYB

O Come, O Come, Emmanuel
Alternate title: Veni, Veni, Emmanuel
Score: BB, SLT, THE
Sound: CYB, HYM, LUT

O Yemaya
Score/CD: SFE

On the Dusty Earth Drum
Alternate titles: Jesus, Stand Among Us, Glory Be to Jesus, Holy
Spirit, Hear Us
Tune: Bemerton (Caswall)
Score: SLT, THE
Sound: CYB, SLT

Pastures of Plenty
Score: sheetmusiccatalog.com/
CD: Woody Guthrie. *This Land Is Your Land*. Smithsonian
Folkways.

Pié Jesu
Score: music-scores.com/faure/composer.php
Lyrics and Sound: windy.vis.ne.jp/art/lib/freq4.htm
CD: Gabriel Fauré. *Gabriel Fauré: Requiem and Other Choral Music*. Requiem.

Praise God from Whom All Blessings Flow
Alternate titles: All People That on Earth Do Dwell, Doxology
Tune: Old Hundreth
Score: BB, BH, SLT, THE, TPH
Sound: CYB, HYM

Samhain Hymn
Score/CD: SFE

Sing of Living, Sing of Dying
Score: SLT

Sung at Harvest
Score: *Sing Through the Seasons: Ninety-Nine Songs for Children*. Rifton, NY: Plough Publishing House, 1972.
The melody for "Come Thou Font of Every Blessing" can be used for these words as well.

Sunshine on My Shoulders
Lyrics: cowboylyrics.com/lyrics/denver-john/sunshine-on-my-shoulders-11304.html
Score: sheetmusicplus.com/
CD: John Denver. *John Denver's Greatest Hits*. RCA.

This Is the Truth That Passes Understanding
Alternate titles: O Son of God, Our Captain of Salvation, Our Nation, God, Its Heart to Thee Upraiseth
Score: SLT, TPH
Sound: CYB

This Little Light of Mine
Score: SLT
Lyrics and Sound: walkthroughlife.com/midis/kidsmidis/thislilight.htm

'Tis a Gift to Be Simple
Alternate title: Simple Gifts
Score: SLT, THE
Sound: SLT

Turn! Turn! Turn!
Lyrics: musicaememoria.com/turn_turn_turn.htm
Score: Pete Seeger. *Turn! Turn! Turn! (To Everything There Is a Season)*. New York: TRO, 2000.
Chord progressions: getsome.org/guitar/olga/chordpro/s/Pete.Seeger/TurnTurnTurn.chopro
Sound: datasync.com/~lee120fs/pagem.htm
CD: Pete Seeger. *If I Had a Hammer: Songs of Hope & Struggle.* Smithsonian Folkways.

We Gather Together
Tune: Kremser
Score: BB, BH, SLT, THE, TPH
Sound: CYB, HYM

What Is Remembered Lives
Score/CD: SFE

Index